AMERICAN CONSTITUTIONALISM

AMERICAN CONSTITUTIONALISM

FROM THEORY TO POLITICS

Stephen M. Griffin

PRINCETON UNIVERSITY PRESS   PRINCETON, NEW JERSEY

Library of Congress Cataloging-in-Publication Data

Griffin, Stephen M., 1957–
American Constitutionalism :
from theory to politics / Stephen M. Griffin
p.   cm.
Includes bibliographical references and index.
ISBN 0-691-03404-4
ISBN 0-691-00240-1 (pbk.)
1. United States—Constitutional law. 2. United States—
Politics and government. 3. Constitutional law—
Philosophy. I. Title.
KF4550.G74   1996
342.73'001—dc20   [347.30201]   96-3337 CIP

This book has been composed in Galliard

Princeton University Press books are printed
on acid-free paper and meet the guidelines
for permanence and durability of the Committee
on Production Guidelines for Book Longevity
of the Council on Library Resources

Second printing, and first paperback printing, 1998

http://pup.princeton.edu

Printed in the United States of America

10   9   8   7   6   5   4   3   2

For Marianne Lynch Griffin
and Clifford S. Griffin

Contents

Preface _____

THIS BOOK is an original contribution to American constitutional theory in the form of a short introduction to the subject. A number of considerations led me to write the book as an introduction. One is simply that no one has yet written an introduction to the field. While there are some helpful collections of articles, no general introduction is available at present.[1] Another is that despite the continuous stream of articles and books on constitutional theory, few scholars have bothered to inquire into the nature of the field. What *is* constitutional theory? This is the question I started with several years ago.[2]

At the same time, this book is a *critical* introduction. I had no intention of writing a textbook that simply summarized the views of other scholars. I take a position on the subject matter of constitutional theory, how that subject matter should be approached, and I offer my own arguments on many of the issues constitutional scholars have discussed in the last several decades.

While I hope students find this book useful, it is written primarily for scholars in law, political science, and philosophy. In particular, I attempt to cross the boundary that separates constitutional theory in law and political science. While political scientists who contribute to constitutional theory often discuss the work of legal scholars, legal scholars do not often return the favor. My attempt to integrate law and political science is, however, more a matter of orientation than a detailed consideration of the work of specific scholars. In a way I find difficult to define, I try to take the idea of politics seriously and to keep in mind that legalistic interpretations of American constitutionalism have their limits.

As a consequence, the organization of the book and the treatment of a number of topics differs significantly from other works in the field. Constitutional theories offered by legal scholars rarely pay much attention to

[1] For edited collections of articles, see John H. Garvey and T. Alexander Aleinikoff, eds., *Modern Constitutional Theory: A Reader* (St. Paul: West Publishing Company, 1989); Michael J. Gerhardt and Thomas D. Rowe, Jr., *Constitutional Theory: Arguments and Perspectives* (Charlottesville, Va.: Michie Company, 1993).

While there is an introduction to constitutional interpretation, it is in the form of a traditional legal casebook. See Walter F. Murphy, James E. Fleming, and William F. Harris, II, eds., *American Constitutional Interpretation* (Mineola, N.Y.: Foundation Press, 1986).

[2] See Stephen M. Griffin, "What Is Constitutional Theory? The Newer Theory and the Decline of the Learned Tradition," *Southern California Law Review* 62 (1989): 493.

the concept of the state, focus on the importance of institutions, discuss behaviorist research on judicial decisionmaking, or raise issues connected with constitutional crises and reform efforts, but these topics are all considered here. Nevertheless, legal scholars will find that much of the book, especially chapters 3 through 5, covers the familiar issues that they regard as the core of constitutional theory.

The main point I wish to stress, no matter what the orientation of the reader, is that constitutional theory is an independent field of inquiry. Constitutional theory is not, for example, dependent on Supreme Court decisions to set its agenda. Nor is constitutional theory primarily an aspect of legal or political philosophy. Constitutional theory is an inquiry of the middle range and is first and foremost about constitutionalism, a distinctive political practice that deserves closer study than it has so far received. While this book is not a comprehensive guide to American constitutional theory, I attempt to achieve four objectives: (1) to ask the right questions; (2) to provide a helpful general approach to American constitutional theory through an account of American constitutionalism; (3) to provide a fair-minded description of the best arguments in constitutional theory; and (4) where there is an impasse in the debate or the arguments are unclear, to suggest how further progress might be made.

I want to note a few important aspects of the scope and nature of my inquiry. Since there are many introductions to jurisprudence and political philosophy, I generally do not discuss those subjects except when they relate directly to the topic at hand.[3] There are, of course, many works discussing the doctrines of American constitutional law, and I had no intention of adding to their number in writing this book. I do assume a basic working knowledge of American constitutional law and history. For example, when I refer to decisions of the Supreme Court, I do not summarize the facts or engage in a detailed discussion of the Court's opinion. A knowledge of these matters is taken for granted.

One might approach constitutional theory by examining each major theory put forward by individual scholars, but I have organized the book around a set of topics common to many theories. One might also discuss the theoretical questions raised by particular constitutional clauses such as the Due Process clause, the Equal Protection clause, and the First Amendment. When scholars offer a "theory" of a particular clause, however, my opinion is that the discussion is more often doctrinal than theoretical.

---

[3] Two interesting books by John Arthur provide accessible introductions to the philosophical questions posed by Supreme Court decisions and contemporary constitutional theory. See John Arthur, *The Unfinished Constitution: Philosophy and Constitutional Practice* (Belmont, Calif.: Wadsworth Publishing Company, 1989); John Arthur, *Words That Bind: Judicial Review and the Grounds of Modern Constitutional Theory* (Boulder: Westview Press, 1995).

Such doctrinal analyses make assumptions that constitutional theory should put in question.

Finally, I think a special effort should be made to avoid the understandable sentimentality that often colors many discussions of the Constitution. Scholars may be patriotic, but they should not be blind to the weaknesses of American constitutionalism and the discontinuities in the American constitutional tradition. The study of the Constitution could benefit from the spirit expressed in the words of William Butler Yeats: "Cast a cold eye On life, on death."

In a book that stresses the role that institutions play in our constitutional order, it is only fitting that I recognize the support provided by the law schools at the University of Kansas, New York University, the University of Chicago, and Tulane University. I am grateful for the support that all these institutions have provided, especially the summer research grants provided by Dean John Kramer at Tulane.

My thanks also goes to individuals who have taken the time to listen to my ideas over the years: Frank Cross, Lawrence Solum, John Stick, Cass Sunstein, Mark Graber, Rex Martin, Robert Rowland, William E. Nelson, and especially Sanford Levinson. A number of individuals provided very useful comments on the manuscript: Clifford S. Griffin, Mark Osiel, Lloyd Bonfield, Mark Graber, Howard Gillman, Jack Rakove, Mark Tushnet, Joachim Zekoll, Sanford Levinson, Gary Jacobsohn, and Rex Martin. Earlier versions of various chapters were presented at conferences of the American Political Science Association, the Georgetown Discussion Group on Constitutional Law, Tulane's Murphy Institute of Political Economy, the NYU Legal History Colloquium, and the 17th IVR World Congress in Bologna. I first began conceiving the essential ideas of the book in the winter of 1987–88 after attending a thought-provoking NEH summer seminar at New York University conducted by William E. Nelson and Gordon S. Wood.

Portions of the book were originally published in several articles: "Constitutionalism in the United States: From Theory to Politics," *Oxford Journal of Legal Studies* 10 (1990): 200, reprinted here by permission of Oxford University Press; "Bringing the State into Constitutional Theory: Public Authority and the Constitution," *Law and Social Inquiry* 16 (1991): 659, and "How to Analyze the American State," *Law and Social Inquiry* 16 (1991): 731, both articles copyright 1991 American Bar Foundation; "Pluralism in Constitutional Interpretation," *Texas Law Review* 72 (1994): 1753, published originally in the *Texas Law Review*.

I would like to give a special acknowledgment to two works that had a strong influence on this book that may not be apparent from the text or the notes. The late Judith Shklar's insistence that we should turn our attention to the relationship between law and politics rather than law and morality struck me with unusual force at an early stage of my reading and encouraged me to concentrate just as much on American politics as on constitutional law in understanding American constitutionalism.[4] A seminal article by Sanford Levinson also had a significant impact on my thinking by demonstrating that there were alternative ways to view the history of American constitutionalism.[5]

For all things, especially her love, faith, and support, I thank my wife, Starlynn.

[4] See Judith N. Shklar, *Legalism: Law, Morals, and Political Trials* (Cambridge: Harvard University Press, 1986).

[5] See Sanford Levinson, "The Specious Morality of the Law," *Harper's*, May 1977, p. 35.

AMERICAN CONSTITUTIONALISM

Introduction _____

CONSTITUTIONAL THEORY is not a new term, but the enterprise of academic constitutional theory is a new phenomenon. For most of American constitutional history, constitutional theory simply denoted an inquiry into the more general and abstract questions posed by constitutional law. The emergence of constitutional theory as a distinct field of scholarly inquiry occurred only in the aftermath of landmark decisions of the Warren and Burger Courts, such as *Brown v. Board of Education* and *Roe v. Wade*.[1]

Why did *Brown* and *Roe* encourage constitutional *theory* in particular, rather than more vigorous efforts to understand constitutional law? It appears that a need for theory arises when long-standing assumptions about a particular practice are overturned or put in question. Decisions of the Warren and Burger Courts challenged such assumptions by pursuing a steady course of activism in striking down state and federal legislation, by reviving the substantive due process doctrine, and by employing reasoning that was questionable at best. Since many scholars found the consequences of the decisions to be desirable, however, this created a conflict that they sought to alleviate by elaborating theories of judicial review and constitutional interpretation. By the mid-1980s, it was apparent that the debate over these theories had created a self-sustaining scholarly enterprise, one that was independent to a certain extent of Supreme Court decisions.

While it is now clear that constitutional theory is a separate field of scholarly inquiry, scholars have not paid much attention to defining it as such. The origin of contemporary constitutional theory as a reaction to controversial Supreme Court decisions suggests that we can define it in relation to constitutional law. Constitutional theory can be understood as a second-order inquiry into the validity of the first-order judgments that are made in constitutional law. Constitutional theory is a second-order inquiry in that it asks questions about how to arrive at first-order judgments. In this definition, constitutional theory stands to constitutional law as metaethics stands to ethics.

This definition is suggestive, but it is ultimately flawed as a way to understand constitutional theory. The definition assumes that the practice

_____

[1] See *Brown v. Board of Education*, 347 U.S. 483 (1954); *Roe v. Wade*, 410 U.S. 113 (1973).

of constitutional law is fundamental for constitutional theory.[2] But the questions posed by the American constitutional tradition range far beyond the confines of constitutional law. There are important theoretical questions about American constitutionalism that have nothing to do with Supreme Court decisions. The nature of American constitutionalism, the validity of the doctrine of popular sovereignty, and the relationship of the Constitution to American political development are all examples. These questions do not normally arise in any court case because they concern the appropriate purpose and design of the constitutional system as a whole.

For purposes of this book, then, I understand American constitutional theory as addressing any theoretical issue raised by the distinctive practice of American constitutionalism. American *constitutionalism* is the primary object of study here, not constitutional law.

In light of the Constitution's role in American politics and history, three broad questions suggest themselves as the subject matter of constitutional theory. First, how did we get from the adoption of the Constitution of 1787 to the present? What is the relationship between the present Constitution and that older version of the same document? Further, what does this relationship tell us about the nature of American constitutionalism? Second, what is the relationship between the Constitution and the constitutional-political system in which it is embedded? For example, how has the Constitution contributed to American political development? Third, what are the issues raised by the development of constitutional law by the Supreme Court? As the order of these questions indicates, I do not begin this book with the issues raised by judicial review and constitutional interpretation. These issues are important, but they are distinctly secondary to the task of reaching an understanding of the nature of American constitutionalism and the process of constitutional change. Thus I begin discussing judicial review in chapter 3 only after completing the explorations of American constitutionalism in chapter 1 and how the Constitution relates to political institutions in chapter 2.

In attempting to answer these questions, it is important to use an interdisciplinary approach to the extent that it is possible. From my perspective, an interdisciplinary approach is simply a requirement of sound scholarship. One should try to take into consideration all relevant scholarly work, no matter if that work is done by political scientists, legal scholars, historians, or philosophers. I attempt, in particular, to take proper ac-

---

[2] For examples of definitions of constitutional theory that make such an assumption, see H. N. Hirsch, *A Theory of Liberty: The Constitution and Minorities* (New York: Routledge, 1992), p. 28; Mark Tushnet, "Constitutional Theory," in Leonard W. Levy, Kenneth L. Karst, John G. West, Jr., eds., *Encyclopedia of the American Constitution, Supplement I* (New York: Macmillan, 1992), p. 120.

count of relevant work by political scientists. Their work strongly influences the treatment of the topics in chapters 2, 3, and 4.

On the other hand, I understand constitutional theory as an inquiry in the middle range between actual political-legal decisionmaking and the more abstract territory occupied by political and legal philosophy. One consequence is that I do not discuss the contributions to constitutional theory of each of the significant approaches to legal theory such as critical legal studies, law and economics, critical race theory, feminist legal theory, the law and literature movement, and so on. These legal theories are better discussed directly rather than in terms of what they have to say about the Constitution (and each could be the topic of a separate book).[3] In addition, I believe that all of these theories at least implicitly employ the kind of legalistic or Supreme Court–centered approach that I criticize at various points in this book.[4]

As mentioned above, the guiding idea of this book is that the best way to understand the Constitution and the American constitutional tradition is through the study of the idea of constitutionalism. Constitutionalism should be appreciated as a dynamic political and historical process rather than as a static body of thought laid down in the eighteenth century. This is not a call to ignore the designs of the founding generation. It is rather an attempt to describe American constitutionalism in a way that will enable us to comprehend the development of the Constitution over time and the complex constitutional system of the present. To that end, I will offer some informal remarks to preview the argument in chapter 1 that influences many of the discussions in subsequent chapters.

The key to understanding American constitutionalism is to appreciate it as a somewhat implausible political practice. Many scholars have made two observations about American constitutionalism: it attempts to use words to create a political order, and the artfully designed system of institutions specified in the Constitution works to maintain that order by di-

---

[3] In particular, readers familiar with contemporary theories of constitutional interpretation will note the absence in chapter 5 of any discussion of the relevance of theories developed in the context of literary interpretation. In my judgment, the use of literary theory to illuminate constitutional interpretation is largely a dead end, given the significant differences between interpreting literary texts and the political-legal enterprise of interpreting the Constitution. For helpful introductions to this approach, see Gregory Leyh, ed., *Legal Hermeneutics: History, Theory, and Practice* (Berkeley: University of California Press, 1992); Sanford Levinson and Steven Mailloux, eds., *Interpreting Law and Literature: A Hermeneutic Reader* (Evanston, Ill.: Northwestern University Press, 1988).

[4] I regret, however, that I could not include a discussion of the relevance of public choice theory to constitutional theory. There is an excellent introduction to public choice theory that includes discussions of issues relevant to constitutional theory. See Daniel A. Farber and Philip P. Frickey, *Law and Public Choice: A Critical Introduction* (Chicago: University of Chicago Press, 1991).

viding and checking political power. The latter observation is thus used to explain how the former is possible. The problem is that this story does not really explain how constitutionalism is plausible given the pressures exerted by politics and the forces of historical change.

The basic idea of American constitutionalism is conducting government under the provisions of a fundamental law. The Constitution can control the state over many generations because it is phrased in general language and adopted through a special political process that gives it a legitimacy above and beyond any ordinary law. The difficulty is explaining exactly how this is supposed to work.

Suppose political actors care more about their immediate interests than about preserving the carefully balanced constitutional scheme. Suppose also that the general language of the Constitution is susceptible to a variety of reasonable interpretations. Further suppose that historical change makes the original meaning of the Constitution difficult to recapture and also creates a pressing need for fundamental policy shifts. In these circumstances, it is possible for the entire government to be controlled by a party interested in pursuing a policy that is at odds with the Constitution. In such a situation, there is no apparent way to enforce the original meaning of the Constitution. The Constitution can be frustrated by political interests.

The problem of constitutionalism is more subtle than this blunt reasoning suggests. Since the general language of the Constitution can be interpreted in different ways, it will not necessarily be apparent to anyone that its meaning has changed. Those in favor of a policy that arguably violates the Constitution will of course argue that the policy is consistent with the document once it is understood properly. If the policy is favored by an overwhelming majority, the constitutional issue may not even be recognized and debated. Party politics and historical change thus pose serious difficulties for the idea of controlling government through a constitution.

These difficulties arise because American constitutionalism is based on a questionable analogy between the Constitution and ordinary law. The task of controlling government and, ultimately, national politics through a constitution is not the same as controlling individual behavior through ordinary laws. In the constitutional case, the stakes are much higher and the language and enforceability of the document are much less certain. American constitutionalism seeks to control democratic politics, something that is not easily controlled or influenced.

These informal remarks will be made more concrete in chapter 1. But it should be apparent that understanding American constitutionalism as a dynamic process involves asking some basic questions. How should constitutionalism be defined? How is it supposed to work? What led the founding generation to believe that the Constitution would function in the manner intended? Answering these questions will force us to connect the abstract concept of constitutionalism with the particular approach to politics prevalent in the founding era and enable us to construct a theory of constitutional change that will situate the Constitution in the continuous flow of American political development. This political and historical approach to the study of American constitutionalism and constitutional theory thus avoids the static recital of the thought of the founding generation followed by the jarring leap to the late twentieth-century United States that characterizes much of contemporary constitutional scholarship. Chapter 1 thus provides an introduction to American constitutionalism through a discussion of three topics: the idea of American constitutionalism, the doctrine of popular sovereignty, and the process of constitutional change.

Chapter 2 considers the relationship between the Constitution and political institutions by exploring Madison's theory of how the Constitution would control factious majorities, the Constitution and the concept of the state, and the relation of the Constitution to American political development. The discussion of this last topic serves to complete the theory of constitutional change offered in chapter 1.

Chapters 3 through 5 consider most of the issues that are normally thought to make up the core of contemporary constitutional theory. Chapter 3 discusses the role of the Supreme Court in American democracy by examining the establishment of judicial independence in the founding era, the role of judicial review in the modern state, and contemporary arguments concerning judicial review and American democracy.

Chapters 4 and 5 can be considered a single unit and are divided for purposes of convenience. They both discuss the theoretical issues raised by decisions of the Supreme Court in constitutional cases. Chapter 4 examines the institutional setting of the Court's decisionmaking process by focusing on the task American constitutionalism sets for the Court and the external theories of judicial decisionmaking favored by political scientists working in the behaviorist tradition. Chapter 5 is devoted to a lengthy discussion of theories of constitutional interpretation. I approach this intricate debate by first proposing a pluralistic theory of constitutional interpretation that is based on the account of American constitutionalism in chapter 1. I then review the contemporary debate between interpretivism-noninterpretivism and originalism-nonoriginalism, examine the relationship between democratic principles and theories of interpretation, explore the problem of history in constitutional interpretation, discuss the debate over interpreting the Fourteenth Amendment between proponents of the fundamental rights perspective and their originalist opponents, and examine republicanism as an example of a constitutional philosophy.

Chapter 6 considers the theoretical issues raised by periods of constitutional crisis such as Watergate, thus returning to the structural questions introduced in chapter 2. It also considers recent proposals for constitutional reform, including criticism of the separation of powers, and the proposed amendments for term limits and a balanced budget. Chapter 6 concludes with some reflections on the future of American constitutionalism.

Three themes run through much of this book. The first, and most important, is that there can be no genuine advance in many of the standard debates in constitutional theory without formulating an account of American constitutionalism—what it is and how it is supposed to work—and a theory of constitutional change. The second theme is a steady push, particularly in chapters 2 and 5, against constitutional perfectionism, the idea that the Constitution has come through American history unscathed or, at least, without significant flaws. The third theme is that we should add issues of constitutional structure and reform to the agenda of constitutional theory. As illustrated in chapters 2 and 6, the most pressing questions for contemporary American constitutionalism have to do with constitutional powers, representation, and legitimacy, rather than rights, adjudication, and doctrine.

One

American Constitutionalism

As WITH THE ERA of nation building that followed the end of World War II, the end of the Cold War saw a burst of constitution making worldwide. Eastern European countries such as Poland and the Czech Republic, the various states that formerly made up the Soviet Union, and South Africa all acquired new constitutions.[1] Constitutionalism is a strong and vital political practice that is not confined to the North Atlantic countries where its modern form originated in the eighteenth century.

As the country with the oldest single-document constitution, the United States can take justifiable pride in these developments, as they are inspired in part by the examples set by the adoption of state constitutions in the revolutionary era and the 1787 Constitution.[2] Yet when the United States celebrated the bicentennial of the Constitution in 1987, the festivities, while widespread, were marked by the awed self-congratulation and public indifference characteristic of earlier anniversaries.[3] The relationship of Americans to their most basic law has been ambivalent. The Declaration of Independence and the Gettysburg Address have more popular appeal than the lawyerly Constitution. Even the bicentennial of the Bill of Rights did not excite much popular involvement.

The Constitution is apparently revered, but it is not celebrated. It is at once part of American history and a timeless ideal, seemingly outside the flow of political events and social change. During the bicentennial, for example, constitutional scholar Walter Berns stated that "the remarkable thing about the Constitution is how little it has had to be changed or, for that matter, adapted."[4] In response, historian Gordon Wood observed that the Constitution, like other political institutions, was the product of

---

[1] For a review of developments in Eastern Europe, see A. E. Dick Howard, ed., *Constitution Making in Eastern Europe* (Washington, D.C.: The Woodrow Wilson Center Press, 1993).

[2] See Louis Henkin, "A New Birth of Constitutionalism: Genetic Influences and Genetic Defects," *Cardozo Law Review* 14 (1993): 536–37.

[3] See Michael Kammen, *A Machine That Would Go Of Itself: The Constitution in American Culture* (New York: Alfred A. Knopf, 1986), pp. 127–55, 282–312; Michael Kammen, *Mystic Chords of Memory: The Transformation of Tradition in American Culture* (New York: Alfred A. Knopf, 1991), p. 695.

[4] Walter Berns, *Taking the Constitution Seriously* (New York: Simon and Schuster, 1987), p. 238.

"incremental developments through time," and that "[t]he president's cabinet, the independent regulatory agencies, the structure and practices of political parties, the practice of judicial review, indeed most of the means by which we carry on our governmental business, are all unmentioned in the Constitution and are the products of historical experience."[5] More pointedly, the late Justice Thurgood Marshall argued that the Constitution devised by the Framers "was defective from the start, requiring several amendments, a civil war, and momentous social transformation to attain the [present] system of constitutional government."[6]

This bicentennial debate is significant because it raises perhaps the most crucial issue in American constitutional theory. What is the relationship between the present Constitution and the Constitution of 1787? As Wood and Marshall suggest, it is surely not just a matter of enumerating the amendments to the Constitution. If there is more to it, however, how do we account for constitutional change that appears to occur outside what lawyers call the "four corners" of the document? Since the bicentennial, constitutional scholars have become increasingly aware of the importance of developing a theory of constitutional change.[7]

In this chapter we will examine what might be called the large-scale structure of the American constitutional universe. Arriving at an understanding of constitutional change is the key to this inquiry. What are the chief elements of American constitutionalism and how has it changed over time? Are we still living with the same basic constitutional order established during the founding period or has it changed in fundamental ways? How should the Constitution be defined? What is the role of the Supreme Court in American constitutionalism and how does the Court fit into a theory of constitutional change? These are some of the main questions we will be considering in this chapter. The account of the structure of American constitutionalism and the theory of constitutional change offered in

---

[5] Gordon S. Wood, "The Fundamentalists and the Constitution," *New York Review of Books*, February 18, 1988, pp. 39–40.

[6] Thurgood Marshall, "Reflections on the Bicentennial of the United States Constitution," *Harvard Law Review* 101 (1987): 2. For commentary, see Sanford Levinson, *Constitutional Faith* (Princeton: Princeton University Press, 1988), pp. 180–91; Raymond T. Diamond, "No Call to Glory: Thurgood Marshall's Thesis on the Intent of a Pro-Slavery Constitution," *Vanderbilt Law Review* 42 (1989): 93.

[7] For a useful introduction to these issues, see Sanford Levinson, ed., *Responding to Imperfection: The Theory and Practice of Constitutional Amendment* (Princeton: Princeton University Press, 1995). See also Bruce Ackerman, *We the People: Foundations*, vol. 1 (Cambridge: Harvard University Press, 1991); John R. Vile, *Constitutional Change in the United States* (Westport, Conn.: Praeger, 1994); Morton J. Horwitz, "Foreword: The Constitution of Change: Legal Fundamentality Without Fundamentalism," *Harvard Law Review* 107 (1993): 32; Lawrence Lessig, "Understanding Changed Readings: Fidelity and Theory," *Stanford Law Review* 47 (1995): 395.

this chapter and the next form the basis for many of the discussions in subsequent chapters.

Accounts of American constitutionalism are often too static. There are many descriptions in the literature of the idea of constitutionalism in the eighteenth century, but far fewer descriptions of how American constitutionalism has changed over time. To set the static picture of American constitutionalism in motion, we must explore the relationship between the Constitution and the conception of politics held by those who framed and ratified the document. This is the primary purpose of the first section on the idea of American constitutionalism. The second section on the doctrine of popular sovereignty is not, strictly speaking, relevant to the theory of constitutional change, but this doctrine must be considered by any credible account of American constitutionalism. The third section sets out the theory of constitutional change, which is developed further and completed in chapter 2.

The Idea of American Constitutionalism

Article VI of the United States Constitution proclaims it to be "the supreme law of the land."[8] This signals the primary characteristics of American constitutionalism. It is based on a written document that is the fundamental law of the republic. These two characteristics are reinforcing—the Constitution of 1787 can be law because it is not based on oral tradition or a fragmentary written record. It was established all of a piece at a definite time and place.

Early definitions of "constitution" did not focus on this distinctive American idea that a constitution was a single fundamental law. A well-known eighteenth-century British definition was that "By constitution we mean . . . that assemblage of laws, institutions and customs, derived from certain fixed principles of reason, directed to certain fixed objects of public good, that compose the general system, according to which the community hath agreed to be governed."[9] In this definition, a constitution is not

[8] Here and elsewhere in the book when the Constitution is quoted, the capitalization in the engrossed copy has been modernized. For commentary on the differences between the engrossed copy that is on display at the National Archives and the printed copies used in ratifying the Constitution, see Akhil Reed Amar, "Our Forgotten Constitution: A Bicentennial Comment," *Yale Law Journal* 97 (1987): 281.

[9] This definition by Bolingbroke is quoted in Gerald Stourzh, "*Constitution*: Changing Meanings of the Term from the Early Seventeenth to the Late Eighteenth Century," in Terence Ball and J.G.A. Pocock, eds., *Conceptual Change and the Constitution* (Lawrence: University Press of Kansas, 1988), p. 43.

This definition is still in use. For one contemporary example, see Roger Scruton, "Safer unstated," *The Times Literary Supplement*, March 9–15, 1990, p. 252.

understood to be a single document, but a set of documents that relate to the system of government of a given community. Any law that relates to the general system of governance is part of the constitution.

By contrast, the American idea of a constitution, developed during the revolutionary period, was that of a single law that had a special status as a paramount or fundamental law. The crucial American move was not to reduce the fundamental law to written form—written laws that could be characterized as fundamental already existed in Great Britain. The crucial move was the development of a theory that would justify the supreme status of a constitution over other laws.[10]

Americans gradually established an original method of constitution making to justify the special status of a constitution during the revolutionary period. The first state constitutions and the Articles of Confederation were written and adopted by the assemblies and legislatures that happened to be sitting at the time. This method of constitution making was criticized on the ground that it did not distinguish the constitution from ordinary legislation because the same method of enactment was used in both cases. The American innovation of the constitutional convention developed to meet this criticism was based on what historian R. R. Palmer calls "the people as a constituent power."[11] A constitution had to be created in a special convention called for that purpose. The idea was that the entire people, through the mechanism of the convention and subsequent popular ratification, were the creators of the constitution. The constitutional convention was thus linked intimately with the doctrine that the people were the sole sovereign in American government.[12]

The adoption of the 1787 Constitution by the Federal Convention and its subsequent ratification by conventions in the thirteen original states exemplified this new method of constitution making. It is important to emphasize that the 1787 Constitution had no modern precedent.[13] No country had ever adopted a single-document constitution that had the status of supreme law. Americans had previous experience with colonial charters and state constitutions so they could reasonably believe that their attempt to frame the structure of government through a fundamental law might work. As noted, however, these charters and state constitutions were not adopted in the same way as the federal Constitution and were

---

[10] See Stourzh, "*Constitution*," in Ball and Pocock, eds., *Conceptual Change and the Constitution*, pp. 47–48.

[11] R. R. Palmer, *The Age of Democratic Revolution: The Challenge* (Princeton: Princeton University Press, 1959), p. 215.

[12] For general discussion, see ibid., pp. 213–35. See also Gordon S. Wood, *The Creation of the American Republic, 1776–1787* (New York: W. W. Norton, 1969), pp. 259–343.

[13] See Judith N. Shklar, "A New Constitution for a New Nation," in A. E. Dick Howard, ed., *The United States Constitution: Roots, Rights, and Responsibilities* (Washington, D.C.: Smithsonian Institution Press, 1992), p. 136.

not designed for the purpose of framing a union of disparate states. The Articles of Confederation were a better precedent for a federal constitution, but the Articles were not adopted by conventions and did not create an effective national government. It is worth asking, then, what led Americans to believe that the Constitution would work?

The basis for this belief was that although the Constitution would have the status of supreme or fundamental law, it would operate in the same manner as other laws. American constitutionalism is based on an analogy between a constitution and ordinary law. Just as it is desirable to restrain and empower individuals by subjecting them to the rule of law, so it is desirable to restrain and empower the state.[14] The idea of conducting government under law is the core of American constitutionalism. The Constitution and ordinary law are thought to be analogous because they are both written and enacted according to authoritative procedure. The eighteenth-century lawyers and men of affairs who wrote and ratified the Constitution presumably had a good grasp of how law could influence individual behavior. This experience, along with the experience acquired under state constitutions, led them to believe that the new federal government could be influenced in much the same manner.

There are significant points of disanalogy, however, between the Constitution and other laws. The Constitution is the framework for the entire government and, as such, provides the structure for national politics as a whole. Furthermore, through its provisions affecting the states and by virtue of its example, the Constitution has a profound influence on the framework for government provided by every state constitution.[15] Obviously no single ordinary law is comparable to the Constitution in these respects.

In addition, the Constitution is written in more general terms than most laws or common-law rules. The Constitution can be specific, as

[14] This definition of constitutionalism is inspired in part by H.L.A. Hart's argument that law can facilitate as well as limit conduct. See H.L.A. Hart, *The Concept of Law* (Oxford: Oxford University Press, 1961), pp. 26–33. For the point that constitutions are enabling devices, see Stephen Holmes, *Passions and Constraint: On the Theory of Liberal Democracy* (Chicago: University of Chicago Press, 1995), pp. 6–8, 101–2.

The idea of constitutionalism as limited government is, of course, widely accepted. See Carl J. Friedrich, *Constitutional Government and Democracy: Theory and Practice in Europe and America* (Waltham, Mass.: Blaisdell Publishing, 1950), p. 35; Charles Howard McIlwain, *Constitutionalism Ancient and Modern* (Ithaca: Cornell University Press, 1940), p. 24; Harvey Wheeler, "Constitutionalism," in Fred I. Greenstein and Nelson W. Polsby, eds., *Handbook of Political Science* (Reading, Mass.: Addison-Wesley, 1975), p. 36; Stephen L. Elkin, "Constitutionalism: Old and New," in Stephen L. Elkin and Karol Edward Soltan, eds., *A New Constitutionalism: Designing Political Institutions for a Good Society* (Chicago: University of Chicago Press, 1993), p. 21.

[15] For example, only Nebraska, with its unicameral legislature, deviates in a significant fashion from the three governmental branches established by the Constitution.

when it establishes the qualifications and manner of election for representatives and senators in Article I. As has been noted so many times, however, the Constitution uses general language both in granting and in limiting the power of government. The Congress is given the power to "provide for the common defence and general welfare of the United States," "to regulate commerce . . . among the several states," and "to make all laws which shall be necessary and proper for carrying into execution the foregoing powers."[16] The grant of power to the President is less specific. The President is vested with "the executive power."[17] Article IV provides that "the citizens of each state shall be entitled to all privileges and immunities of citizens in the several states" and "the United States shall guarantee to every state in this Union a republican form of government."[18] This short list does not begin the exhaust all of the provisions of the 1787 Constitution that have been the subject of controversy from the beginning of President George Washington's first administration in 1789.[19]

Finally, a crucial difference between the Constitution and other laws is that the Constitution cannot be enforced in the same way other laws can.[20] When an individual violates a law, the government stands ready to enforce the law and remedy the violation. There is no parallel to this situation in the constitutional sphere. There is no agency external to the federal government that stands ready to enforce the Constitution when a branch of that government violates the Constitution. We may immediately think of judicial enforcement of the Constitution, but this response misses the point. Just as it is possible for any individual to violate the law, it is possible for any branch of government (including the judiciary) to violate the Constitution. The difference is that although the government stands ready to enforce the law against any individual, there is no government agency with a similar power to enforce the Constitution. The checks and balances the Constitution provides are no remedy when all branches are in violation of the Constitution. The Constitution does not have a police force.

These three points of disanalogy raise serious problems for the idea that the Constitution can serve as a fundamental law. Since the Constitution structures the political universe, it will be subject to pressure as various

---

[16] U.S. Const., Article I, section 8.

[17] U.S. Const., Article II, section 1.

[18] U.S. Const., Article IV, sections 2, 4.

[19] Many of the provisions of the Bill of Rights, of course, are equally general if not more so. Our purpose here is to illustrate how the problem of using general language influences even the framework of government provided by the 1787 Constitution.

[20] This point is clearly recognized and discussed in Sylvia Snowiss, *Judicial Review and the Law of the Constitution* (New Haven: Yale University Press, 1990), pp. 5–6, 198–99.

political actors seek to use it to their advantage. These political conflicts and the general language of the Constitution guarantee controversy and uncertainty over the meaning of its provisions. The lack of sure enforcement means violations of the Constitution may go unaddressed, unacknowledged, or even unnoticed. In short, these points of disanalogy between the Constitution and ordinary law give political actors the motive, means, and opportunity to render the Constitution ineffective as a fundamental law.

Fortunately, all of these problems can be mitigated if a certain kind of politics prevails. If political actors treat the Constitution in a noninstrumental fashion as a guide to political action, then the Constitution can structure national politics. If substantial agreement exists on what the Constitution means, its general language will structure political controversy rather than become a part of it. If all the branches of government agree that one branch should have the final say in questions of constitutional interpretation, then enforcement of the Constitution is possible.

The viability of the Constitution was thus dependent on a particular kind of politics. It is important, therefore, to consider the state of politics when the Constitution was adopted. At the time, American politics was in transition from an older hierarchical model of politics to a more democratic model.[21] The Framers of the Constitution aspired to the older model while recognizing the new democratic tendencies accelerated by the American Revolution. The Constitution was not designed to halt this process but to control it.[22]

Nevertheless, the Framers expected that the kind of politics they were familiar with would continue, at least on the national level. That politics was based on personal contacts among public-spirited white men of similar education, wealth, and circumstance. As issues presented themselves for resolution, this virtuous elite would, after judicious deliberation, reach a consensus on a course of action. This was not a politics of political parties, well-organized interests, universal white male suffrage, or in which men of limited education and means could serve as representatives. Yet this was precisely the direction in which American politics moved during the first several decades of the republic.[23]

---

[21] For general discussion, see Stanley Elkins and Eric McKitrick, *The Age of Federalism* (New York: Oxford University Press, 1993); Richard Hofstadter, *The Idea of a Party System: The Rise of Legitimate Opposition in the United States, 1780–1840* (Berkeley: University of California Press, 1969); Gordon S. Wood, *The Radicalism of the American Revolution* (New York: Alfred A. Knopf, 1992).

[22] See Wood, *The Radicalism of the American Revolution*, pp. 95–124, 230.

[23] Ibid., pp. 243–70, 287–305. See also Edmund S. Morgan, *Inventing the People: The Rise of Popular Sovereignty in England and America* (New York: W. W. Norton, 1988), pp. 291–92, 304–6.

There is a close relationship between the idea of American constitutionalism and this Federalist conception of politics. The Federalist conception of politics made it easy to overlook the differences between the project of restraining and empowering individuals by law and restraining and empowering the state through the Constitution. Surely the elite that was responsible for writing the Constitution would treat it as a guide to political action. Surely they would agree on the meaning of its provisions or work out disagreements amicably when problems of interpretation arose. There is less evidence that the Framers came to grips with the problem of interpretive disagreement among the branches of the federal government. But with President Washington at the helm and men of good will in the other branches, surely such disagreements would not be serious.

Of course, this serene vision did not come to pass. There was disagreement over what the Constitution meant almost from the beginning of the national government and there was no apparent way to resolve the disputes that would preserve an interpretive consensus. The most serious early constitutional quarrel arose when Alexander Hamilton made his proposal to establish a national bank in 1790. In opposing this proposal, James Madison set forth the theory of strict construction of the Constitution in arguing that Congress did not have the power to establish a bank.[24] More important, the kind of politics that Federalists were familiar with was rapidly disappearing as party-political disagreements became increasingly common in the 1790s. If these disagreements were not checked in some fashion, there would be no clear distinction between the law of the Constitution and the politics the Constitution was meant to control.

Several constitutional developments that began in the 1790s can be understood as the response of the founding generation to their new political circumstances. Somehow a sharp boundary had to be established between the Constitution and politics. Here the example set by ordinary law was extremely suggestive. Although the Constitution was a special kind of law, it could be understood through the methods used to construe ordinary laws. The answer the founding generation hit on was to define the difference between the Constitution and politics as the difference between law and politics.[25] This answer appears to simply restate the original idea of constitutionalism of controlling politics through a fundamental law. The critical move was to make this theoretical distinction operational and effective by narrowing the scope of the law derived from the Constitution, that is, constitutional law.

[24] See Elkins and McKitrick, *Age of Federalism*, pp. 223–34.

[25] For general discussion, see Morton J. Horwitz, *The Transformation of American Law 1870–1960* (New York: Oxford University Press, 1992), p. 193; Jennifer Nedelsky, *Private Property and the Limits of American Constitutionalism* (Chicago: University of Chicago Press, 1990), pp. 187–99.

The scope of constitutional law was narrowed by denying, in effect, that significant differences existed between the Constitution and ordinary law. Since significant differences did not exist, the judiciary, the branch of government with the greatest legal expertise, had the special responsibility of interpreting the Constitution. Lawyers of the founding generation argued that the Constitution should be interpreted according to the principles used to construe other legal documents. They placed the Constitution within the framework of the common law, perhaps the most important kind of law in America at this time.[26] The Federalist conception of politics, a conception that emphasized the importance of a guiding virtuous elite, was now seen as applicable only to the judiciary.[27] Since political actors would inevitably treat the Constitution instrumentally, the only source of constitutional meaning that was independent of politics was the impartial judiciary. The judiciary was, however, the weakest branch of the federal government. One price of a legalized and judicially enforceable Constitution was a narrowed scope for constitutional values. In addition, the differences between the Constitution and ordinary law ensured that the goal of legalizing the Constitution could never be achieved fully. There would always be important differences between the constitutional law created by the judiciary and other kinds of law.

Thus, the Constitution was legalized. It was made enforceable in ordinary courts of law and interpreted as any other legal document.[28] This legalization appeared to be consistent with the original idea of constitutionalism because it emphasized the importance of the Constitution as law. But this legalization was not without costs. The legalization of the Constitution was based on denying the importance of the differences between the Constitution and ordinary law. Since the differences still existed, the legalization of the Constitution warped the original idea of constitutionalism. The judiciary was apparently committed to enforcing the entire Constitution, but it became clear that not all constitutional provisions could be reduced to cognizable legal principles. The scope of the Constitution was restricted as the judiciary bypassed constitutional disputes that resisted resolution through the means appropriate to ordi-

---

[26] For discussions of the developments in the 1790s and after, see William E. Nelson, "The Eighteenth-Century Background of John Marshall's Constitutional Jurisprudence," *Michigan Law Review* 76 (1978): 893; H. Jefferson Powell, "The Political Grammar of Early Constitutional Law," *North Carolina Law Review* 71 (1993): 949; H. Jefferson Powell, "The Principles of '98: An Essay in Historical Retrieval," *Virginia Law Review* 80 (1994): 689.

[27] This point is detailed in Wood, *Radicalism of the American Revolution*, pp. 322–25.

[28] See Gordon S. Wood, "Judicial Review in the Era of the Founding," in Robert A. Licht, ed., *Is the Supreme Court the Guardian of the Constitution?* (Washington, D.C.: AEI Press, 1993), pp. 163–66.

nary law.[29] In addition, since constitutional disputes were seen first and foremost as legal disputes, constitutional law became a form of expert knowledge that required legal training. This tended to exclude the public from the development of constitutional meaning, reducing the democratic potential of the Constitution. Finally, by giving the judiciary the special duty to interpret the Constitution, the legalization of the Constitution encouraged a profoundly misleading distinction between formal or legal constitutional change through amendment or Supreme Court precedent and informal or political change.

American constitutionalism is thus best understood as an instance of the interpenetration of law and politics.[30] The attempt to evade the differences between the Constitution and ordinary law introduced significant tensions into American constitutionalism that persist to this day. Many of the subsequent discussions in this book will illustrate these tensions. The legalization of the Constitution is at once a significant source of the strength of American constitutionalism and a significant source of its weakness. Legalizing the Constitution made it enforceable, but also made large areas of the constitutional order subject to ordinary political change. The line between politics and the legalized Constitution is under constant stress as lawyers and judges seek to preserve and extend the legalized Constitution and resist the pressures toward informal change generated by American politics. Both aspects of American constitutionalism must always be kept in view if we are to understand it properly.

This highly schematic account of American constitutionalism will be developed further in this chapter and the next. The discussion of constitutional change in this chapter will describe the narrowed scope of constitutional law provided by the legalized Constitution. The description of the interaction between the Constitution and American political development in chapter 2 will illustrate the impact of ordinary political change on the Constitution.

The idea of American constitutionalism as a unique mixture of law and politics will structure the treatment of a number of topics in this book. The debate over the democratic legitimacy of judicial review discussed in chapter 3 will show that it has been influenced by whether the participants describe constitutional decisions as predominantly legal or political. The account of constitutional adjudication advanced in chapter 4 will rely on this idea of American constitutionalism to establish the terrain in which the Supreme Court must operate. Chapter 5 will show how the legalized

[29] The "political question" doctrine is a good example. For discussion, see Laurence H. Tribe, *American Constitutional Law*, 2d ed. (Mineola, N.Y.: Foundation Press, 1988), pp. 96–107.

[30] See Stuart A. Scheingold, *The Politics of Rights* (New Haven: Yale University Press, 1974), p. 16.

Constitution led to a pluralistic theory of constitutional interpretation. These different discussions will all illustrate that American constitutional theory is best conceived as the study of American constitutionalism as a distinctive political practice.

The Sovereignty of the People

The sovereignty of the people is a key element of American constitutionalism. The Constitution begins with the words "We The People," signifying that it is the American people as a whole who "ordain and establish this Constitution for the United States of America."[31] As we have seen, the ratification of the Constitution through constitutional conventions enabled the founding generation to implement the abstract idea that only the people could adopt a fundamental law. Yet the doctrine of popular sovereignty has never had an entirely clear meaning in the American constitutional tradition.[32] Despite the presumed exclusiveness of the people's sovereignty, the federal government, state governments, and other self-governing groups such as Indian tribes also claim that they are sovereign, at least for certain purposes. In fact, their claims of sovereignty are more than that; they have been legally recognized. In various cases, the Supreme Court has held that all of these entities are sovereigns.[33]

How can this be the case? The dispute over the nature of sovereignty was the most basic issue that divided American colonists from their British rulers. Most colonists accepted the idea, conventional in the political theory of the time, that there must be a supreme, indivisible, final, and absolute power in every government. The British asserted that the sovereign in the empire was the king-in-Parliament and that this sovereign ruled America as well as Britain. The American response was to deny the king and Parliament full sovereignty over colonial matters. The logic of sovereignty eventually pushed Americans to realize that there was no halfway house between British rule and rule by the American people.[34]

After the decision for independence, the question arose as to whether the Continental Congress or the new state governments would assume

[31] U.S. Const., preamble.

[32] For general discussion, see Powell, "The Political Grammar of Early Constitutional Law," pp. 985–87.

[33] On the continued existence of state sovereignty and the sovereignty of the national government, see Akhil Reed Amar, "Of Sovereignty and Federalism," *Yale Law Journal* 96 (1987): 1425–26. For discussion of cases concerning the limited but real sovereignty of Indian tribes, see Tribe, *American Constitutional Law*, pp. 1468–74.

[34] See Samuel H. Beer, *To Make a Nation: The Rediscovery of American Federalism* (Cambridge: Harvard University Press, 1993), pp. 146–53, 163–94; Wood, *Creation of the American Republic*, pp. 344–54.

the mantle of sovereignty. One answer was that each state government was now sovereign in the full sense. On this understanding, the Articles of Confederation merely established a league of states, and the Continental Congress was an assemblage of ambassadors. Another answer was that the sovereign people had invested authority in the Continental Congress, which then authorized the former colonies to create new state governments. There were practical problems with both answers. The states could not in fact act as sovereigns in the full sense because they could do very little by themselves. For example, they could only deal with foreign states through the Continental Congress. For its part, the Continental Congress could only act if the states cooperated.[35]

In the debate over ratification of the Constitution, the Federalists gave new emphasis to the idea of popular sovereignty. Neither state governments or the new federal government were to be sovereign. Instead, the American people as a whole was the true sovereign, parceling out authority to the different levels and branches of government.[36] Since its clear articulation by the Federalists in the ratification struggle, the doctrine of popular sovereignty has been an unquestioned building block of the American constitutional order. Nevertheless, a serious reexamination of the doctrine is long overdue.[37] While the idea of government by the people is obviously crucial to American constitutionalism, the question we ask here is whether the concept of sovereignty and thus the doctrine of popular sovereignty add anything useful or important.

We should start by asking whether the concept of sovereignty makes sense in American circumstances. It is somewhat puzzling that the American revolutionaries, fired by republican ideals, were concerned with the concept of a sovereign. As Judith Shklar remarks, "sovereignty has scarcely any meaning at all apart from absolute monarchy."[38] Of course,

---

[35] For discussion of these complications, see Beer, *To Make a Nation*, pp. 137, 196–202; Jack P. Greene, *Peripheries and Center: Constitutional Development in the Extended Polities of the British Empire and the United States, 1607–1788* (New York: W. W. Norton, 1986), pp. 178–80; Morgan, *Inventing the People*, pp. 263–65; Jack N. Rakove, *The Beginnings of National Politics: An Interpretive History of the Continental Congress* (Baltimore, Md.: Johns Hopkins University Press, 1979), pp. 163–91.

[36] See Elkins and McKitrick, *Age of Federalism*, pp. 11–13; Wood, *Creation of the American Republic*, pp. 596–600.

[37] A common distinction made in discussions of the concept of sovereignty is that between internal and external sovereignty. Internal sovereignty is the kind we are concerned with here, that is, the sovereignty that obtains within the territory of a given state. External sovereignty refers to the relationships between sovereign states. The discussion that follows does not apply to external sovereignty. For this distinction, see Charles R. Beitz, "Sovereignty and Morality in International Affairs," in David Held, ed., *Political Theory Today* (Stanford: Stanford University Press, 1991), p. 236.

[38] Judith N. Shklar, *Men and Citizens: A Study of Rousseau's Social Theory* (Cambridge: Cambridge University Press, 1985), p. 168.

Americans in the latter half of the eighteenth century may not have had a choice in the matter. The concept of sovereignty was part of their mental furniture and they felt compelled to respond to British assertions that the king and Parliament were sovereign. Yet this commonsense observation suggests just how much Americans were used to being part of a monarchical government.

The problem posed by the persistence of the concept of sovereignty was that although the founding generation was accustomed to being part of a government that included a monarch, they were, after all, republicans. They believed that the people should rule, however indirectly, and most of them rejected the idea of establishing a new monarchy in America. But the concept of sovereignty was retained. The founding generation disagreed about the nature and location of sovereignty, but not over whether the concept was relevant to their new political circumstances.

As we have noted, the Federalists insisted that the people as a whole were sovereign, and this argument apparently prevailed in the ratification debates. Yet the acceptance of the Federalist position did not stop a growing debate over how the Union was formed and whether the states or the federal government were sovereign.[39] Since this dispute was arguably the basis of the Civil War, it is one of the most important constitutional questions in American history. The debate over whether, as President Ronald Reagan asserted, "'the states created the Federal government,'"[40] or whether the federal government created the states continues to this day.[41] The puzzle is why the debate began at all if everyone already agreed on the doctrine of popular sovereignty. If the people were the ultimate sovereign, then neither the states or the federal government could claim ultimate sovereign power for themselves. If Americans believed in the sovereignty of the people, why did the Civil War occur?

To make sense of this situation, we must probe deeper into the concept

[39] See Greene, *Peripheries and Center*, pp. 212–17.

[40] Quoted in Beer, *To Make a Nation*, p. 2.

[41] For recent presentations of the nationalist viewpoint that the American people, acting through the Continental Congress, created the states, see generally Beer, *To Make a Nation*; Richard B. Morris, *The Forging of the Union 1781–1789* (New York: Harper and Row, 1987); Rakove, *The Beginnings of National Politics*. For continuing doubts about the strength of the nationalist position, see Herman Belz, "The South and the American Constitutional Tradition at the Bicentennial," in Kermit L. Hall and James W. Ely, eds., *An Uncertain Tradition: Constitutionalism and the History of the South* (Athens: University of Georgia Press, 1989), p. 24; Greene, *Peripheries and Center*, pp. 178–80.

See also the discussion in *U.S. Term Limits v. Thornton*, 115 S. Ct. 1842 (1995) invalidating state-imposed term limits on members of Congress). In 1994, Colorado was one of a number of states that passed resolutions stating that "[t]he scope of power defined by the 10th Amendment means that the federal government was created by the states specifically to be an agent of the states." Quoted in Dirk Johnson, "'Conspiracy Theories' Impact Reverberates in Legislatures," *New York Times*, July 6, 1995, p. A10.

of sovereignty. Why is this concept important? The eighteenth-century British doctrine of sovereignty tells us that when we locate the sovereign, we locate the supreme, indivisible, and unlimited source of power in a state. This tells us something useful about that state. It gives us the location of state power, of the monopoly on coercion that is thought to be a necessary characteristic of a state.[42] British ideas about sovereignty developed in the context of a seventeenth-century civil war and the doctrine that sovereignty lies in the king-in-Parliament, suitably elaborated, tells us something significant about the outcome of that struggle.[43]

The problem this poses for eighteenth-century American debates about sovereignty is that the political context in which the British doctrine emerged is lacking. At the time the Constitution was ratified, Americans had recently finished fighting a revolutionary war to establish a republic, not a constitutional monarchy. In addition, winning the war did not require building a strong, centralized state. The Continental Congress, Continental Army, and the separate state governments won the war with only a limited amount of ceding of authority.

This different political context produced a different concept of sovereignty. Americans did not see the point of placing sovereignty in a law-making body or in the government generally. As republicans, it seemed natural to conclude that the people were sovereign. Arguably, however, the most consistent response to the absence of the circumstances that produced the British doctrine of sovereignty would have been to abandon the concept altogether.[44] Of course, this did not occur. The concept of sovereignty is still used and there is an apparent consensus on the doctrine of popular sovereignty. Yet, as we have noted, this doctrine, apparently agreed to by all, has not forestalled a continuing debate over the location of sovereignty. What has gone wrong?

To appreciate the underlying issue, we should focus on the concept of political authority.[45] The British doctrine of parliamentary sovereignty at least focuses our attention on the location of political authority in a state, an approach that addresses the basis of subsequent American disputes over the location of sovereignty in the states or federal government. Of course, the British doctrine does not apply in the American context. But the British do seem to focus on the right issue. Suppose a constitution does not resolve the issue of what governmental body shall have supreme political authority. It is reasonable to expect that a struggle for power will

---

[42] See Wood, *Creation of the American Republic*, p. 382.

[43] See Greene, *Peripheries and Center*, pp. 56–57.

[44] A few contributors to the debates of the time suggested abandoning the concept. See Greene, *Peripheries and Center*, pp. 137–38.

[45] See Beitz, "Sovereignty and Morality in International Affairs," in Held, ed., *Political Theory Today*, p. 238.

ensue until there is a resolution that all can accept, whether it occurs through force of arms or otherwise. In such a situation, the location of supreme political authority is uncertain and the political order is likely to be unstable.[46]

This description fits the circumstances of the United States before the Civil War. There was a continuing argument about the location of sovereignty because the Constitution had not resolved the question of whether the states or the federal government should have supreme political authority.[47] The Supremacy Clause of Article VI was set against the Tenth Amendment and the doctrine of state sovereignty. The Virginia and Kentucky Resolutions of 1798, authored by James Madison and Thomas Jefferson, respectively, argued that the Union was a compact of separate states and this theory was opposed by nationalists such as Justice Joseph Story.[48] As historian Kenneth Stampp notes, "The language of state sovereignty had become deeply embedded in the American vocabulary. . . . The term 'sovereign' was associated with the states far more than with the federal government."[49] Americans seemed caught in a never-ending argument as to the nature of the Union.

Arguably, however, the Federalists had provided a coherent doctrine of sovereignty that could settle this argument. Reflecting a widespread understanding, Justice Anthony Kennedy recently stated that "[t]he Framers split the atom of sovereignty. It was the genius of their idea that our citizens would have two political capacities, one state and one federal, each protected from incursion by the other."[50] The basic idea here is clear enough in *The Federalist*. Madison argued that the republican form of government embodied in the Constitution derived "all its powers directly or indirectly from the great body of the people,"[51] and that the people had granted a limited set of powers to the new federal government, reserving the balance of sovereign power to the states.[52] This implicitly entailed abandoning the idea that sovereignty was indivisible. The Framers thus

---

[46] See the discussion of Jean Bodin's theory of sovereign power in Holmes, *Passions and Constraint*, pp. 103–4.

[47] See Greene, *Peripheries and Center*, pp. 212–17.

[48] On the ambiguity of the Constitution and the role of the Virginia and Kentucky Resolutions in developing states' rights views, see Richard E. Ellis, *The Union at Risk: Jacksonian Democracy, States' Rights, and the Nullification Crisis* (New York: Oxford University Press, 1987), pp. 4–5. On Story's nationalist views, see Beer, *To Make a Nation*, pp. 325–28.

[49] Kenneth M. Stampp, "The Concept of a Perpetual Union," *Journal of American History* 65 (1978): 28.

[50] *U.S. Term Limits*, 115 S. Ct. at 1872.

[51] James Madison, The Federalist No. 39, in Jacob E. Cooke, ed., *The Federalist* (Middletown, Conn.: Wesleyan University Press, 1961), p. 251.

[52] See Madison, The Federalist Nos. 39–40, 45–46, 51, in Cooke, ed., pp. 250–67, 308–23, 347–53.

created a new form of government, which Madison described as a "compound republic," in which "the power surrendered by the people, is first divided between two distinct governments, and then the portion allotted to each, subdivided among distinct and separate departments."[53]

On this Madisonian understanding, sovereignty lies with the people, who then delegated power to the federal and state governments. The problem here is that Madison's carefully balanced theory did not survive the sectional stresses that led eventually to the Civil War.[54] Historian Jack Greene notes that in "the early decades of the republic . . . the notion of coordinate sovereignty in which the balance of authority lay with the states rapidly came to predominate over the concept of popular sovereignty."[55] By the nullification crisis of 1832–33, Madison could barely get anyone to comprehend his original theory of divided sovereignty based on the people.[56] The dissolution of the Madisonian understanding suggests that the idea of a delegation of power from the people is ultimately an abstraction unless it is actually the case that the people can step in to resolve conflicts between the different levels of government.

The doctrine of popular sovereignty could not resolve the arguments over nullification, secession, and states rights because there was no practical way to implement the doctrine. There was no institution the people as a whole could use to settle disputes between the federal and state governments. The constitutional convention provided a way to operationalize popular sovereignty in creating the Constitution, but there was no way to use the convention as a continuous means of settling disputes. This suggests that when a claim of sovereignty is made, the validity of the claim should be judged on whether the individual, group, or institution in question actually wields political authority.

The difficulty with the course of the debate over the concept of sovereignty during the founding era is that Americans simply substituted the people for the British parliament as their sovereign without significant reflection on the question of political authority.[57] There were good reasons for Americans to think they could make popular sovereignty work. They invented the constitutional convention as a way to distinguish between fundamental and ordinary law. Once the Constitution was ratified and the government began operating, however, the power of popular sovereignty as an order-creating doctrine necessarily began receding into the

---

[53] Madison, The Federalist No. 51, in Cooke, ed., p. 351.

[54] See also the discussion in chapter 2, section three.

[55] Greene, *Peripheries and Center*, p. 213.

[56] See the very useful discussion in Drew R. McCoy, *The Last of the Fathers: James Madison and the Republican Legacy* (New York: Cambridge University Press, 1989), pp. 119–62.

[57] For relevant commentary on this point, see Samuel P. Huntington, *Political Order in Changing Societies* (New Haven: Yale University Press, 1968), p. 7.

background. The task now was not to create a fundamental law but to provide the authority to govern. Popular sovereignty and constitutional conventions had no role here.

We are now in a position to offer a test for validating claims of sovereignty. Validating claims of sovereignty is a matter of discovering whether the asserted location of sovereignty matches a concrete set of institutions that exercise political authority. The assertion that the king is sovereign is true if and only if there is a monarch that effectively wields political authority. This provides a way to assess the validity of the doctrine of popular sovereignty. The assertion that sovereignty lies with the people is valid if the people actually rule, that is, if a direct democracy exists with appropriate institutions. This has never been true in the United States. At best, the U.S. has a representative democracy. By this test, sovereignty in the U.S. lies with the national government, although the question is complicated by the federal structure of government.

This test for validating claims of sovereignty tells us something important about the doctrine of popular sovereignty and American political thought. It was common in the revolutionary era for Americans to reject the need for representative institutions properly understood. Some Americans either wanted to rule directly or to arrange representative institutions so that they would be immediately responsive to popular will, through means such as annual elections and giving specific instructions to representatives.[58] This did not work very well and is not a feasible means to order the institutions of a large republic. Yet the rejection of this populist mode of republicanism in the Constitution did not lead to the rejection of popular sovereignty. Indeed, the Constitution was sold on the basis that all of the authority of the new government flowed from the people.[59] The persuasive appeal of the doctrine of popular sovereignty tells us that for most Americans, representative government is always a second-best way to run a democracy. The doctrine expresses a revolutionary (now reactionary) impulse in favor of direct democracy founded on consensus and against the institutions of the modern democratic state.[60]

The wish for direct democracy, however, does not translate into an effective solution for the problem of political authority. The doctrine of popular sovereignty could not solve the very real problems of political authority inherent in the Constitution, problems that led to the Civil War. Popular sovereignty helps Americans to avoid important practical ques-

---

[58] See Morgan, *Inventing the People*, pp. 210–11, 257–58; Wood, *Creation of the American Republic*, pp. 363–89.

[59] See Wood, *Creation of the American Republic*, pp. 532–36.

[60] For an insightful presentation of this theme, see James A. Morone, *The Democratic Wish: Popular Participation and the Limits of American Government* (New York: Basic Books, 1990).

tions of political authority, questions that became more urgent in the twentieth century as the federal government was forced to take on greater responsibilities.[61]

When we assess the usefulness of the concept of sovereignty, we should keep in mind that this concept originated in a nondemocratic system of government and when the principles and institutions of twentieth-century democracy did not exist. It is highly questionable whether this concept is relevant in analyzing our contemporary democracy. Sovereignty is the right to rule and democracy undermines the very idea of "rule" by dissolving the permanent difference between rulers and ruled that characterized aristocratic and oligarchic regimes.

Political authority in the United States is diffused and the doctrine of popular sovereignty does not help us understand the constitutional system that ensures this diffusion. The doctrine should be abandoned in favor of the concept of political authority. When we seek the location of political authority in America in a practical sense, a plausible answer is that authority lies in a complex governmental system in which the people participate. There is no one locus for political authority. Saying that all political authority lies in the people, however, is clearly inaccurate. Popular sovereignty points toward an ideal of direct democracy that has never existed in the United States and avoids crucial issues of state authority.

Some scholars nonetheless contend that the doctrine of popular sovereignty is a useful fiction.[62] It is true that there can be no objection if the doctrine is used simply as a synonym for democratic government. As we shall see in subsequent chapters, however, the doctrine has had a deleterious influence on American constitutional theory. It has served as an intellectual crutch, a substitute for a robust understanding of contemporary American democracy. It enables constitutional scholars, especially those in law schools, to ignore important questions about the principles and evolution of American democracy.[63] Appeals to the doctrine are routine in the debate over the legitimacy of judicial review, a debate we will review in chapter 3. The doctrine is also important in the debate over theories of constitutional interpretation, as we shall see in chapter 5.

The Problem of Constitutional Change

As we saw in the introduction to this chapter, constitutional change poses a puzzle for constitutional scholars and jurists. Evaluating the relationship of the present Constitution to the Constitution of 1787 evokes widely

---

[61] See the discussion in chapter 2.

[62] See Holmes, *Passions and Constraint*, p. 9; Morgan, *Inventing the People*.

[63] We will take up these questions in the second section of chapter 3.

varying responses. The apparent permanence of the Constitution and the institutions it established suggests to scholars like Berns that it has changed very little in two centuries.[64] But the significance of particular amendments (notably the Fourteenth Amendment) and the obvious importance of Supreme Court decisions to any proper understanding of what the Constitution means encourage the notion of a living Constitution, one that has adapted successfully to changing historical conditions.[65] Recently, constitutional scholars have become interested in developing theories of constitutional change that revolve around Article V and the distinction between providing an interpretation of the Constitution and changing it through amendment.[66] On this understanding, while the Constitution has no doubt adapted to change in part through judicial interpretation, some changes not reflected in the text and some Supreme Court decisions are so significant that they count as additional amendments to the document.

Our discussion of constitutional change will challenge all of these received positions in varying degrees. The problem of constitutional change is indeed the key to understanding the large-scale structure of American constitutionalism. How has constitutional change occurred? How has the Constitution been affected by the political, social, economic, and cultural changes since its adoption? What is the role of the Supreme Court in constitutional change? How do we define the Constitution? The discussion below is divided into sections providing an overview of the problem of constitutional change, exploring constitutional change in the light of the experience of the states and the New Deal, examining an important recent theory of constitutional change, discussing the question of how to define the Constitution, and exploring the implications of the problem of constitutional change for our understanding of American constitutionalism.

The most important points made in the following discussion can be stated briefly. First, the Constitution has changed since its adoption in ways not fully captured by amendments made under Article V or judicial interpretations of the text. These changes, however, should not be thought of as *legal* changes, changes that have the same legal status as amendments made under Article V. Nor are they best understood as extraconstitutional changes, as if there were a clear dividing line between constitutional and extraconstitutional change. As we noted in the first

[64] For another example of this view, see Jeffrey K. Tulis, *The Rhetorical Presidency* (Princeton: Princeton University Press, 1987), pp. 6–9.

[65] See, e.g., Lawrence G. Sager, "The Incorrigible Constitution," *New York University Law Review* 65 (1990): 895–97.

[66] See, e.g., Sanford Levinson, "How Many Times Has the United States Constitution Been Amended?" in Levinson, ed., *Responding to Imperfection*, p. 13. See also Ackerman, *We the People: Foundations*, which is critiqued below.

section to this chapter, the impulse to draw such distinctions is a consequence of the legalization of the Constitution. The lack of any sure institutional mechanism to control the flow of federal constitutional change means that any such distinction dissolves under the pressures of ordinary politics.

Second, the preceding point can be overlooked because the pace of federal constitutional change has varied sharply in different historical periods. The most important factor in determining the pace of constitutional change has been the relative activism of the federal government. The most rapid period of constitutional change thus did not occur until the twentieth century and most of the change in this period occurred outside Article V. Interestingly, the experience of constitutional change in the states is very helpful in understanding twentieth-century federal constitutional change. Unfortunately, this experience has been neglected by constitutional theorists. President Franklin Roosevelt's decision not to ask for constitutional amendments during the New Deal is also crucial in this regard.

Third, the Supreme Court has not and cannot serve as the main gatekeeper of federal constitutional change. The most significant source of constitutional change in the twentieth century has not been amendments under Article V or Court decisions, but changes initiated and carried out by the President and Congress. The Court's limited role in supervising the flow of constitutional change is dictated by its limited role in supervising the twentieth-century activist state.

Fourth, how we define the Constitution and the set of constitutional norms depends on our conceptions of constitutional change and American constitutionalism. The ordinary definition of the Constitution used by lawyers and judges serves well enough for the legalized Constitution. Once we move beyond the legalized Constitution, however, the ordinary definition is unsuited to describing the consequences of constitutional change. Here the idea of the Constitution as a text-based institutional practice works well enough. Finally, it should be kept in mind that the theory of constitutional change presented below will not be complete until the end of chapter 2.

An Overview of the Problem of Constitutional Change

The question of how to provide for change poses difficult choices for those who create a constitution. If the constitution makes change too easy, there is a risk that the constitution will not structure politics, but will be hostage to it. But making change too difficult may cause political instability, may cause the constitution to be ignored, or force change to occur outside the procedure for amendment.[67] The procedure for change that the Framers provided in Article V has operated historically to guard against the former danger much more than the latter. Amendments can be made when two-thirds of both houses of Congress agree and legislatures or conventions in three-fourths of the states concur, or when two-thirds of the legislatures of the states call for a convention to propose amendments and three-fourths of the legislatures or conventions in the states agree to the proposed amendments.[68] Since there has never been a constitutional convention called under Article V, all twenty-six (or twenty-seven depending on the validity of the Twenty-seventh Amendment) amendments to the Constitution have been adopted through the former procedure.[69]

Since the first ten amendments to the Constitution, commonly called the Bill of Rights, were ratified only three years after the Constitution itself, it seems evident that they were part of the same historical process and so are not useful as evidence as to the difficulty of change under Article V. Once these amendments are excluded, the infrequency of change through Article V is apparent. Since 1791, the Constitution has been amended only sixteen (or seventeen) times. The provisions of Article V have undoubtedly played a role in causing this low rate of amendment. Article V requires a supermajority in both houses of Congress before an amendment can be sent to the states. A further supermajority of state legislatures is then required for the amendment to become part of the Constitution. This second round of approval seems especially daunting. By requiring the concurrence of both national and state legislatures, Article V comes close to requiring unanimity to approve any amendment as a practical matter.[70]

In *The Federalist* No. 49, James Madison presented a revealing argument against making constitutional change too easy.[71] Madison argued

[67] See, e.g., Stephen Holmes and Cass R. Sunstein, "The Politics of Constitutional Revision in Eastern Europe," in Levinson, ed., *Responding to Imperfection*, p. 275.

[68] U.S. Const., Article V.

[69] For discussion of the problems surrounding adoption of the Twenty-seventh Amendment, see Sanford Levinson, "Authorizing Constitutional Text: On the Purported Twenty-Seventh Amendment," *Constitutional Commentary* 11 (1994): 101; Michael Stokes Paulsen, "A General Theory of Article V: The Constitutional Lessons of the Twenty-Seventh Amendment," *Yale Law Journal* 103 (1993): 677.

[70] An important recent study confirms that the U.S. Constitution is one of the most difficult constitutions in the world to change. See Donald S. Lutz, "Toward a Theory of Constitutional Amendment," *American Political Science Review* 88 (1994): 355. This study is reprinted in Levinson, ed., *Responding to Imperfection*, p. 237.

[71] See James Madison, The Federalist No. 49, in Cooke, ed., p. 338. For helpful discussions, see Holmes, *Passions and Constraint*, pp. 152–58; McCoy, *The Last of the Fathers*, pp. 47–64; Marvin Meyers, "Founding and Revolution: A Commentary on Publius-Madison," in Stanley Elkins and Eric McKitrick, eds., *The Hofstadter Aegis: A Memorial* (New York:

that frequent recourse to amendment would undermine the stability of the government because it would imply that the Constitution was seriously defective. Madison noted that the Constitution would benefit from "that veneration, which time bestows on every thing," and that this veneration would enhance the stability of the government.[72] The most serious danger of frequent change through amendment was that "of disturbing the public tranquility by interesting too strongly the public passions."[73] Madison thought that the commendable deliberation that had attended the adoption of state constitutions was due to the unique characteristics of the revolutionary era. Since it was unlikely that these circumstances would recur, frequent recourse to amendment would engage the passions of the public, not its reason.[74] Thus, making amendment of the Constitution relatively easy would have the effect of constantly placing the fundamental structure of the government up for grabs as ordinary political struggles were transformed into constitutional crises. While Madison saw that provision had to be made for amendment, he believed that amendment would be appropriate only on "certain great and extraordinary occasions."[75]

Madison's cautious approach toward constitutional amendment is probably the prevailing view today. While concerns are expressed from time to time that the amendment process is too difficult and stifles needed change, the dominant attitude is that it is dangerous to "tinker" with the Constitution and that the de facto near-unanimity requirement imposed by Article V helps preserve the stability of American government. Another common view is that change through judicial adaptation of the Constitution has forestalled any difficulties caused by Article V.[76]

The problem Madison did not confront, however, is what occurs when the difficulty of amendment forces constitutional change to assume other forms. Since the practical effect of Article V was to err on the side of making amendment difficult, the founding generation ran the risk that it might make the Constitution irrelevant as circumstances changed. An answer to this problem can be constructed from the historical record. The notes of Edmund Randolph, a member of the Committee of Detail at the

---

Alfred A. Knopf, 1974), pp. 3–35; Sanford Levinson, " 'Veneration' and Constitutional Change: James Madison Confronts the Possibility of Constitutional Amendment," *Texas Tech Law Review* 21 (1990): 2443.

[72] Cooke, The Federalist No. 49, p. 340.

[73] Ibid.

[74] Ibid., pp. 340–43.

[75] Ibid., p. 339. For an excellent discussion, see Holmes, *Passions and Constraint*, pp. 152–58.

[76] For relevant discussion, see John R. Vile, *The Constitutional Amending Process in American Political Thought* (New York: Praeger Publishers, 1992), pp. 73, 148–50.

Federal Convention, show a belief that only the most important matters should be included in a constitution. "In the draught of a fundamental constitution, two things deserve attention: 1. To insert essential principles only, lest the operations of government should be clogged by rendering those provisions permanent and unalterable, which ought to be accomodated to times and events. and 2. To use simple and precise language, and general propositions . . ."[77]

One purpose of placing only the most fundamental principles in the Constitution was to preserve the difference between the Constitution and ordinary law. Preserving this difference also had implications for the necessity of amendment. Federalists believed that the Constitution should be permanent and unchanging over the decades if not centuries to come, given that it contained the lasting principles by which government should be conducted. It was therefore unlikely that amendments would be necessary, and this argued in favor of making the process of amendment relatively difficult to preserve the permanent character of the Constitution.[78]

The process of change under Article V shows the difficulty of making formal amendments of significance. The important amendments after the Bill of Rights fall into two clusters. The most famous are the Reconstruction Amendments, Amendments 13–15, but the Progressive Era also saw the passage of several amendments within a relatively brief period. Amendments 16 (allowing an income tax), 17 (direct election of the Senate), 18 (prohibition), and 19 (women's right to vote) were ratified from 1913–1920, making these seven years a significant period of constitutional change. Arguably, there were no amendments ratified after the Progressive Era that made significant structural changes to the constitutional system, although a good case can be made that the Twenty-second Amendment limiting the President to two terms had an important effect on that office.

Virtually no one believes that these amendments are the whole story of federal constitutional change. The Constitution of 1787 left a large number of questions unresolved, some of which had to be addressed soon after President Washington took office. Some constitutional precedents were established quickly such as the advisory role of the Cabinet and the President's power to remove executive officers.[79] Other constitutional questions became sources of continuing controversy. The debate over the power of Congress to establish a national bank posed the broader issue of

---

[77] Max Farrand, ed., *The Records of the Federal Convention of 1787*, vol. 2 (New Haven: Yale University Press, 1966), p. 137.

[78] See Philip A. Hamburger, "The Constitution's Accommodation of Social Change," *Michigan Law Review* 88 (1989): 239.

[79] See Alfred H. Kelly, Winfred A. Harbison, and Herman Belz, *The American Constitution: Its Origins and Development*, 6th ed. (New York: W. W. Norton, 1983), pp. 123–27.

how strictly the list of powers granted to Congress should be read. The Virginia and Kentucky Resolutions of 1798 posed the broader issue of the nature of American federalism.

The Louisiana Purchase of 1803 is a good example of early constitutional change. President Jefferson thought at first it was clear that an amendment was required because the Constitution said nothing about the power of the United States to acquire new territory. He stated that asking for an amendment was preferable to assuming the existence of the power through an interpretation of the Constitution. "Our peculiar security," Jefferson argued, "is in the possession of a written Constitution. Let us not make it a blank paper by construction . . ." Nevertheless, Jefferson was eventually persuaded otherwise—after all, the opportunity to acquire the vast Louisiana territory from Napoleon might be lost if they had to wait for an amendment to be approved. So he agreed, in effect, to find the power to make the purchase, saying that " 'the good sense of our country will correct the evil of construction when it shall produce ill effects.' "[80]

These early encounters with the necessity for constitutional change illustrate several aspects of federal constitutional change. Partly because the Constitution adhered to Randolph's criteria, it could not begin to settle the various specific, practical questions that arose once the government began operating. Yet, although amendments to the Constitution were probably made more easily during this period than at any other time in American history, amendments were either not seen as necessary or, as in the case of the Louisiana Purchase, were thought of as impracticable. The Louisiana Purchase is significant because it shows how constitutional change can occur through ordinary political means. Before the Purchase, there was substantial doubt as to whether the Constitution granted the power to acquire new territory. No amendment was proposed under Article V and the Supreme Court was not involved in the Purchase. Yet after the Purchase, the United States acquired other territories without any substantial controversy. Thus, a change in the constitutional powers of government occurred without an amendment or Court decision. Constitutional change was driven by the course of events and supervised by the elected branches.

While the Louisiana Purchase is constitutional change on a relatively small scale, American history provides many examples of large-scale constitutional changes that occurred outside Article V. The examples cited by Gordon Wood in the introduction to this chapter are fairly conventional:

---

[80] Quoted in Everett S. Brown, *The Constitutional History of the Louisiana Purchase 1803–1812* (Clifton, N.J.: Augustus M. Kelley, 1972 [1920]), p. 28. For a valuable discussion, see John Lauritz Larson, "Jefferson's Union and the Problem of Internal Improvements," in Peter S. Onuf, ed., *Jeffersonian Legacies* (Charlottesville: University Press of Virginia, 1993), pp. 356–58.

the president's Cabinet, independent regulatory agencies, political parties, and judicial review.[81] The development of political parties, against the
wishes of the founding generation, is an especially important example of
a significant change in the constitutional system that occurred without
amendment or Supreme Court interpretation.[82] Historian Richard Hofstadter concludes that "it seems doubtful whether this Constitution, devised against party, could have been made to work if such a functional
agency as the party had not sprung into the gap [between the executive
and legislative branches] to remedy its chief remaining deficiencies."[83] To
illustrate the process of large-scale constitutional change, we will focus on
the state constitutional experience and the New Deal.

Exploring Constitutional Change: The State Experience and the New Deal

No account of American constitutionalism or theory of constitutional
change is complete unless it takes into consideration the constitutional
experience of the American states. After all, the United States is not governed by one constitution, but by fifty-one. Constitutional change at the
state level should be of special interest because it departs sharply from
what we have come to think of as the norm. More important, the state
constitutional experience helps illuminate the process of federal constitutional change by demonstrating the constitutional impact of changes in
the responsibilities of government.

In contrast to Madison's caution about tinkering with constitutions,
Americans have continuously changed their state constitutions since the
first wave of post-revolutionary constitution making hit the states in the
early nineteenth century. At the state level, change occurs much more
often in the form of amendments, the entire constitution is sometimes
revised in constitutional conventions, and the constitution becomes, in
adapting to changing circumstances, much longer and more like ordinary
statutes. By 1860, for example, North Carolina was the only state in the
Union with a constitution dating back to 1776, and that constitution had
been revised substantially in 1835.[84] Before the Civil War, many new constitutions were written in response to social and economic change that
resembled statutory codes and contained far more specific, legislative-type

---

[81] The case of independent regulatory agencies as an example of constitutional change is
discussed in chapter 2. The development of judicial review is discussed in chapter 3.

[82] See Hofstadter, *The Idea of a Party System*, pp. 70–73.

[83] Ibid., p. 70.

[84] See Don E. Fehrenbacher, *Constitutions and Constitutionalism in the Slaveholding
South* (Athens: University of Georgia Press, 1989), p. 5.

rules than their eighteenth-century counterparts.[85] The result is that there has been far more formal constitutional change at the state level than at the federal level. Since 1776 the fifty states have operated under 146 constitutions and thirty-one of the fifty states have had two or more constitutions.[86] Over the years, roughly 10,000 amendments to the U.S. Constitution have been *proposed*, but at the state level, more than 5,800 have been *adopted* through 1991.[87]

Constitutional change at the state level departs from Federalist norms in several respects. Amending state constitutions appears to be relatively easy and there is little adherence to the idea of cautious change. Further, constitutions are not regarded as a framework of permanent principles and thus the constitution is transformed into a kind of superstatute. Americans appear to be committed to two completely different models of constitutional change.[88]

Why does state constitutional change differ so radically from the experience at the federal level? There are two differences that require explanation. State constitutions have changed at a faster rate through formal amendment and in adapting to change, they have become more like ordinary statutes. The explanation for the greater rate of change is relatively straightforward. There were important differences in the responsibilities of the state and federal governments in the nineteenth century. The states had primary responsibility for the tasks of government—they pursued mercantilist policies to stimulate economic development, set money and banking policies, subsidized transportation, and dealt with crime, poverty, and various religious and moral issues.[89] In short, state governments performed many more of what we think of as the normal tasks of government, while the federal government, especially in the Jacksonian period and after, was more of a caretaker government with only a rudimentary bureaucracy.[90]

During the nineteenth century, state governments took nearly the full

---

[85] See Kermit L. Hall, *The Magic Mirror: Law in American History* (New York: Oxford University Press, 1989), pp. 102–4.

[86] Kermit L. Hall, "Mostly Anchor and Little Sail: The Evolution of American State Constitutions," in Paul Finkelman and Stephen E. Gottlieb, eds., *Toward a Usable Past: Liberty Under State Constitutions* (Athens: University of Georgia Press, 1991), pp. 394–95.

[87] For the federal figure, see Richard B. Bernstein with Jerome Agel, *Amending America* (New York: Times Books, 1993), p. xii. For the state figure, see Lutz, "Toward a Theory of Constitutional Amendment," p. 359.

[88] See James Willard Hurst, *The Growth of American Law: The Law Makers* (Boston: Little, Brown, 1950), pp. 202–3.

[89] See William E. Nelson, *The Fourteenth Amendment: From Political Principle to Judicial Doctrine* (Cambridge: Harvard University Press, 1988), pp. 27–30.

[90] See Leonard D. White, *The Federalists* (New York: Macmillan, 1948), p. 466; Leonard D. White, *The Jacksonians* (Chicago: Free Press, 1954), pp. 4–5.

brunt of the adaptation in government policy that was required by the developing American economy. State constitutions were rewritten in response to these changes and in response to the normal demands of the electorate on a variety of issues.[91] Many state constitutions acquired articles regulating corporations, labor unions, and systems of higher education—topics unknown to the federal Constitution. Another important force behind frequent constitutional change was popular distrust of state legislatures. Legislatures were distrusted for handing out a variety of special privileges and for loading state governments with debt. In the late nineteenth century state constitutions became even more codelike as constitutional conventions attempted to regulate the legislature in detail.[92]

By contrast, most citizens could live their lives without seeing any federal official other than the postmaster. The federal government was not seen as the appropriate agent of change in response to changing conditions.[93] Hence there was no felt need for changing the federal Constitution. Thus the difference in evolution between state and federal constitutions—state constitutions changed rapidly because there was more governing going on at the state level, while at the federal level, time seemed to stand still.

The American experience with state constitutions is illuminating in several ways. First, it shows that despite conventional wisdom, Americans do not have a consistent philosophy of constitutional change. When change is relatively easy, Americans are not restrained by a taboo against constitutional tinkering. We know very little about how this permissive attitude toward constitutional amendment developed, but it is possible it is the descendant of Anti-federalist beliefs that limits on government should be as specific as possible.[94]

Second, the state constitutional experience indicates that constitutional change usually follows changes in the broader political environment. Social, economic, and technological forces can make demands on political actors that then force changes in the powers and responsibilities of government. This state experience is highly suggestive for any theory of fed-

[91] See Albert L. Sturm, "The Development of American State Constitutions," *Publius* 12 (1982): 63–74.

[92] See Morton Keller, *Affairs of State: Public Life in Late Nineteenth Century America* (Cambridge: Harvard University Press, 1977), pp. 110–14, 319–20. For a specific example of constitutional revision that illustrates these trends, see The Constitution Revision Study Commission, "The Constitution of the State of Oklahoma: Recommendations for Revision," *Oklahoma City University Law Review* 16 (1991): 515.

[93] See Phillip S. Paludan, "The American Civil War Considered as a Crisis in Law and Order," *American Historical Review* 77 (1972): 1021.

[94] This is suggested by Michael Lienesch, *New Order of the Ages: Time, the Constitution, and the Making of Modern American Political Thought* (Princeton: Princeton University Press, 1988), pp. 148–49.

eral constitutional change. That is, it is reasonable to assume that as the federal government acquired new responsibilities in the twentieth century, responsibilities that the states had previously borne by themselves in the nineteenth century, constitutional change had to occur.[95]

Third, and perhaps most important, the state experience suggests the difficulty of adhering to Randolph's criterion that the constitution ought to include essential principles only. The primary way states adapted their constitutions to change was to load them with specific regulatory rules. There was, however, an alternative way to proceed, one that would have preserved the original character of state constitutions as broad frameworks for government. If a state government needed the authority to deal with a new policy problem, a general grant of power could have been made. Why did state constitution makers change the nature of their original revolutionary constitutions by making them into long legislative codes? This question refers to the second difference between the state and federal constitutional experience that we identified earlier.

Answering this question requires exploring the federal experience with constitutional change. As we have already noted, the federal experience looks very different from the state experience at first glance. As we shall see, however, there is a deeper resemblance between state and federal constitutional change.

The best way to explore why federal constitutional change has not revolved around amendments is to examine the New Deal period during which the federal government permanently assumed new powers and responsibilities. The changes made during the New Deal amounted to a "constitutional revolution," one that continues to structure our contemporary constitutional-political system.[96] Yet the most important constitutional changes made during this period left no trace on the text of the Constitution. Most scholars see the Supreme Court as the agent of change since the Court played a key role in the drama of the New Deal, first striking down important legislation in 1935–36 and then, reversing its course, upholding New Deal legislation in 1937. After President Roosevelt had a chance to appoint several justices, the Court changed federal constitutional law even more sharply by explicitly deferring to Congress and state legislatures on matters of social and economic regulation.[97]

Led by President Roosevelt, the New Deal made at least three funda-

<hr/>

[95] See Lutz, "Toward a Theory of Constitutional Amendment," p. 357.

[96] See generally William E. Leuchtenburg, *The Supreme Court Reborn: The Constitutional Revolution in the Age of Roosevelt* (New York: Oxford University Press, 1995). It is important to note that constitutional change continued after the New Deal in World War II and the Cold War. The changes during these periods are explored in chapter 2. Contemporary constitutional developments are reviewed in chapter 6.

[97] See, e.g., ibid., pp. 213–28.

mental changes to the American constitutional order. First, the power and prestige of the presidency was enhanced dramatically by Roosevelt's leadership during the Great Depression. The presidency became a new kind of constitutional office, offering the potential for a president to surmount the separation of powers and become the head of the federal government, if not the nation as a whole.[98] Second, the nature of American federalism was transformed by the new responsibilities assumed by the federal government and the greatly changed relationship between the states and the federal government implied by these new responsibilities.[99] As we shall see, one of the reasons for this change was the inadequacy of state constitutions. The inability of state governments to respond adequately to the Depression caused constitutional power to shift upward to the national level. Third, Congress and the agencies to which it delegated regulatory power acquired virtually plenary authority over the economy and the ability to deal directly with many social problems.[100]

Although these elements of the constitutional revolution of the New Deal were among the most significant changes ever made to the American constitutional order, none of them were ratified through amendments made under Article V. Indeed, most of the significant constitutional changes made in the twentieth century have not occurred through amendment. In exploring why this is the case, it is helpful to focus on the conflict between President Roosevelt and the Supreme Court. Roosevelt's reasons for not asking for amendments to validate the New Deal are instructive, because they apply with equal force to all of the significant constitutional changes that came after the New Deal and show why these changes did not occur through amendment. In response to the Court decisions against the New Deal, Roosevelt seriously considered the option of amending the Constitution from the summer of 1935 until after the

[98] See, e.g., Sidney Milkis, *The President and the Parties: The Transformation of the American Party System since the New Deal* (New York: Oxford University Press, 1993), pp. 150–51; Michael E. Parrish, "The Great Depression, the New Deal, and the American Legal Order," *Washington Law Review* 59 (1984): 726–27.

[99] See, e.g., Parrish, "The Great Depression, the New Deal, and the American Legal Order," p. 727; Harry N. Scheiber, "American Federalism and the Diffusion of Power: Historical and Contemporary Perspectives," *University of Toledo Law Review* 9 (1978): 644–48. For an account of the first two changes from a legal point of view, see Henry Paul Monaghan, "Stare Decisis and Constitutional Adjudication," *Columbia Law Review* 88 (1988): 729–39.

[100] See, e.g., Leuchtenburg, *The Supreme Court Reborn*, pp. 216–28. The last two changes have not been affected significantly by recent Supreme Court decisions suggesting that there are upper limits on the power of Congress in the areas of federalism and social regulation. See *New York v. United States*, 112 S. Ct. 2408 (1992); *United States v. Lopez*, 115 S. Ct. 1624 (1995). As discussed below, the ability of the Court to supervise Congress in these matters is limited by the political constraints on the Court in the post–New Deal period.

presidential election of 1936. He eventually rejected this option for several reasons.[101]

First, after two years of study there was still no agreement on the language of any amendment. Roosevelt's Department of Justice faced serious practical problems in attempting to draft an amendment that would guarantee that the Court would uphold New Deal legislation. There were objections to an amendment whether it was written broadly or narrowly. If it was written broadly, adding it to the Constitution could have unforeseen effects on the scope of government power. On the other hand, there was no guarantee that a narrow amendment could do the job required, given the broad nature of the regulatory powers the government needed to cope with the crisis.[102]

Second, any new amendment would be subject to judicial interpretation. If the amendment was drafted in broad terms, the Court might be able to undermine it through a narrow construction of its ambiguous provisions. If the amendment was drafted narrowly to overturn specific precedents, then it might not apply to all the circumstances in which the government needed new powers.[103]

Third, the amending process mandated by Article V was too cumbersome. It would take much too long and would not have a clear chance of success, since a minority of state legislative houses could defeat any amendment. This difficulty especially concerned Roosevelt. He knew that interest groups would oppose any amendment and they would only have to prevail in one house in thirteen state legislatures to defeat it.[104] Any amendment therefore required an extraordinary degree of national consensus. While Roosevelt may have had that degree of consensus behind him as a national leader, he could not be certain that the consensus would guarantee action on any particular reform issue, especially when it involved an important change to the Constitution.[105]

---

[101] For good analytic accounts of the conflict between Roosevelt and the Court, see Leuchtenburg, *The Supreme Court Reborn*; William Lasser, *The Limits of Judicial Power: The Supreme Court in American Politics* (Chapel Hill: University of North Carolina Press, 1988), pp. 111–60.

[102] See David E. Kyvig, "The Road Not Taken: FDR, the Supreme Court, and Constitutional Amendment," *Political Science Quarterly* 104 (1989): 473–76.

[103] See Leuchtenburg, *The Supreme Court Reborn*, pp. 100, 111.

[104] Ibid., pp. 110–11. See also Kyvig, "The Road Not Taken," pp. 476–78.

[105] Kyvig suggests that the amendment option was more realistic than Roosevelt realized, given the political experience acquired in ratifying six constitutional amendments since 1913 (Amendments 16–21). Kyvig also points out that state conventions could have been used under Article V to ratify an amendment (as they were used to ratify the Twenty-first Amendment, repealing prohibition). Kyvig, "The Road Not Taken," p. 479. None of these amendments, however, raised the truly fundamental constitutional questions that would have been posed by an amendment designed to validate the New Deal.

A fourth reason is suggested by Roosevelt's strategy in the 1936 presidential election. The election was Roosevelt's best chance to win popular support for needed amendments, but he kept the Democratic platform ambiguous on this critical issue. Proposing amendments would constitute not only a criticism of the Court, but would suggest that the Constitution was not adequate to meet the crisis. Because the public respected the Court as an institution and revered the Constitution, this would give Republicans a strong campaign issue. Republicans would be able to cast themselves as defenders of the constitutional faith and denounce the Democrats as destroyers of the Constitution. Roosevelt therefore stifled constitutional debate in the months leading up to the election.[106]

During this period, Attorney General Homer Cummings was encouraging Roosevelt to see the problem in a different light. The problem was not with the Constitution, but merely with the shortsighted interpretation of the Constitution by the Supreme Court. What was required was new personnel on the Court and Roosevelt moved to the Court-packing option.[107] From Roosevelt's point of view, changing the Constitution through amendment became an irrelevant option. Changing the Constitution was too dangerous. The Constitution was better regarded as a document to be revered rather than changed in response to changing conditions.[108] As long as constitutional interpretation was the special province of the Supreme Court, changing justices would always appear easier than changing the Constitution.

The influence of reverence for the Constitution on Roosevelt's strategy for dealing with the Court is interesting because it suggests that Madison's analysis in *The Federalist* No. 49 was correct. Veneration of the Constitution makes it a stable basis for government because it is very difficult to change a revered document. The Constitution is seen as an ideal by which government should be judged and becomes the focus of strong patriotic sentiments. Such sentiments prevent even reasonable constitutional changes when they become necessary because proposed changes imply that the national political order and its values are seriously defective. Since Americans do not believe that the values endorsed by the Framers and solemnly reaffirmed by subsequent generations are defective, this creates an enormous roadblock to adapting the Constitution to historical change.

---

[106] See Lasser, *The Limits of Judicial Power*, pp. 142–45, 152; Leuchtenburg, *The Supreme Court Reborn*, pp. 98–108. See also Michael Nelson, "The President and the Court: Reinterpreting the Court-Packing Episode," *Political Science Quarterly* 103 (1988): 274–78.

[107] See Leuchtenburg, *The Supreme Court Reborn*, pp. 100, 114–27; Kyvig, "The Road Not Taken," pp. 476–77.

[108] Kyvig, "The Road Not Taken," p. 480.

The option available to state governments of responding to change by inserting specific rules into the constitution is thus closed for the federal government. All of the significant constitutional changes that resulted from the assumption of new powers and responsibilities by the federal government in the twentieth century had to occur outside Article V. This bias against change through amendment was further reinforced by the growing institutionalization of American politics, especially after the New Deal. The entrenched power of government bureaucracies, congressional committees, and powerful interest groups became greater over time and made any effort at significant change very difficult.[109] Any amendment that would make an important structural difference to the way government operates is thus bound to attract substantial opposition. Since near-unanimity is required to pass any constitutional amendment, passing a truly significant amendment after the New Deal became extraordinarily difficult.

We are now in a position to bring together our accounts of state and federal constitutional change. So far we have highlighted the differences between the state and federal experience. From the federal perspective, formal constitutional change in the states is fast and furious; while from the state perspective, formal change at the federal level is glacially slow. There is, however, a crucial similarity between the state and federal experience. In both cases, the option of regularly updating the Constitution through amendments that preserve the framework character of the document has not been pursued. The states have been able to change their constitutions through amendment, but the many amendments have transformed their constitutions into superstatutes. Amending the federal Constitution has been so difficult that many of the most significant constitutional changes of the twentieth century have made no impression on the document.

Earlier we asked why the states adapted their constitutions by making them into legislative codes. The New Deal experience points the way to answering this question. Passing a broad amendment to preserve the framework character of the document runs the risk of overreacting to a specific policy problem by changing some fundamental power of government. With a broad amendment there is a greater risk of unforeseen effects. The safe way to proceed is to pass a narrow amendment that deals with the specific problem at hand. In addition, as set out earlier, revision of state constitutions was partly motivated by distrust of state legislatures. The people of the states wanted to make the restrictions on the legislature as specific as possible in order to prevent particular abuses of power.

[109] See John E. Chubb and Paul E. Peterson, "Realignment and Institutionalization," in John E. Chubb and Paul E. Peterson, eds., *The New Direction in American Politics* (Washington, D.C.: Brookings Institution, 1985), p. 6.

Madison's analysis in *The Federalist* No. 49 can also be applied here. If a framework change had to be made to a state constitution each time there was a change in historical circumstance, the entire constitutional structure could too easily be put in question. It would be as if the state were sitting in a continuous constitutional convention. But it is in no one's interest to have the fundamental rules of the political game previously agreed on to be put in question on a continuous basis. The political order would be unsettled by the constant need to enact fundamental changes to the constitution in response to changing historical conditions.[110]

This provides a way to understand the state and federal constitutional experience in theoretical terms. Having a permanent constitution that serves as a framework for government is a laudable goal. But the way the Constitution interacts with the political system guarantees you will only be able to make framework amendments on rare occasions. You can use the formal amendment method of adapting the constitution to historical change only at the price of abandoning the commitment to have a constitution that serves as a framework for government.

It is reasonable to attribute two goals to the founding generation: they wanted the government to be based on and guided by written law, and they wanted to maintain the framework character of the Constitution so it would last through the centuries. The problem is that these two goals are inconsistent when one takes account of the need to adapt the Constitution to changing circumstances. The experience of American constitutionalism shows that you can maintain the written quality of the constitution only at the expense of abandoning the framework character of the document and you can maintain the framework character of the constitution only by abandoning the idea that all important constitutional change must occur through formal amendment.

It is important to note that the option the states have pursued, while being more explicit than the method of change at the federal level, has significant disadvantages. Specifically, it dramatically enhances the antidemocratic character of the constitution by enabling temporary majorities to lock in particular policies that an ordinary legislative majority then cannot change.[111] This severely hampered the ability of state governments to

---

[110] See the discussion in Holmes, *Passions and Constraint*, pp. 152–58. An important article by Russell Hardin arguing that a constitution is not a contract is also relevant to this point. See Russell Hardin, "Why a Constitution?" in Bernard Grofman and Donald Wittman, eds., *The Federalist Papers and the New Institutionalism* (New York: Agathon Press, 1989), pp. 100–120.

[111] One scholar notes the contradictory impulses that shaped state constitution making—constitutional conventions inserted detailed policies into the constitution, but recoiled at making constitutional change as easy as legislative change. The constitutions that resulted were as specific as statutes, but much harder to change. See Janet Cornelius, *Constitution Making in Illinois 1818–1970* (Urbana: University of Illinois Press, 1972), p. 42.

respond to new social and economic problems. The detailed restraints in most state constitutions greatly restricted the ability of the states to respond to the Great Depression and helped create a vacuum in which federal constitutional power had to be exercised.[112] State constitutions continued to receive criticism in the 1950s and 1960s for restricting state economic development.[113]

We have so far bypassed the role of the Supreme Court in adapting the Constitution to historical change. This issue deserves separate treatment because there is an important link between this issue and the account of American constitutionalism advanced in the first section of this chapter. Many different observers have accepted the thesis that judicial interpretation has been the primary means of adapting the Constitution to change outside Article V.[114] According to this thesis, the Supreme Court has served as the gatekeeper for constitutional change. The Court has the power to allow certain changes through the gate while excluding others. The substantial body of constitutional case law built by the Court over the years lends this thesis considerable credibility, as do the occasional instances where the Court reverses course and overrules a past case. This indicates a Court in control of the process of constitutional change.

Despite the plausibility of the gatekeeper thesis, it is profoundly mistaken as an approach to understanding federal constitutional change. Two structural features of American constitutionalism prevent the Supreme Court from being the primary agent of constitutional change. First, the legalization of the Constitution meant that the Court had to act as other courts and wait for actual litigation before rendering a judgment. Thus, in one of the Court's earliest decisions, it declined the power to issue advisory opinions to the other branches of government.[115]

This means that the Court has no involvement with constitutional changes that do not produce litigation. For example, the development of political parties and the change in government power that resulted from the Louisiana Purchase did not involve the Court. The Court also had no opportunity to pass on the constitutionality of the new power of the presidency acquired in the New Deal. Constitutional change thus occurred outside Article V without the participation of the Court. This point can be generalized. When a constitutional change is necessary that is in the interest of Congress, the President, the states, and citizens in general (or the

---

[112] See Hall, "Mostly Anchor and Little Sail," in Finkelman and Gottlieb, eds., *Toward a Usable Past*, p. 408.

[113] See Sturm, "The Development of American State Constitutions," pp. 71–72.

[114] See, e.g., Holmes and Sunstein, "The Politics of Constitutional Revision in Eastern Europe," in Levinson, ed., *Responding to Imperfection*, p. 279; Sager, "The Incorrigible Constitution," pp. 895–97.

[115] See *Hayburn's Case*, 2 U.S. (2 Dall.) 409 (1792).

states and citizens are indifferent), the change will not involve the Court because no one has an incentive to begin litigation.

Usually, however, any significant constitutional change will result in some kind of litigation. But this does not mean that the Court either initiates or is a major contributor to the change. The Court is also disabled from serving as the primary gatekeeper of constitutional change by its own institutional weakness. This weakness takes the form of judicial self-restraint toward exercises of constitutional power that the Court cannot successfully influence. The New Deal experience is instructive. It is inaccurate to say that the Court approved of the new powers and responsibilities of the federal government as if the Court had a real choice to continue to keep a watchful eye over the constitutionality of economic and social regulation. In fact, the Court recused itself from any significant role in reviewing state and federal legislation affecting the economy. As a prominent constitutional scholar notes, "[i]n the years after 1937, the Supreme Court essentially offered the Congress *carte blanche* to regulate the economic and social life of the nation, its actions subject only to the requirements of the Bill of Rights."[116]

In the constitutional crisis that followed the Court's actions striking down New Deal legislation in 1935–36, it became apparent that the Court did not have the option of serving as the gatekeeper of constitutional change.[117] After 1937 the Court adopted the position that a proper understanding of the Constitution required it to stay out of deciding the constitutionality of economic and regulatory legislation altogether. The same pattern was apparent with respect to the enormous expansion in presidential power in foreign affairs. The Court has either taken an entirely hands-off approach to foreign affairs cases, regarding them as presenting "political questions," or it has usually deferred to presidential authority.[118] The result is the same—an expansion in the power of the other two branches results not in the Court adapting the Constitution to the new reality, but in the Court getting out of the way. Congress and the President, not the Court, initiated the constitutional changes in question and brought them to fruition. The Court's role was distinctly secondary.

The idea of the Supreme Court as the gatekeeper of constitutional change is inherently implausible. Once the fluid nature of constitutional change outside Article V is understood, the gatekeeper idea can be valid only if the Court is the most powerful branch of government. The Court

---

[116] Tribe, *American Constitutional Law*, p. 386.

[117] See Leuchtenburg, *The Supreme Court Reborn*, pp. 231–36; Parrish, "The Great Depression, the New Deal, and the American Legal Order," p. 734.

[118] See generally Michael J. Glennon, *Constitutional Diplomacy* (Princeton, N.J.: Princeton University Press, 1990); Harold Hongju Koh, *The National Security Constitution* (New Haven: Yale University Press, 1990). We will return to this point in chapter 2.

must have a right of approval over any change in government power that is arguably constitutionally significant. Otherwise, it would lose control over the flow of constitutional change. Of course, the Court has never possessed this kind of power.[119]

It is important to keep in mind that many of the most famous Supreme Court decisions, including *Lochner v. New York* and post–New Deal opinions such as *Brown v. Board of Education* and *Roe v. Wade* are cases affecting the power of state governments, not the federal government.[120] Truly significant Court decisions limiting the power of Congress and the President in the post–New Deal era are rare.[121] After the New Deal the Court became a specialist, largely concerning itself with whether state legislation satisfied the standards found in the Bill of Rights and Civil War Amendments.[122] The impressive body of constitutional case law that resulted is thus based on a comparatively small portion of the Constitution. Moreover, this case law affects only a very small portion of the total policy output of all of the branches and agencies of the federal government. To the extent that this output is based on the constitutional changes initiated during the New Deal, the Court cannot be said to be supervising the power of the federal government under the Constitution. The Court therefore cannot be the gatekeeper of constitutional change and judicial interpretation cannot be the primary means of adapting the Constitution to change outside Article V.

What, then, accounts for the widespread impression to the contrary? Part of the answer lies in the substantial body of case law affecting the states, the point we have just noticed. Of course, this case law cannot be the source of the ongoing changes occurring in the executive and legislative branches. The main problem with the conventional analysis of constitutional change, however, is the failure to appreciate the differences identified in the first section between the Constitution and ordinary law. The difference that is of special relevance to understanding constitutional change is that the Constitution cannot be enforced as ordinary laws can.

---

[119] In this regard, see the comments of Sidney George Fisher, writing just after the beginning of the Civil War. Fisher argued against the immutability of the Constitution: " 'If the Constitution be immutable, what was law in 1787, must be law as long as the Constitution lasts. To maintain it, therefore, the Judiciary must be stronger than the people, stronger than the representatives of the people. In a popular government this is impossible.' " Quoted in Paul W. Kahn, *Legitimacy and History: Self-Government in American Constitutional Theory* (New Haven: Yale University Press, 1992), p. 71.

[120] See *Lochner v. New York*, 198 U.S. 45 (1905); *Brown v. Board of Education*, 347 U.S. 483 (1954); *Roe v. Wade*, 410 U.S. 113 (1973).

[121] For relevant commentary, see William N. Eskridge, Jr. and Philip P. Frickey, "Foreword: Law as Equilibrium," *Harvard Law Review* 108 (1994): 42–56, 87–95.

[122] See Lawrence Baum, *The Supreme Court*, 5th ed. (Washington, D.C.: Congressional Quarterly Press, 1995), pp. 195–99.

The separate branches of government are all simultaneously responsible for obeying and enforcing the Constitution. As long as they have some popular support, they can be held accountable for changing the Constitution only when they so choose. Thus, for example, if the executive branch wishes to alter its powers and responsibilities and the legislative branch agrees or is indifferent, there is not much the Supreme Court can do. If the Court does take a hard line against changes that the elected branches think are necessary, the Court knows quite well that the objecting justices can eventually be replaced by justices who are more compliant.[123]

The legalized Constitution misleads scholars into thinking that amendment through Article V and judicial interpretation are the only possible means of constitutional change. The idea of the legalized Constitution was based on treating the Constitution as if it were another kind of ordinary law. The Constitution was held to be enforceable by the courts and interpreted according to the same methods used for other kinds of law. Since the Constitution structures politics and government, giving the judiciary the unique power to enforce the Constitution is tantamount to making the judiciary the most powerful branch of government. Since this is not tenable politically, the scope of constitutional law is necessarily narrow.

This is what is meant by the move from "theory" to "politics." American constitutionalism has moved from the theory that the entire Constitution could remain separate from politics to a situation where the meaning of most of the Constitution is determined through ordinary politics. This implication of the legalized Constitution was not obvious until the federal government became a truly activist, interventionist state in the twentieth century. The experience of the New Deal made it apparent that the judiciary can enforce only a small portion of the Constitution. The meaning of most provisions in the Constitution is thus determined in the course of the interaction between the executive and legislative branches. While it is possible for these branches to change their interpretations of the Constitution through legalistic procedures involving carefully reasoned written arguments (as change is supposed to occur in the judicial branch), change does not most often occur in this manner. Instead, these branches alter the Constitution in the course of ordinary political struggles, without much attention to legal and constitutional values that lawyers and judges think important.

As a final matter, how do we know that there have been significant constitutional changes in the twentieth century outside of Article V,

---

[123] Or, as in the case of the invalidation of the legislative veto, *INS v. Chadha*, 462 U.S. 919 (1983), the decision will simply be evaded. See Louis Fisher, "The Legislative Veto: Invalidated, It Survives," *Law and Contemporary Problems* 56 (1993): 273.

changes that are still ongoing? There is a near-consensus among constitutional scholars that fundamental constitutional changes occurred during the New Deal. In making this point, however, the state experience with constitutional change is especially useful. The state experience shows that changes in the powers and responsibilities of government lead to continuous constitutional change, change that has been expressed in the states primarily through formal amendment. The lack of any taboo against constitutional tinkering in the states implies that if constitutional change through Article V was relatively easy, there would have been many amendments to the Constitution made in response to the activism of the federal government in the twentieth century. For example, President Roosevelt might well have decided to ask for amendments if the procedure for change had been easier. In light of this state experience, the lack of any amendments to validate the New Deal does not mean that constitutional change did not occur. It implies rather that constitutional change assumed other forms. The course of constitutional change during the New Deal and other important periods of change in the twentieth century flowed through the President and Congress, not the Supreme Court and the legalized Constitution.

Exploring Constitutional Change: Ackerman's Theory

The legal scholar Bruce Ackerman has recently produced an important theory of constitutional change that deserves separate consideration.[124] Although we will not be able to consider all of Ackerman's many interesting ideas and arguments, we will focus on his central idea of America as a dualistic democracy and a key claim that follows from this idea.[125]

Ackerman believes that the Constitution established a dualistic democracy in the United States. Ackerman's conception of dualism must be distinguished carefully from two more familiar and uncontroversial ideas about American constitutionalism. One familiar idea is that of the difference between ordinary law and constitutional law, which we explored in the first section of this chapter. Another familiar idea is the contrast be-

---

[124] See Ackerman, *We The People: Foundations*. See also Bruce Ackerman, "Higher Lawmaking," in Levinson, ed., *Responding to Imperfection*, p. 63; Bruce Ackerman and David Golove, "Is NAFTA Constitutional?" *Harvard Law Review* 108 (1995): 799; Bruce Ackerman and Neal Katyal, "Our Unconventional Founding," *University of Chicago Law Review* 62 (1995): 475.

[125] In particular, Ackerman's theory of constitutional interpretation and the Supreme Court's role are not considered here. Among Ackerman's more valuable ideas not considered here are his treatment of constitutional history as a succession of constitutional regimes and his argument that we should avoid treating cases such as *Lochner v. New York* in an anachronistic fashion. See Ackerman, *We The People: Foundations*, pp. 59–67.

tween amendments to the Constitution that happen through the process specified in Article V and those constitutional changes that occur outside Article V. Ackerman's conception of dualism is related to this second idea, but it is considerably more complex and controversial.

Ackerman's conception of dualism draws a distinction between normal and constitutional politics and a related distinction between ordinary lawmaking and higher lawmaking. These distinctions are intended to capture something important about American constitutionalism.[126] As we noted in our discussion above, constitutional change in America has an episodic quality. Truly fundamental alterations to the constitutional structure occur infrequently and do not necessarily result in formal amendments to the Constitution. Ackerman's theory is ultimately an attempt to justify and make sense of this characteristic of American constitutionalism. He contends plausibly that there have been only three truly fundamental (or, in his terms, transformative) moments of constitutional change in American history: the original adoption of the Constitution and the Bill of Rights, Reconstruction, and the New Deal. These moments are all examples of higher lawmaking, a special kind of politics that involves the entire American people acting in their capacity as sovereign. On the other hand, there have been many more periods of constitutional politics, when a heightened awareness and debate of constitutional issues nevertheless does not result in transformative moments of higher lawmaking. These failed constitutional moments include the Populist and Progressive Eras of the late nineteenth and early twentieth centuries and the civil rights movement of the 1960s.[127]

Ackerman's dualistic theory thus cuts across the familiar contrast between change through and change outside Article V. Some amendments to the Constitution are the result of higher lawmaking and are thus transformative amendments, while others are not. Some constitutional changes outside Article V nonetheless count as transformative "amendments" to the Constitution, amendments that have the same legal status as those that have been formally approved through Article V. The latter claim is crucial to the entire theory. The only transformative constitutional moment that did not result in the original adoption of the Constitution or amendments to that document is the New Deal. Ackerman nevertheless sees the changes made during the New Deal as having the same legal status as the Constitution and Reconstruction Amendments. To place all of these moments of constitutional change on the same plane, Ackerman seeks to undermine the conventional legal understanding of the founding and Reconstruction. Ackerman's key claim is that all of the

---

[126] Ibid., pp. 6–7.
[127] Ibid., pp. 40–50, 81–86, 92–94, 108–13.

transformative constitutional moments in American history occurred outside the process specified in Article V.

This claim seems easily demonstrated by the original adoption of the Constitution, which of course occurred before Article V was in effect. But Ackerman's argument goes deeper. For him, all of the transformative constitutional moments occurred illegally in a certain sense. That is, while they resulted in legal constitutional change through the mechanism of higher lawmaking, they occurred outside the accepted means of making such changes. Reconstruction and the New Deal occurred outside Article V, while the founding occurred outside the means specified in the Articles of Confederation.[128]

While Ackerman's theory is intriguing, it should be noted that the basis for justifying the theory is never made explicit. For example, does Ackerman's theory rest solely on an appeal to the thought of the founding generation, or does it have a basis that is independent of an appeal to original intent? Ackerman states that his theory is a model of American constitutionalism that is "designed to capture the distinctive spirit of the American Constitution."[129] This leaves the basis for justification unclear. Ackerman does, however, spend a great deal of time justifying his theory through a discussion of *The Federalist*, so it is fair to test his claims on that basis.

Ackerman claims that the essays of James Madison and Alexander Hamilton in *The Federalist*, particularly those of Madison, show that his theory of constitutional change outside Article V was embraced by the founding generation.[130] Ackerman sees a number of essays as a response to two objections raised by the Anti-federalists—that the Constitution was illegal because the Federal Convention adopted an entirely new plan for government rather than simply amending the Articles of Confederation and that the process for ratification in Article VII of the Constitution did not conform with the Articles of Confederation, which required the unanimous consent of the states before amendments could be approved.[131] As Ackerman sees it, in these essays Madison and Hamilton produced the theory of constitutional politics and higher lawmaking in order to justify the departure from the process of change specified in the Articles of Confederation (although these terms are Ackerman's).[132]

[128] Ibid., pp. 44–57, 315–16.

[129] Ibid., p. 6.

[130] Ibid., pp. 165–99.

[131] For a valuable discussion of these objections, see Richard S. Kay, "The Illegality of the Constitution," *Constitutional Commentary* 4 (1987): 57. For a vigorous defense of the legality of the Constitution, see Akhil Reed Amar, "The Consent of the Governed: Constitutional Amendment Outside Article V," *Columbia Law Review* 94 (1994): 462–87. Ackerman responds to Amar in Ackerman and Katyal, "Our Unconventional Founding."

[132] Ackerman, *We The People: Foundations*, pp. 167–69.

Madison confronted the Anti-federalist objections in *The Federalist* No.
40, which Ackerman quotes at length. Madison reflected on the practical
situation in which the Federal Convention found itself. There was widespread agreement that the country was in a crisis produced by the deficiencies of the government under the Articles of Confederation. In these circumstances, delegates from several states met at Annapolis in 1786 and
called for the Articles to be revised. After most states elected delegates to
the Philadelphia convention, the Confederation Congress issued a call for
a convention to revise the Articles. Madison argued that in such a situation, "forms ought to give way to substance" and, if necessary, changes
must "be instituted by some *informal and unauthorised propositions*, made
by some patriotic and respectable citizen or number of citizens."[133]

As we saw in our discussion in the first section, Americans agreed in the
founding era that it was appropriate for conventions to make new constitutional arrangements. Madison argued that since the Constitution was to
be submitted to conventions, it would thus be approved or disapproved
by the people as a whole.[134] If the people approved the Constitution, this
would have the effect of blotting out any "antecedent errors and irregu-
larities" that occurred at the Federal Convention.[135] It is important to
note that Madison earlier disposed of the objection that ratification of the
Constitution by convention should be unanimous by noting that Rhode
Island sent no delegates to the Convention and thus adhering to the requirement of unanimity would enable that state to hold the remaining
states hostage to its approval.[136]

Ackerman contends that each time Americans confronted the need to
transform their constitutional order, they found themselves in the same
situation which Madison analyzes in this essay. There is, however, one
significant difference between the founding and subsequent periods of
constitutional change in this respect. Subsequent periods of change such
as Reconstruction and the New Deal have always occurred in the shadow
of Article V and, unfortunately for Ackerman's theory, there is no reason
to think Madison and Hamilton believed it would be otherwise. Although
it is not apparent from Ackerman's discussion, both Madison and Hamilton discussed Article V and indicated that they thought it was the appropriate way to change the Constitution.[137] This is confirmed by the fact that

---

[133] James Madison, The Federalist No. 40, in Cooke, ed., p. 265 (emphasis in original).
[134] Ibid., pp. 265–66.
[135] Ibid., p. 266.
[136] Ibid., p. 263.
[137] See James Madison, The Federalist No. 43, in Cooke, ed., p. 296; Alexander Hamilton, The Federalist No. 85, in Cooke, ed., pp. 591–93. For a reliable discussion of *The
Federalist* essays on Article V, see Vile, *The Constitutional Amending Process in American
Political Thought*, pp. 34–42.

the founding generation used Article V to amend the Constitution no less than twelve times in nearly as many years. Ackerman might reply that none of these amendments involved a true transformative change. The Bill of Rights, however, is usually thought of as fundamental to our constitutional order. The ratification of the Bill of Rights complied with the provisions of Article V in all respects.

Ackerman also attempts to use *The Federalist* No. 49, which we analyzed earlier, to support his theory. He refers several times to Madison's statement "that a constitutional road to the decision of the people, ought to be marked out, and kept open, for certain great and extraordinary occasions."[138] As we have seen, this essay presents an argument against making constitutional change too easy. Madison does not draw a distinction here between normal and constitutional politics in Ackerman's sense. The most natural reading of this passage is that Madison is referring to change through Article V, which he believes will be infrequent.

Ackerman emphasizes the importance of Hamilton's famous essay on the judiciary in *The Federalist* No. 78, and claims that it supports his theory. Hamilton argued that the independence of the judiciary from the other branches of government is necessary to protect the Constitution against sudden inclinations of the public to violate its provisions. Hamilton noted that although the people may "alter or abolish the established constitution whenever they find it inconsistent with their happiness," it is binding on them until they change it "by some solemn and authoritative act."[139] Ackerman makes much of Hamilton's omission of the word "legal" in describing the means of constitutional alteration. He thinks this shows that Hamilton believes that a process for constitutional change exists outside Article V.[140] Again, however, the most natural reading of this passage is that Hamilton is referring to Article V. It would be out of place for Hamilton to introduce a theory of constitutional change in the context of a discussion of how the judiciary can protect the Constitution.

Since Ackerman is not willing to rely on Article V as the only legal road to constitutional change, he faces the problem of devising his own roadmap of higher lawmaking. How do we distinguish moments of higher lawmaking that result in transformative constitutional amendments from failed constitutional moments?[141] But this question makes it even more apparent that Ackerman cannot appeal to *The Federalist* to justify his theory. Ackerman's answer that higher lawmaking consists of distinct

[138] James Madison, The Federalist No. 49, in Cooke, ed., p. 339. For Ackerman's frequent use of this passage, see *We The People: Foundations*, pp. 179, 191, 197.

[139] Alexander Hamilton, The Federalist No. 78, in Cooke, ed., pp. 527–28.

[140] Ackerman, *We The People: Foundations*, p. 195.

[141] Ibid., pp. 196–97.

phases of signaling transformative change, proposing that change, mobilizing the people to deliberate over the change, and legal codification of the accepted change, has no connection to the thought of the founding generation.[142]

Although Ackerman's theory finds no support in *The Federalist*, his account of American constitutional history remains challenging. Ackerman builds not only on the apparent illegality of the Constitution but also on the uncomfortable fact that the Reconstruction Amendments would not have been ratified without the forced acceptance of the former states of the Confederacy.[143] While Ackerman always attempts to be sensitive to historical and political context, his contention that these transformative moments rested on non–Article V illegality is overly legalistic. Analyzing these moments as legal or illegal commits a kind of category mistake.[144] As Madison noted in *The Federalist* No. 40, the inadequacies of the Articles of Confederation created a political and constitutional crisis which the members of the Federal Convention hoped to solve. Despite their deviation from the process of amendment specified in the Articles, the Confederation Congress passed the proposed Constitution on to the states and the states proceeded to elect delegates to ratifying conventions. This process could have broken down at any stage if enough citizens were convinced that the question of legality was important. This did not happen, however. The political context in which the Federal Convention was held and the Constitution was ratified rendered such concerns moot.[145]

The same holds true for the Reconstruction Amendments. While there are no provisions in Article V respecting the forced acceptance of amendments, there are no provisions in the entire Constitution adequate to the exigencies of secession and the Civil War. In mandating the acceptance of amendments, Republicans in Congress may have been operating outside Article V, but then again, the southern states had been operating outside of the Union.[146] The Civil War created a political and constitutional crisis in which actions such as the forced acceptance of amendments

---

[142] Ibid., pp. 266–67.

[143] See the discussion in chapter 2, section three.

[144] For relevant discussion, see Frederick Schauer, "Amending the Presuppositions of a Constitution," in Levinson, ed., *Responding to Imperfection*, pp. 153–54.

[145] See Bernstein, *Amending America*, p. 26. See also Ackerman and Katyal, "Our Unconventional Founding." This curious article argues simultaneously that the Federalist advocates of the Constitution did not claim that it was legal or illegal and that this shows that adoption of the Constitution was, in fact, illegal. The evidence the authors produce, however, supports the conclusion that the concept of legality is irrelevant to understanding the process by which the Constitution was ratified.

[146] See James M. McPherson, *Battle Cry of Freedom: The Civil War Era* (New York: Oxford University Press, 1988), p. 699.

became necessary.[147] It is beside the point to argue over whether these actions were legal or illegal because the War altered the grounds on which such a debate could be conducted.

In addition, our earlier review of constitutional change during the New Deal casts considerable doubt on Ackerman's thesis that President Roosevelt followed a theory of higher lawmaking and pursued change outside Article V. Part of the reason Roosevelt rejected proposing amendments was that he became convinced he was not asking for fundamental alterations to the Constitution. The problem was with the Supreme Court's interpretation of the Constitution, not with the Constitution itself. In particular, Roosevelt did not highlight constitutional issues during the election of 1936, as Ackerman's theory requires. Throughout the Court-packing crisis that followed the election, Roosevelt often downplayed the constitutional issues behind his proposal to put more justices on the Court.[148] These are not the actions of someone seeking a transformative constitutional moment.

There is no doubt that there have been important periods of constitutional politics in American history, periods in which constitutional questions became the overriding issues of the hour and fundamental changes were made to the constitutional system. But there have been many more of these moments than Ackerman is willing to admit. In particular, both the Progressive Era and the civil rights movement (which Ackerman counts as failed constitutional moments) transformed the constitutional order through amendments made under Article V, statutes of fundamental importance, and alterations in the relationship of governing institutions. Any adequate theory of constitutional change must account for all of the important periods of change in American history.

The questionable aspects of Ackerman's theory suggest also that it is a mistake to attempt to transmute constitutional change outside Article V into legal change. We should not understand constitutional change outside Article V in terms of the concept of amendment. Given the context produced by the legalized Constitution, calling significant constitutional changes "amendments" implies that such changes have the same legal

---

[147] See the discussion in Laurence H. Tribe, "Taking Text and Structure Seriously: Reflections on Free-Form Method in Constitutional Interpretation," *Harvard Law Review* 108 (1995): 1292–94. Tribe criticizes in detail the argument made in Ackerman and Golove, "Is NAFTA Constitutional?"

[148] See Stephen Skowronek, *The Politics Presidents Make: Leadership from John Adams to George Bush* (Cambridge: Harvard University Press, 1993), pp. 320–21. See also the sources cited in note 106.

It should be noted that Ackerman's accounts of Reconstruction and the New Deal are difficult to assess on the basis of his first of three projected volumes because he does not set out his argument in detail. An assessment of Ackerman's argument on these periods cannot be made properly until his second volume is published.

status as amendments made under Article V. Once it is understood that the legalized Constitution limits the sphere in which the Constitution can be enforced in the same manner as ordinary law, changes outside this sphere cannot be legal in the way required by Ackerman's theory. Understanding the legalized Constitution means accepting the reality that significant constitutional changes can occur through ordinary politics outside the realm of constitutional law.

Defining the Constitution

At first glance, defining the Constitution appears an easy task. The document, after all, is under glass at the National Archives.[149] But the preceding discussion of constitutional change should have made us sensitive to why defining the Constitution continues to puzzle those who study American constitutionalism. The more the Constitution changes through means other than amendment, the less we can say that the document under glass comprises the sum total of the Constitution. This is why we did not begin our discussion of constitutional change by defining what the Constitution is—the difficulty of defining the Constitution can be appreciated only after the problem of constitutional change is understood. The task of defining the Constitution is also complicated by the need to distinguish carefully between attempts to describe and explain the constitutional system and attempts to trace the boundaries of the normative order established by the Constitution.

To fix ideas, we will define the Constitution as the content of the 1787 document as ratified and validly amended plus valid precedents interpreting the document issued by the federal judiciary. This is what is studied in law schools and political science departments as "constitutional law" (although courses concentrate on Supreme Court decisions) and it would probably be accepted by most lawyers and judges as a conventional definition of the Constitution. Note that this is a normative and legal definition because it purports to tell us what our obligations are under the law.

Although this definition may seem uncontroversial, it has been criticized implicitly on the ground that just as Supreme Court precedent can be part of the Constitution, certain actions of the executive and legislative branches can attain constitutional status. Various scholars have argued that some presidential practices and federal laws have the status of "framework legislation."[150] One scholar defines framework legislation as follows:

---

[149] Although, perhaps, not forever. The Constitution and other founding documents are threatened by the deterioration of their casing. See Warren E. Leary, "Threat Is Posed to America's Charter Documents," *New York Times*, April 1, 1995, p. 7.

[150] Gerhard Casper, "Constitutional Constraints on the Conduct of Foreign and Defense

"[f]ramework legislation is different from ordinary legislation in that it does not formulate specific policies for the resolution of specific problems, but rather attempts to implement constitutional policies."[151] Examples of framework legislation include the National Security Act of 1947, the Congressional Budget and Impoundment Control Act of 1974, the National Emergencies Act of 1976, and the War Powers Resolution of 1973.[152]

The idea of framework legislation is intriguing and captures an important difference between laws enacted to implement the Constitution (such as laws specifying the jurisdiction of federal courts), and legislation directed at specific policy problems. Yet a question can be raised as to whether these laws truly have constitutional status in the same sense as the text of the Constitution and federal court precedents. Some of the laws listed above have been the subject of constitutional controversy and actual litigation. While none of these laws has been held unconstitutional, the idea that they have the same status as Supreme Court precedents implies that the Court would give them greater deference as compared with other laws. While it is difficult to test this proposition, it seems questionable.[153] Certainly the Court has not recognized such a doctrine.

The conventional definition of the Constitution can also be criticized in light of the preceding discussion of constitutional change. We established that important changes to the Constitution have occurred through means other than amendment and judicial interpretation. Yet the conventional definition does not recognize such changes. This suggests revising the conventional definition to include truly fundamental changes such as the party system and those that followed the New Deal.[154] Again, however, this revised definition can be questioned on the ground that it is uncertain

---

Policy: A Nonjudicial Model," *University of Chicago Law Review* 43 (1976): 481–82. See also Ackerman and Golove, "Is NAFTA Constitutional?" pp. 915–16; Kenneth W. Dam, "The American Fiscal Constitution," *University of Chicago Law Review* 44 (1977): 272–73; Stephen R. Munzer and James W. Nickel, "Does the Constitution Mean What It Always Meant?" *Columbia Law Review* 77 (1977): 1046–50; Peter M. Shane, "Voting Rights and the 'Statutory Constitution,'" *Law and Contemporary Problems* 56 (1993): 243.

[151] Casper, "Constitutional Constraints on the Conduct of Foreign and Defense Policy," p. 482.

[152] For this list and other examples, see the discussion in Koh, The National Security Constitution, pp. 69–72.

[153] There are, arguably, examples of framework legislation that have been held to be unconstitutional. See *INS v. Chadha*, 462 U.S. 919 (1983)(invalidating the legislative veto) and *Bowsher v. Synar*, 478 U.S. 714 (1986)(holding unconstitutional the Gramm-Rudman-Hollings Act to control the deficit). It seems unlikely that the Court gave the statutes involved in these cases greater deference than statutes involved in other cases.

[154] This revised definition expresses an important element of Ackerman's theory. It has also been advanced by the noted legal realist Karl Llewellyn. See Karl N. Llewellyn, "The Constitution as an Institution," *Columbia Law Review* 34 (1934): 1.

whether the legal system recognizes such changes as part of the Constitution. The Court, for example, does not have a doctrine that recognizes "quasi-amendments" to the Constitution. In addition, the revised definition is even more indeterminate than the idea of framework legislation (where we worked from a fairly definite list). The revised definition so blurs the difference between ordinary political practices and the Constitution that we are left with an undifferentiated soup of supposed "fundamental" practices without a clear way to distinguish them from enforceable constitutional norms.[155]

We seem to be left with a quandary—a sense that the conventional definition does not capture the full reality of constitutional change, against the criticism that expanding the conventional definition runs the risk of obscuring the clear status of the text as supreme law. This problem has been the basis for a long debate over whether the Constitution is better characterized as written or unwritten.[156]

To make sense of this quandary, we must appreciate that the suggested revisions to the conventional definition do not necessarily conflict with it. We can understand the suggested revisions as attempts to describe and explain the Constitution we have by noticing that norms not in the text are functionally equivalent to norms in the text. The account of constitutional change presented earlier illustrates the increasing importance of such functionally equivalent norms as the federal government became more activist in the twentieth century. The difference between the set of norms in the Constitution and the set of all norms that are functionally equivalent to those in the Constitution is a measure of how much constitutional change has occurred off-text. Some scholars have seen a convergence in this respect between the "written" American Constitution and the "unwritten" British constitution. As the British constitution became more written and formalized over time, the American Constitution became encrusted with political compromise and judicial interpretation.[157]

The conventional definition is still valid, however, as long as it is understood in the context of the legalized, normative Constitution. As we saw in the first section, lawyers and judges are most familiar with the legalized Constitution and the conventional definition captures their understand-

---

[155] For similar criticisms of Llewellyn, see Herman Belz, "History, Theory, and the Constitution," *Constitutional Commentary* 11 (1994): 45; Munzer and Nickel, "Does the Constitution Mean What It Always Meant?" pp. 1033–36.

[156] This way of describing the debate is not used here because the idea of the unwritten Constitution is an overly simple way of approaching issues that must be considered in detail, as with the concept of framework legislation. For a valuable discussion of the written-unwritten distinction, see Michael Foley, *The Silence of Constitutions* (London: Routledge, 1989), pp. 3–11.

[157] See Carl J. Friedrich, *The Impact of American Constitutionalism Abroad* (Boston: Boston University Press, 1967), p. 12.

ing of the boundaries of the constitutional world. It is possible that the statutes most important to the legalization of the Constitution, such as those pertaining to the jurisdiction of the federal judiciary, may also have constitutional status in a normative sense. If Congress attempted to change the jurisdiction of federal courts in a fundamental way, it is possible that the Supreme Court might treat the statutes in question as functionally equivalent to constitutional norms, given that they implement Article III of the Constitution. This addition aside, however, the conventional definition holds up well from a normative perspective.

We are still left with the issue of how to define the Constitution when our concern is to describe and explain how it has changed over time. So far we have appealed simply to the idea of fundamental norms or norms that are functionally equivalent to those in the text. The best descriptive definition of the Constitution offered so far is that it is "a text-based institutional practice in which authoritative interpreters can create new constitutional norms."[158] As we will further detail in chapter 2, these norms are part of the structure of the state. Since authoritative interpreters can create new constitutional norms, the text of the Constitution is only one source of those norms. For the purposes of describing and explaining how the Constitution has changed over time, then, the Constitution is best understood as a text-based institutional practice.

Implications for American Constitutionalism

In Michael Kammen's history of the public understanding of constitutionalism, his main theme is the tendency of Americans to see the Constitution as "a machine that would go of itself."[159] The metaphor suggests that the Constitution can run the political system without any further refinement or external intervention. This way of thinking has no doubt been encouraged by the relative infrequency of important amendments to the Constitution and the apparent permanence of the institutions it established.

We are now in a position to appreciate why this metaphor is false. The difficulty of amendment forced federal constitutional change to assume a protean character. If the responsibilities of the federal government change, the relevant constitutional norms change also. If the text of the Constitution is frozen in place due to the difficulty of amendment, then the constitutional change simply assumes a different form. The change

[158] Munzer and Nickel, "Does the Constitution Mean What It Always Meant?" p. 1045.
[159] Kammen, *A Machine That Would Go Of Itself,* p. 18 (quoting James Russell Lowell).

may occur through a new statute, a Supreme Court decision, or an adjustment in political practice. The examination of the relationship between the Constitution and American political development in chapter 2 will enable us to explore this process in greater detail.

To understand the large-scale structure of American constitutionalism, imagine a large sphere containing a smaller sphere. The large sphere is the entire constitutional domain, including constitutional norms not created through the original adoption of the Constitution, Article V, or judicial interpretation. The smaller sphere is the domain of the legalized Constitution, the domain identified most readily by lawyers and judges as *the* Constitution. Here constitutional change is understood in terms of amendments made under Article V, judicial interpretations, and perhaps statutes of fundamental importance.

The path these spheres trace in political space and historical time cannot be followed unless both are kept in view. If the legalized Constitution attempts to occupy space claimed by the elected branches, then its small sphere contracts further. If the elected branches are irresolute on a particular constitutional issue and cast it into the hands of the Supreme Court, the sphere of the legalized Constitution expands. But the form and nature of the legalized Constitution cannot be understood without taking into consideration its larger companion.

The theory of constitutional change offered in this chapter suggests that in an important respect, constitutionalism as the founding generation understood it is incompatible with the modern democratic regulatory-welfare state. The founding generation expected that the federal government would be one of enumerated powers only. At least some of them believed that all branches of government, not just the Supreme Court, should interpret the Constitution in order to give effect to its provisions. But establishing a legalized Constitution required the Court to have monopoly power on issuing legal interpretations of the Constitution. If the Court declares a government action constitutional or not, that is taken to be the last word in a legal sense. This means that the idea of the Constitution as an enforceable higher law is only preserved to the extent that the Court gives full effect to all of its provisions. Yet, as we observed in our discussion of the New Deal, the Court responded to the advent of the modern democratic state by recusing itself from deciding crucial issues of constitutional power. This means that government power in those areas is no longer subject to constitutional constraints, unless we think of the legislative and executive branches as willing to place principled checks on themselves.

It appears that the eighteenth-century idea of constitutionalism is inextricably linked with the concept of the minimal state. In our political system, the minimal state translates into the kind of federal government that existed in the nineteenth century, one that lets the states take the lead and stays in the background, at least in matters of domestic policy.[160] Once the federal government was no longer a minimal state, the eighteenth century idea of limiting and empowering government through a careful enumeration of constitutional power was no longer viable. Control of the modern democratic state is achieved primarily through the normal operation of the political system, not through the legalized Constitution. In this respect, democracy has replaced constitutionalism as the means of constituting government.

[160] See, e.g., James Madison, The Federalist No. 45, in Cooke, ed., p. 313.

Two

The Constitution and Political Institutions

WAR is in many respects the ultimate test of the modern state.[1] The Constitution clearly provides the power to prepare for and fight wars that may be necessary to defend the republic. Article I gives Congress the power "to declare war," "to raise and support armies," "to provide and maintain a navy," and "to make rules for the government and regulation of the land and naval forces."[2] Article II provides that "the President shall be Commander in Chief of the army and navy of the United States."[3] Yet these clauses do not provide for many of the situations that may arise with respect to the defense of American territory and interests. What if the United States is attacked when Congress is not in session? No doubt the President has the power to repel sudden attacks in his capacity as Commander in Chief. Suppose, however, that the armed forces that exist are insufficient to meet the emergency. What constitutional power does the President possess in such a situation?

This was the situation faced by President Abraham Lincoln at the attack on Fort Sumter in April 1861. Congress had adjourned the previous month, yet some response was necessary. To bridge the gap in constitutional power, Lincoln called for thousands of volunteers, increased the size of the army and navy, authorized a blockade of rebel ports, had money paid from the Treasury on his own authority, and suspended the writ of habeas corpus in particular instances.[4] Although the Constitution did not clearly provide the authority for any of these measures, the emergency forced Lincoln to act as if he had the power to do so.

---

[1] See, e.g., Stephen Skowronek, *Building a New American State: The Expansion of National Administrative Capacities, 1877–1920* (Cambridge: Cambridge University Press, 1982), p. 10.

[2] U.S. Const., Article I, sec. 8.

[3] U.S. Const., Article II, sec. 2.

[4] See Alfred H. Kelly, Winfred A. Harbison, and Herman Belz, *The American Constitution: Its Origins and Development*, 6th ed. (New York: W. W. Norton, 1983), pp. 300–302. For other commentaries on Lincoln's exercise of power, see Phillip Shaw Paludan, *The Presidency of Abraham Lincoln* (Lawrence: University Press of Kansas, 1994), pp. 69–82; Michael Les Benedict, "The Constitution of the Lincoln Presidency and the Republican Era," in Martin L. Fausold and Alan Shank, eds., *The Constitution and the American Presidency* (Albany: State University of New York Press, 1991), p. 45.

The constitutional problem that Lincoln faced as chief executive re-curred each time the United States fought a major war. In World War I, President Woodrow Wilson received an almost unlimited delegation of power from Congress to conduct the war as he saw fit. President Franklin Roosevelt received similar delegations of power during World War II and, like Lincoln, exercised what he regarded as inherent presidential authority to reorganize the executive branch, direct the national economy, and aid the allies even in the absence of legislation authorizing such acts.[5]

The recurrence of serious constitutional problems each time the United States fights a major war is a dramatic example of the difference between providing a constitutional framework of government powers and building competent government institutions.[6] While there is no doubt that the Constitution gave the federal government the power to wage war, the mere provision of constitutional powers did not guarantee that the government would be able to use those powers effectively. To bridge the gap between the grant of power and the effective use of power, institu-tions are required to operationalize constitutional powers and make them meaningful.[7] Much of the history of the relationship of the Constitution to American political institutions is the story of how this gap was bridged, very gradually in the nineteenth century and with increasing urgency and effort in the twentieth century.[8]

The relationship between the Constitution and political institutions, as well as American political development, has not been a traditional focus of constitutional theory. Theories of judicial review and constitutional inter-pretation have received far more attention from scholars. In part this is because constitutional theory has been oriented toward answering the im-portant normative questions raised by Supreme Court cases. Questions

---

[5] See Kelly, Harbison, and Belz, *The American Constitution*, pp. 448–53, 550–62.

[6] For commentary on this problem in relation to the Vietnam War, see Stanley I. Kutler, *The Wars of Watergate* (New York: Alfred A. Knopf, 1990), p. 79.

[7] This is the import of Woodrow Wilson's well-known observation that "[i]t is getting to be harder to *run* a constitution than to frame one." Woodrow Wilson, "The Study of Ad-ministration," *Political Science Quarterly* 2 (1887): 200 (emphasis in original). For an at-tempt to legitimate the modern administrative state under the Constitution, see John A. Rohr, *To Run a Constitution: The Legitimacy of the Administrative State* (Lawrence: Uni-versity Press of Kansas, 1986).

[8] This chapter draws on recent work on the concept and history of the state by historians and social scientists and the "new institutionalism" in political science. See, e.g., Peter B. Evans, Dietrich Rueschemeyer, and Theda Skocpol, eds., *Bringing the State Back In* (New York: Cambridge University Press, 1985); James G. March and Johan P. Olsen, *Re-discovering Institutions: The Organizational Basis of Politics* (New York: Macmillan, 1989); Eric Nordlinger, *On the Autonomy of the Democratic State* (Cambridge: Harvard Univer-sity Press, 1981); Martin Shefter, *Political Parties and the State: The American Historical Experience* (Princeton: Princeton University Press, 1994); Skowronek, *Building a New American State*.

raised by the interaction of the Constitution with political institutions seem more of historical interest and raise descriptive-explanatory issues as well as normative concerns. Nevertheless, these questions are worthy of attention and are important to understanding American constitutionalism. How did the founding generation understand the relationship between the Constitution and politics? Did the founding generation succeed in designing a system of government capable of responding to the political problems of their day? What is the relationship between the Constitution and the state? What influence has the Constitution had on the development of American politics and governing institutions?

These questions deserve a permanent place on the agenda of American constitutional theory, especially if that theory is to be responsive to the challenging issues of constitutional reform posed by contemporary American politics.[9] This chapter explores the relationship between the Constitution and political institutions by examining Madison's famous theory of how the Constitution would respond to American political circumstances by curbing factious majorities, the Constitution and the concept of the state, and the interaction between the Constitution and American political development. The discussion of American political development in the third section will complete the theory of constitutional change offered in chapter 1.

Madison and the Problem of Faction

The Constitution sets out an institutional structure for government. The preamble states the general purposes those institutions serve. These purposes, however, do not reveal fully the goals of the Federalists. The Constitution was adopted not only to fulfill abstract purposes, but also as a response to the political circumstances of the 1780s. Moreover, the purpose of the Constitution was not simply to establish a more effective government than that provided by the Articles of Confederation, but to change the structure in which politics took place and perhaps to change politics itself.

By common scholarly agreement, James Madison's essays in *The Federalist* are the best single starting point in understanding this political-institutional aspect of the Constitution.[10] Madison's essays are famous because they present an account of what the Constitution is *for* in a broad sense;

---

[9] We will take up issues of constitutional reform and continue the discussion begun in the third section of this chapter in chapter 6.

[10] This scholarly agreement, however, is a product of the twentieth century. See the discussion in Douglass Adair, *Fame and the Founding Fathers* (New York: W. W. Norton, 1974), pp. 75–92. For a qualified and original dissent from this agreement, see Albert

that is, what it is supposed to accomplish, given the circumstances of the new republic. Madison was well prepared for the Federal Convention and this preparation helped him to keep up with the rapid rate at which *The Federalist* was produced during the winter of 1787–88. Although Madison wrote essays on a number of topics, we will concentrate here on how he thought the Constitution responded to a single problem—the deficiencies of state legislation resulting from the politics of faction.[11]

In a manuscript completed just before the Federal Convention, titled "Vices of the Political System of the United States," Madison laid out the defects of government under the Articles of Confederation and detailed problems in the state legislative process. Problems of the Confederation occupied the first eight points of his analysis.[12] But he also devoted substantial attention to the problems of state government. Madison complained of the "multiplicity of laws in the several states," their "mutability," and, most important, their "injustice," which he regarded as the most alarming defect. The injustice of state laws was most alarming because it called into question the principle of republican government that the majority should rule because they are the safest guardians of the public good and private rights.[13]

Madison argued that the injustice of state laws resulted from problems with the state legislatures and with the people themselves. Men sought positions in the state legislatures out of ambition and personal interest rather than devotion to the public good. This led state representatives to act contrary to the interest of their constituents and sacrifice the public good to their own interest. If this was the case, however, why

---

Furtwangler, *The Authority of Publius: A Reading of the Federalist Papers* (Ithaca: Cornell University Press, 1984).

There are, of course, many studies of *The Federalist* and Madison's The Federalist No. 10. Some of the most helpful studies in addition to Adair's are cited in the notes below. Two good general studies are David F. Epstein, *The Political Theory of The Federalist* (Chicago: University of Chicago Press, 1984) and Morton White, *Philosophy,* The Federalist, *and the Constitution* (New York: Oxford University Press, 1987). For a recent, comprehensive treatment of the issues surrounding The Federalist No. 10, see Alan Gibson, "Impartial Representation and the Extended Republic: Towards a Comprehensive and Balanced Reading of the Tenth *Federalist* Paper," *History of Political Thought* 12 (1991): 263.

On Madison's thought generally during this period, see the excellent work by Lance Banning, *The Sacred Fire of Liberty: James Madison and the Founding of the Federal Republic* (Ithaca: Cornell University Press, 1995).

[11] For the importance of Madison's discussion of this problem, see Paul A. Rahe, *Republics Ancient and Modern: Classical Republicanism and the American Revolution* (Chapel Hill: University of North Carolina Press, 1992), pp. 582–83.

[12] See "Vices of the Political System of the United States," in Marvin Meyers, ed., *The Mind of the Founder: Sources of the Political Thought of James Madison* (Hanover: University Press of New England, 1981), pp. 57–61.

[13] Ibid., pp. 61–62.

would their constituents not detect this lack of devotion to the public interest? Madison stated that elections did not solve this problem because "base and selfish measures" are "masked by pretexts of public good and apparent expediency."[14]

The most important cause of the injustice of state laws was the influence of factious majorities.[15] The problem of faction was the subject of what is now the most famous essay in *The Federalist*: Madison's *Federalist* No. 10.[16] Madison begins this essay by repeating the complaints about state governments discussed in his "Vices" manuscript—that they are unstable, that the public good has been disregarded in the conflicts of rival parties, and that measures have been too often decided by an interested majority not acting for the public good. Evidently "a factious spirit has tainted our public administrations."[17]

Madison defines a faction as "a number of citizens, whether amounting to a majority or minority of the whole, who are united and actuated by some common impulse of passion, or of interest, adverse to the rights of other citizens, or to the permanent and aggregate interests of the community."[18] Note that this definition is normative or ethical, rather than numerical.[19] Even if 90 percent of the citizens in the United States believe a certain measure is necessary, they are nonetheless a faction if that measure violates the rights of other citizens or is contrary to the public good. A faction is not limited to what we would call a special or narrow interest group. Since Madison is concerned with the problem of majority factions, the kind of faction he has in mind is a large party of citizens whose designs are hostile to private rights or the public good.

Factions are caused by the differing interests in society and are ultimately grounded in the fallible opinions of men and the liberty they have to exercise those opinions. There is thus no question of eliminating the causes of faction, the issue is rather one of control.[20] Madison was most specific about the various kinds of factions in his "Vices" manuscript. "All

---

[14] Ibid., p. 62.

[15] Ibid., pp. 62–63. Madison concentrates on the problem posed by factious majorities because factious minorities can be controlled by being outvoted by the majority. See James Madison, The Federalist No. 10, in Jacob E. Cooke, ed., *The Federalist* (Middletown, Conn.: Wesleyan University Press, 1961), p. 60.

[16] Many analyses of The Federalist No. 10 treat it as an abstract discussion of the advantages of large versus small republics. By contrast, we will examine Madison's reasoning in the light of his concern with the deficiencies of politics and government in the states. In this regard, see Jack N. Rakove, "The Madisonian Moment," *University of Chicago Law Review* 55 (1988): 479–80.

[17] James Madison, The Federalist No. 10, in Cooke, ed., p. 57.

[18] Ibid.

[19] On this point, see White, *Philosophy, The Federalist, and the Constitution*, p. 187.

[20] James Madison, The Federalist No. 10, in Cooke, ed., p. 58.

civilized societies are divided into different interests and factions, as they happen to be creditors or debtors—rich or poor—husbandmen, merchants or manufacturers—members of different religious sects—followers of different political leaders—inhabitants of different districts—owners of different kinds of property," and so on.[21] In *The Federalist* No. 10, Madison gave special stress to the differing distribution of property, saying that it is "the most common and durable source of factions." "Those who are creditors, and those who are debtors . . . [a] landed interest, a manufacturing interest, a mercantile interest, a monied interest" all have different views as to what government should do and this "involves the spirit of party and faction in the necessary and ordinary operations of Government."[22]

For Madison's argument to work, he must link the existence of factions to the passage of unjust state legislation. Why do factions have so much influence in state government? The import of Madison's argument is that factions have easy access to government when that government has a limited sphere, both in terms of territory and the number of citizens in its jurisdiction. State governments are too small to resist the influence of faction.[23]

Madison then makes an argument respecting how representatives should decide issues in a republic. He argues that "[n]o man is allowed to be a judge in his own cause," and so, "with equal, nay with greater reason, a body of men, are unfit to be both judges and parties, at the same time; yet, what are many of the most important acts of legislation, but so many judicial determinations, not indeed concerning the rights of single persons, but concerning the rights of large bodies of citizens; and what are the different classes of legislators, but advocates and parties to the causes which they determine?"[24]

This argument draws an explicit analogy between the judicial and the legislative process.[25] But it may be doubted whether the two are really analogous. A judicial determination in a given case is one made under law and it requires a neutral or impartial judge because otherwise there would not be an authoritative means of resolving the dispute. By contrast, legislation that, for example, favors debtors over creditors is not adopted under an existing rule of law. Rather, the point of the legislation

---

[21] "Vices of the Political System of the United States," in Meyers, ed., *The Mind of the Founder*, pp. 62–63. Madison gave the same analysis of faction that was in the "Vices" manuscript at the Federal Convention in a speech of June 6, 1787. Ibid., pp. 71–72.

[22] James Madison, The Federalist No. 10, in Cooke, ed., p. 59.

[23] Ibid., pp. 63–64.

[24] Ibid., p. 59.

[25] For discussion, see Gibson, "Impartial Representation and the Extended Republic," p. 276.

is to establish what the rules are. Madison says that "justice" ought to decide the issue between debtors and creditors, but this ignores the question of whether there is a preexisting legal standard to resolve the issue. In any case, in a free republic of the kind Madison endorses, controversies over the content of such rules can legitimately exist. Ordinary politics revolves around the determination of these issues. Madison here assumes without argument a background of specific, uncontroversial, and preexisting rights that will be infringed by legislation sponsored by a particular faction.[26]

The analogy to the judicial process suggests that someone must be the neutral arbiter between the various factions. But Madison immediately denies this. "It is in vain to say, that enlightened statesmen will be able to adjust these clashing interests, and render them all subservient to the public good. Enlightened statesmen will not always be at the helm."[27] Here Madison may still be thinking of the circumstances of state legislatures. The problems attending state governments cannot be solved merely by postulating the existence of wise legislators.[28]

Since factions cannot be eliminated in a free government, the question is which system of government can do the best job controlling the effects of faction. Madison in effect likens state governments to small representative republics or even pure (what we now call direct) democracies. The extended republic promised by the Constitution will best minimize the problem of faction because such a republic has three advantages over the states.[29] First, the republic will be able to draw representatives from a wide area and so provide men "whose enlightened views and virtuous sentiments render them superior to local prejudices."[30] It is possible that men of local prejudices will be elected, but the real issue is whether this is more likely in small or extensive republics. Extended republics have the advantage here for two reasons. First, they are more likely to produce candidates of the appropriate character because they have more people. The second

[26] See Jennifer Nedelsky, *Private Property and the Limits of American Constitutionalism* (Chicago: University of Chicago Press, 1990), p. 185.

[27] Madison, The Federalist No. 10 in Cooke, ed., p. 60.

[28] There is an important disagreement in the literature over the meaning of this passage. Some scholars take it as obvious that Madison is denying the notion that the successful operation of the federal government depends on men of the right character. One scholar refers to this notion as an "ancient heresy." Rahe, *Republics Ancient and Modern*, p. 1057 n. 60. See the discussion below at notes 35–36. But Madison's meaning here is not clear. Is he discussing state governments, the federal government, or both? Note also that this passage occurs before Madison begins discussing the means of controlling the effects of faction. What Madison says after this passage concerning the importance of men of the right character might therefore be given more weight than the "enlightened statesmen" remark.

[29] See Madison, The Federalist No. 10 in Cooke, ed., pp. 64–65.

[30] Ibid., p. 64.

reason is that since in an extended republic each representative will be chosen by a greater number of citizens in large districts, it will be more difficult for representatives of inferior character to be elected. Men of more "diffusive and established characters" will be chosen.[31]

The second advantage of an extended republic is the security provided by the greater variety of parties and factions. The more limited the sphere of government, the smaller the number of factions. This means that a majority of the same party or faction will be formed more frequently and so they can more easily oppress others.[32] The third advantage of an extended republic is closely related to the second. The large size of the Union will pose greater obstacles to factions. A faction may grow and flourish in a particular state or even in a group of states, but it "will be unable to spread a general conflagration through the other States." Madison summarizes the last two advantages as follows: "Extend the sphere, and you take in a greater variety of parties and interests; you make it less probable that a majority of the whole will have a common motive to invade the rights of other citizens; or if such a common motive exists, it will be more difficult for all who feel it to discover their own strength, and to act in unison with each other."[33]

As historian Edmund Morgan has pointed out, the great size of the extended republic is the key to all three advantages.[34] Representatives of the proper character are more likely to emerge because of the large size of the districts from which they are elected. The large size of the republic simultaneously guarantees a wide variety of factions and parties and makes it more difficult for them to cooperate against the public good. The extended republic promised by the Constitution thus best minimizes the problem of faction.

One of the contemporary debates over the interpretation of Madison's thought concerns the importance of men of the right character to his theory of government. As we saw in chapter 1, a number of historians emphasize that Madison and the other Federalists expected the government to be composed of men like themselves—educated and wealthy gentlemen.[35] Madison's remarks in *The Federalist* No. 10 appear to support this idea. Yet other scholars discount this aspect of Madison's thought.

---

[31] Ibid., pp. 62–63.

[32] Ibid., pp. 63–64.

[33] Ibid., p. 64. The second and third advantages of the extended republic were reiterated by Madison in another famous essay, The Federalist No. 51. See Cooke, ed., pp. 351–53.

[34] See Edmund S. Morgan, "Safety in Numbers: Madison, Hume, and the Tenth *Federalist*," *Huntington Library Quarterly* 49 (1986): 104–10.

[35] See Stanley Elkins and Eric McKitrick, *The Age of Federalism* (New York: Oxford University Press, 1993), p. 703; Gordon S. Wood, *The Creation of the American Republic 1776–1787* (New York: W. W. Norton, 1969), pp. 471–518.

They note Madison's realistic appraisal that any representative may act from ambition and self-interest and place more emphasis on the structural aspects of the new constitutional order such as separation of powers and federalism as the means of controlling faction.[36]

While it is unlikely that this debate will ever be settled conclusively, the question we should ask is why scholars are so concerned with this issue. It seems that what is at stake is the applicability of Madison's theory of government to our present circumstances. No one today believes America should be ruled by a wealthy, propertied, classically educated, agrarian male elite. To the extent Madison's theory depends on such an elite, it appears that his theory, along with much of Federalist thought, is irrelevant to understanding the twentieth-century constitutional order. Downplaying Madison's reliance on representatives of the right character still leaves us a theory that recognizably relates to the government we have.

In any event, we should not allow this debate and other debates concerning the thought of the founding generation to distract us from evaluating their arguments. Scholars have tended to focus on what the founding generation *meant*, without going on to ask whether they were *right*. Was Madison right? Were factious majorities one of the most serious dangers faced by the new republic? Did Madison propose a viable solution to this problem? One difficulty in assessing Madison's argument is that he did not offer a detailed analysis of the injustice of the state laws or what justice required in the abstract from the legislative process.[37] Madison's concern is sometimes summed up as "the tyranny of the majority," but this is misleading, overlaid as this phrase is with contemporary associations of civil liberties.[38] Madison was concerned with violations of rights, but it was largely the rights of private property, not what we now call civil rights or civil liberties.[39] The constant jockeying for advantage and special privileges that seemed to be the bread and butter of state legislatures dismayed him.

[36] See Samuel H. Beer, *To Make A Nation: The Rediscovery of American Federalism* (Cambridge: Harvard University Press, 1993), pp. 280–82; Nedelsky, *Private Property and the Limits of American Constitutionalism*, pp. 175–77; Rahe, *Republics Ancient and Modern*, pp. 586–605; Jeffrey K. Tulis, *The Rhetorical Presidency* (Princeton: Princeton University Press, 1987), pp. 38–39, 176–77; Lance Banning, "The Hamiltonian Madison: A Reconsideration," *The Virginia Magazine of History and Biography* 92 (1984): 12–16.

For a careful presentation of an intermediate view, see Rakove, "The Madisonian Moment," pp. 480–85.

[37] For an account of what Madison meant by justice, see Banning, *The Sacred Fire of Liberty*, p. 101.

[38] It is important to note that Madison eventually realized that determined minorities could threaten rights and the public good just as easily as factious majorities. See ibid., pp. 374–75.

[39] See, e.g., ibid., pp. 135–36.

Historian Gordon Wood suggests that the factions that so concerned Madison were in reality the first stirrings of what we would regard as normal interest-group politics.[40] Of course, Madison did not necessarily view all interest groups as factions. His definition made clear that it was only when the group in question was adverse to private rights or the public good that they became a faction. But without a consensus on what constitutes such adversity, there is no way to determine which groups or majorities are factions other than through the messy process of democratic politics. In addition, while we now regard political parties as being essential to democratic politics, Madison almost certainly would have regarded them as factions.[41] The logic of Madison's argument is thus hostile to what we would regard as the legitimate exercise of democratic rights by political groups.

Madison believed that the solution to the problem of faction lay in the extended republic, a republic composed of such a variety of factions that their efforts would either cancel each other or, given the great size of the United States, disable them from any attempt at cooperation. Given contemporary technology, it is now much easier than it was in Madison's day for interest groups to exchange information and cooperate to achieve their ends. Even before Madison's death in 1836, however, it was clear that the extended republic had not prevented the formation of factions and interests that had real influence in the federal government. As we shall see below, the lack of attention in the Constitution to matters of administrative capacity facilitated the colonization of the government by special interests. It appears that the experience of the United States shows that an enlarged sphere of government does not by itself guarantee that the impact of factions will be minimized.

The Constitution and the Concept of the State

While studying *The Federalist* is one important way of understanding the relation of the Constitution to the operation of American government, it is not the best way. The founding generation did not ignore the lessons of experience and neither should we. To understand the relation of the Constitution to American political development and governing institutions, we must take account of what has occurred since 1789. Doing this means coming to grips with the concept of the state. Unfortunately, the concept of the state has never been popular in American public rhetoric or consti-

---

[40] See Gordon S. Wood, *The Radicalism of the American Revolution* (New York: Alfred A. Knopf, 1992), pp. 243–305, 361–69.

[41] See Richard Hofstadter, *The Idea of a Party System: The Rise of Legitimate Opposition in the United States, 1780–1840* (Berkeley: University of California Press, 1969), pp. 64–73.

tutional theory. The very name of the country, the United "States" of America, does not seem to admit the existence of a national government. The only incarnations of the state Americans traditionally recognize are the separate territorial governments (e.g., the "State" of Delaware), or the national government as an international actor, competing with other states for power and prestige.[42]

The failure to understand the national government as a state may derive in part from the colonial rejection of the British concept of parliamentary sovereignty. As we saw in chapter 1, Americans came to believe that sovereignty or the right to rule rests only with the people. As we also saw, however, the doctrine of popular sovereignty cannot be implemented as a mode of political authority for a modern government. The practical effect of popular sovereignty and the division of government power it encourages is to deny legitimate authority to the government as a whole. The British concept of sovereignty at least acknowledges the necessity of providing government a measure of political authority. Any active government with important, permanent tasks must have some measure of political authority to enable it to make effective decisions. If the constitutional structure does not enable the government to summon authority from the public, then policy problems may go unaddressed, may be shifted to institutions that are not responsible to the public, or may have to be resolved in a crisis.

Another reason Americans were able to avoid regarding the national government as a state was that for much of the nineteenth century, that government had very few responsibilities. The United States was far away from the antagonisms that led to the development of strong national states in Europe. *The Federalist* and foreign observers such as Alexis de Tocqueville and James Bryce all remarked on the absence of any need for Americans to maintain a permanent military establishment.[43] On the other hand, state governments had the political authority necessary to meet the needs of the people and claimed primacy in sovereignty in the years before the Civil War.

The history of the American national state thus begins when the responsibilities of the federal government began to expand. This expansion was driven partly by the same forces that led to the development of strong national states in Europe: the need to accommodate the social and economic changes resulting from industrialization and the necessity of ad-

[42] See Theda Skocpol, *Protecting Soldiers and Mothers: The Political Origins of Social Policy in the United States* (Cambridge: Harvard University Press, 1992), pp. 42–43.

[43] See Alexander Hamilton, The Federalist No. 8, in Cooke, ed., p. 49; Alexis de Tocqueville, *Democracy in America* (Garden City, N.Y.: Doubleday, 1969), pp. 168, 170, 222, 278; James Bryce, *The American Commonwealth*, vol. 1 (New York: Macmillan, 1921), pp. 309–10.

vancing American interests in the international arena. Americans could no longer ignore the need to grant the federal government some measure of political authority to cope with the policy problems that arose in the late nineteenth century.[44] It is at this point that the concept of the state becomes useful in exploring the subsequent developments in government institutions.

While there are different definitions of the state, they do not vary much in their essential terms. The modern democratic state is a collective of public institutions, rules, and individuals holding offices that maintains a monopoly on the creation of the legal order and the most effective means of coercion in a geographically defined territory.[45] Americans usually use the terms *government, political system,* or *polity* to refer to the entity defined here as a state. These terms can be substituted for the concept of the state if certain caveats are kept in mind, but the significance of those caveats suggests that we should use a new term. *Political system* and *polity* are too broad since they include the mass public which is not part of the state (despite the doctrine of popular sovereignty). The term *government* is too easily identified with the individuals who hold power at the moment, rather than with the permanent institutions of government.[46]

The concept of the state is useful because it reminds us that grants of constitutional power are useless in the absence of the means to make them effective. Focusing on the state thus appropriately emphasizes the important role institutions play in operationalizing the Constitution. Recent work on the state has emphasized the importance of institutional constraints on individual behavior and the pervasive role that past choices in state building play in the present.[47] In addition, the concept of the state emphasizes the permanent nature of the national state, once it was created in the United States, focuses attention on the structure in which politics takes place, makes it easier to conceive of institutions as having their own interests apart from or against the public, and aids our understanding that the various branches of the federal government often act as a single entity on many policy questions, despite the formal division of power in the Constitution. If all this is kept in mind, the term *government* can be used. It seems more appropriate, however, to refer to the national state.

[44] On the importance of the 1877–1920 period to the development of the national state, see Skowronek, *Building a New American State,* pp. 10–18.

[45] This definition attempts to capture common elements in many definitions. For discussion, see John A. Hall and G. John Ikenberry, *The State* (Minneapolis: University of Minnesota Press, 1989), pp. 1–2.

[46] See Robert R. Alford and Roger Friedland, *Powers of Theory: Capitalism, the State, and Democracy* (New York: Cambridge University Press, 1985), pp. 1, 41.

[47] See Stephen Krasner, "Approaches to the State: Alternative Conceptions and Historical Dynamics," *Comparative Politics* 16 (1984): 224–25.

The concept of the state highlights two significant aspects of the gap between the constitutional grant of power and the effective exercise of governmental power. States are supposed to have a monopoly on the legal use of coercion, but the Civil War aside, it is questionable whether the national state had a monopoly on the most effective means of coercion during the entire nineteenth century. Before the Civil War the federal government had an extremely small army that was incapable of routinely enforcing national laws.[48] The law of slavery actually delegated state power to punish slaves to private individuals. Vigilante justice was not uncommon in the U.S. and lynch law in the South lasted well into the twentieth century.[49] After the Civil War the U.S. Army was somewhat larger, but private armies employed by corporations were just as effective in suppressing strikes and maintaining order in local communities.[50] The historian E. J. Hobsbawm notes that during the latter half of the nineteenth century, "[t]he United States, alone among the states of the bourgeois world, was a country of private justice and private armed forces."[51] The institutional structure of the federal government was so weak in the nineteenth century that it is questionable whether it satisfied the minimum conditions for being a state.

The lack of attention in the Constitution to matters of public administration is another aspect of the gap between constitutional power and its effective exercise which is highlighted by the concept of the state. The Constitution contemplated the existence of "executive departments," but says nothing as to their composition or how they are to carry out their duties.[52] In addition, there was a constitutional commitment to separating the powers (or functions) of government. This created problems because modern administrative agencies combine legislative, executive, and judicial powers.[53] The Constitution was written before the need for compe-

---

[48] See William E. Nelson, *The Fourteenth Amendment: From Political Principle to Judicial Doctrine* (Cambridge: Harvard University Press, 1988), pp. 29–30. See also Paludan, *The Presidency of Abraham Lincoln*, pp. 71–72.

[49] See Lawrence Friedman, *Crime and Punishment in American History* (New York: Basic Books, 1993), pp. 86, 179–92.

[50] See Nell Irvin Painter, *Standing at Armageddon: The United States 1877–1919* (New York: W. W. Norton, 1987), p. 112.

[51] E. J. Hobsbawm, *The Age of Capital 1848–1875* (New York: New American Library, 1975), p. 157.

[52] U.S. Const., Article II, sec. 2.

[53] See David H. Rosenbloom, "Democratic Constitutionalism and the Evolution of Bureaucratic Government: Freedom and Accountability in the Administrative State," in Peter F. Nardulli, ed., *The Constitution and American Political Development: An Institutional Perspective* (Urbana: University of Illinois Press, 1992), pp. 122–23; Peter L. Strauss, "The Place of Agencies in Government: Separation of Powers and the Fourth Branch," *Columbia Law Review* 84 (1984): 575–82.

tent bureaucracies was widely understood and this slowed the development of a national state that had the ability to act autonomously. The absence of experienced bureaucratic institutions thus played an important role in shaping the evolution of the national state.[54]

The Constitution and American Political Development

No student of constitutional law would deny that the Constitution has had a profound influence on the development of American government. Just such a denial, however, might be made by some students of American politics and it is important to understand why. The importance of the Constitution to American political development is not a self-evident proposition. Observing the vast changes in American politics over the past two centuries, particularly in the development of political parties not foreseen in the Constitution, some may wonder how large a role the document has played in structuring the nation s political life. One could reason as follows. If the Constitution remains largely static in the face of a changing political system (an assumption supported by the infrequency of amendment), then it is difficult to see how it has a key role in the development of that system. Alternatively, if the Constitution is shown to be a flexible document that adapts to political change as it occurs, then it seems to play no role in structuring that change. The Constitution simply goes where the political system wants it to go.[55]

Both of these skeptical arguments are equally unattractive because they deny the Constitution any role in structuring American politics. Yet arriving at a satisfactory statement of the Constitution's influence on American political development is not easy. The difficulties arise in part from the issues we explored in chapter 1. One problem is that the legalized Constitution encourages a legalistic approach to constitutional change, an approach that identifies the Supreme Court as the primary agent of change. As we saw in our discussion of constitutional change in chapter 1, however, the Court cannot serve as the primary agent of constitutional change. Focusing on the question of the relationship of the Constitution to American political development makes this even more apparent. As we shall see, Congress and the President are quite capable of initiating important constitutional changes on their own. We will highlight this point in the discussion below by focusing most of our attention on constitutional

[54] See the discussion in Skowronek, *Building a New American State*, pp. 19–23.

[55] See the discussion in Peter F. Nardulli, "The Constitution and American Politics: A Developmental Perspective," in Nardulli, ed., *The Constitution and American Political Development*, pp. 3–9.

changes in the elected branches, although we will also note the role the federal judiciary has played in the American state.

The best way to grasp the relationship between the Constitution and American political development is to review the history of American government from a broad constitutional perspective, using the definition of the Constitution as a text-based institutional practice set out in chapter 1. Of course, American political development is highly complex and we can only skim the surface of its history here. Any adequate account must pay attention to at least three different dimensions of analysis.[56] First, the influence of the governing arrangements established in the text of the Constitution must be taken into account. Throughout American history, the values suggested by the document have provided a succession of normative orderings, ideologies inspired by the text and the constitutional tradition in which it is embedded.[57] Second, the development of the institutions of the national state must be examined, including changes in the relationship and structure of Congress, the Presidency, and the Supreme Court, as well as the executive bureaucracy and administrative agencies. Third, the way society organizes itself for politics is crucial to understanding American political development. Thus, the development of political parties must be taken in account, as well as the seismic forces unleashed by critical or realigning national elections.[58] The task of describing American political development is further complicated by other important factors, such as the influence of the institution of slavery and sectional politics.

A description of American political development could thus fill several volumes and we can only address a few topics. Yet such a discussion is essential to any proper understanding of American constitutionalism. It is therefore necessary to proceed, even as we keep in mind that any comprehensive account of the Constitution and American political development would have to be worked out in much greater detail. We will focus on three topics: the relationship of the Constitution to the problem of slavery, the Civil War, and the role of the Civil War in the creation of the national state; the mismatch that first developed in the late nineteenth century between the demands made on the American state and the capacity of the state to handle policy problems; and the development of

[56] These three dimensions of analysis are suggested by Stephen Skowronek, *The Politics Presidents Make: Leadership from John Adams to George Bush* (Cambridge: Harvard University Press, 1993), pp. 9–10.

[57] For a suggestive treatment of the succession of normative orderings, see Paul W. Kahn, *Legitimacy and History: Self-Government in American Constitutional Theory* (New Haven: Yale University Press, 1992).

[58] For a recent review of theories of realignment, see Byron E. Shafer, ed., *The End of Realignment? Interpreting American Electoral Eras* (Madison: University of Wisconsin Press, 1991).

the national state in the wake of the Great Depression and World War II. In discussing the last topic, we will focus in particular on changes in the presidency.[59]

To an important degree, American political development before the Civil War was dominated by constitutional considerations. The most important constitutional question before the Civil War was whether the Constitution would be successful in creating a workable federal structure that would not be torn apart by sectional stresses.[60] The Constitution failed this test. As we saw in chapter 1, the doctrine of popular sovereignty helped Federalists avoid the question of whether ultimate political authority lay in the states or the federal government. The Constitution was a compromise on this issue and the issue of slavery—not in the sense of embracing a third alternative, but in the sense that the document pointed both toward the states and the federal government as supreme, both toward the protection of slavery and the promise of its inevitable decline.[61] It is always necessary to keep in mind that many of the members of the Federal Convention, including George Washington and James Madison, were slaveholders and that the proslavery delegates were just as much Framers of the Constitution as the antislavery delegates.

The attitude of the founding generation toward slavery was clouded by wishful thinking that the abolition of the slave trade allowed by the Constitution after 1808 would result in the elimination of slavery.[62] Once it became clear that slavery would not be eliminated that easily, various members of the founding generation such as James Madison and Thomas Jefferson (and later, for a time, Abraham Lincoln), saw the colonization of Africa by the slaves as the only viable solution. The reasoning behind this scheme establishes a crucial point about early American constitutionalism. As the founding generation and its inheritors understood the matter, a republican, liberal, and democratic constitutional order was not possible unless the American population was white. Racial prejudice made it impossible to accept slaves from Africa as equals, as required by the premises of the constitutional order.[63] White supremacy was thus an integral as-

---

[59] Discussion of this last topic will continue in chapter 6 as we consider questions raised by periods of constitutional crisis and proposals for constitutional reform.

[60] See David M. Potter, *The Impending Crisis 1848–1861* (New York: Harper and Row, 1976), p. 479.

[61] On the Constitution as a compromise on slavery, see David Brion Davis, *The Problem of Slavery in the Age of Revolution 1770–1823* (Ithaca: Cornell University Press, 1975), pp. 106–7, 124–25, 130–31.

[62] See Peter Kolchin, *American Slavery 1619–1877* (New York: Hill and Wang, 1993), pp. 79–80.

[63] See William W. Freehling, *The Road to Disunion: Secessionists at Bay 1776–1854* (New York: Oxford University Press, 1990), pp. 122–26 (views of Jefferson): Drew R. McCoy, *The Last of the Fathers: James Madison and the Republican Legacy* (Cambridge:

sumption of the 1787 Constitution.[64] Democracy for whites was not possible unless blacks were literally excluded by being repatriated to Africa. The acceptance of some form of equality for African-Americans during Reconstruction thus altered a significant element of the original constitutional order.

The sectional stresses caused by the institution of slavery played a role in the destruction of the first two party systems in the 1820s and 1850s and caused a series of constitutional crises—the Missouri Compromise of 1820, the nullification crisis of 1832–33, and the Compromise of 1850—that eventually resulted in a civil war between the states.[65] The continuing controversy over slavery showed that the American constitutional order was unstable in a fundamental sense. From the introduction of the Wilmot Proviso in 1846 to the end of Reconstruction three decades later, the United States was almost continuously in a political uproar as one constitutional crisis succeeded the next.[66]

The crises and increasingly desperate attempts at compromise in the

---

Cambridge University Press, 1989), p. 5 (views of Madison); Potter, *The Impending Crisis*, pp. 344–46 (views of Lincoln). See also George M. Fredrickson, *White Supremacy: A Comparative Study in American and South African History* (New York: Oxford University Press, 1981), pp. 143–45.

[64] For useful discussions of the relationship of the 1787 Constitution to slavery, see Paul Finkelman, "Slavery and the Constitutional Convention: Making a Covenant With Death," in Richard Beeman, Stephen Botein, and Edward C. Carter II, eds., *Beyond Confederation: Origins of the Constitution and American National Identity* (Chapel Hill: University of North Carolina Press, 1987), p. 188; Herbert J. Storing, "Slavery and the Moral Foundations of the American Republic," in Robert H. Horwitz, ed., *The Moral Foundations of the American Republic*, 3d ed. (Charlottesville: University Press of Virginia, 1986), p. 313; William M. Wiecek, "The Witch at the Christening: Slavery and the Constitution's Origins," in Leonard W. Levy and Dennis J. Mahoney, eds., *The Framing and Ratification of the Constitution* (New York: Macmillan, 1987), p. 167.

On the general theme of multiple American traditions that include white supremacy, see the important article by Rogers Smith, "Beyond Tocqueville, Myrdal, and Hartz: The Multiple Traditions in America," *American Political Science Review* 87 (1993): 549. For a defense of Lincoln's view that the Declaration of Independence was part of the Constitution and thus that equality was a constitutional aspiration from the beginning of the republic, see Paludan, *The Presidency of Abraham Lincoln*, pp. 17–20.

[65] On the relationship of slavery to the end of the first two-party systems, see William Nisbet Chambers, *Political Parties in a New Nation: The American Experience 1776–1809* (New York: Oxford University Press, 1963), pp. 198–200 and Richard P. McCormick, "Political Development and the Second Party System," in William Chambers and Walter Dean Burnham, eds., *The American Party System* (New York: Oxford University Press, 1975), p. 113. On the series of crises before the Civil War, see Wiecek, "The Witch at the Christening," in Levy and Mahoney, eds., *The Framing and Ratification of the Constitution*, pp. 183–84.

[66] See Arthur Bestor, "The American Civil War as a Constitutional Crisis," in Lawrence M. Friedman and Harry N. Scheiber, eds., *American Law and the Constitutional Order: Historical Perspectives* (Cambridge: Harvard University Press, 1978), pp. 219–34.

1850s revealed that the "United States" was essentially a league of states without a central authority powerful enough to resolve a question that could not be settled by compromise. Even the federal courts were dragged into the slavery crisis, as Congress repeatedly tried to have them settle the matter, with the resulting disaster of the *Dred Scott* case.[67] This attempt to resolve the crisis "was an implicit admission that political processes had broken down, and that the dominant political question of the period had proved beyond the capacity of the political system to resolve."[68] Partly because of the ambiguity of the Constitution and influence of events such as the nullification crisis, doctrines such as interposition, nullification, and secession that were inimical to the constitutional order could not be effectively discredited. By December 1859, the House of Representatives barely functioned as a deliberative body, as many members came armed, with the expectation that the war would start in the Capitol itself. As southern states seceded a year later, it was clear to many that the constitutional experiment had failed.[69]

Scholars have disagreed over whether the Civil War was a "Second American Revolution," a fundamental break in American history.[70] Regardless of how we analyze the degree of change brought by the war, it is an error to see it simply as a serious disagreement within the boundaries set by the Constitution.[71] The Civil War, which cost over 620,000 lives, decimated the South's economy, and affected national development well into the twentieth century, was a discontinuity in the American constitutional tradition. Americans do not slaughter each other for the sake of legal arguments. Events such as the Civil War are the result of profound political and moral conflicts. The war eventually became a remorseless struggle to end slavery and destroy the Old South, establish a national guarantee of civil rights, and terminate the agrarian republic of the founding generation. As historian James McPherson notes, "[w]ith complete sincerity the South fought to preserve its version of the republic of the founding fathers—a government of limited powers that protected the rights of property and whose constituency comprised an independent gentry and yeomanry of the white race."[72] These values, preserved in the Constitution, were destroyed by the Civil War.

[67] See *Dred Scott v. Sandford*, 60 U.S. 393 (1856).

[68] William M. Wiecek, *The Sources of Antislavery Constitutionalism in America 1760–1848* (Ithaca: Cornell University Press, 1977), p. 285.

[69] See Potter, *The Impending Crisis*, pp. 389, 448–84.

[70] See James M. McPherson, *Abraham Lincoln and the Second American Revolution* (New York: Oxford University Press, 1991), pp. 3–22.

[71] For this view, see, e.g., Morton Keller, "Powers and Rights: Two Centuries of American Constitutionalism," in David Thelen, ed., *The Constitution and American Life* (Ithaca: Cornell University Press, 1988), pp. 22–24.

[72] James M. McPherson, *Battle Cry of Freedom: The Civil War Era* (New York: Oxford University Press, 1988), pp. 860–61.

The end of the Civil War did not mark an end to the series of constitutional crises the United States experienced in the mid-nineteenth century. Under the Military Reconstruction Act of 1867, the South was occupied by thousands of federal troops commanded by officers who had the power to dismiss local officials and state governors.[73] President Andrew Johnson attempted to subvert congressional Reconstruction by refusing to enforce the law, and became the only president to be impeached and nearly convicted for his failure to carry out his constitutional duties. The Thirteenth, Fourteenth, and Fifteenth Amendments to the Constitution would not have been ratified under normal conditions and were forced on the southern states as a condition of readmission.[74] Southerners refused to accept the evident implications of the war and continued the struggle after 1865 in guerrilla fashion. "More so than at any other time in the history of the United States, terrorism and murder became a frequent adjunct of the political process."[75] Federal authorities were unable to stem this wave of terror and by 1875, the forces of white resistance were strong enough so that Democrats could openly crush the Mississippi Republican party without fear of retribution.[76] Reconstruction culminated in the presidential election crisis of 1876, which the Constitution exacerbated by failing to provide any mechanism for judging disputed returns and allowing for no delay in inauguration. Northern whites now allowed southern whites to institute a new version of white supremacy.[77]

Historians do not agree on the implications of the Civil War for the development of the national state.[78] The administrative capacity of the federal government at the beginning of the nineteenth century was very low and the competence of national administration actually decreased in

[73] See Morton Keller, *Affairs of State: Public Life in Late Nineteenth Century America* (Cambridge: Harvard University Press, 1977), p. 207.

[74] See Richard B. Bernstein with Jerome Agel, *Amending America* (New York: Times Books, 1993), pp. 102–3, 109, 115.

[75] Keller, *Affairs of State*, p. 224.

[76] See Eric Foner, *Reconstruction: America's Unfinished Revolution 1863–1877* (New York: Harper and Row, 1988), pp. 425–26, 442–44, 558–63.

[77] See Harold M. Hyman and William M. Wiecek, *Equal Justice Under Law: Constitutional Development 1835–1875* (New York: Harper and Row, 1982), p. 493.

[78] For the view that the Civil War and Reconstruction marked the beginning of the modern national state, see generally Foner, *Reconstruction*; McPherson, *Battle Cry of Freedom*, pp. 450–53.

For the view that the Civil War made little difference to the national state, see generally Harold M. Hyman, *A More Perfect Union: The Impact of the Civil War and Reconstruction on the Constitution* (Boston: Houghton Mifflin, 1975); Keller, *Affairs of State*.

For intermediate views on this issue, see generally Richard Franklin Bensel, *Yankee Leviathan: The Origins of Central State Authority in America, 1859–1877* (Cambridge: Cambridge University Press, 1990); Harry N. Scheiber, "American Federalism and the Diffusion of Power: Historical and Contemporary Perspectives," *University of Toledo Law Review* 9 (1978): 636–40.

the decades prior to the war.[79] Secession suddenly removed most of the Democratic party in Congress and allowed Republicans to pass historic legislation on tariffs, banking, building a national railroad, higher education, and land grants to western settlers. The war also expanded the federal bureaucracy, but most of the administrative agencies created during the war were dismantled at its end, preventing any permanent gain in bureaucratic competence.[80] The profound localism and antigovernment attitudes typical of nineteenth-century politics outlasted the war by many decades and stifled modernization of the federal bureaucracy.[81] After the war, Congress controlled national policymaking and dominated the departments of the executive branch through its committees and use of patronage.[82] Undoubtedly the Civil War inspired some reformers to believe that the federal government could be an activist government if given the chance, but Reconstruction also disillusioned many Americans as the federal government often seemed ineffective and corrupt in its efforts to change the South.[83]

According to political scientist Stephen Skowronek, the integrative institutions of government during the nineteenth century were the federal judiciary and political parties. The American state was one of "courts and parties."[84] In the absence of a state bureaucracy that had the capacity to penetrate to the local level, the federal courts and the network of state parties had the ability to address issues of importance, distribute government benefits, and organize citizens for politics. In contrast to the dismantling of federal agencies after the end of the Civil War, the jurisdiction and activity of the federal courts steadily increased. Employing the courts enabled Congress to avoid the costs and problems attendant on creating large bureaucracies.[85] But the courts were also trying to fill the "void in governance" left by an inadequate state structure.[86] There seemed to be no limit to the kind of regulatory and administrative tasks the courts would take on—they regulated public utilities, engaged in land-use planning, supervised the collection of local taxes, and tried to prevent the waste of public funds.[87] As this list indicates, the activism of the federal courts was mainly directed at state and local governments.

[79] See Leonard D. White, *The Federalists* (New York: Macmillan, 1948), p. 466; Leonard D. White, *The Jacksonians* (Chicago: Free Press, 1954), pp. 4–5.

[80] See Hyman, *A More Perfect Union*, pp. 380–82.

[81] See Keller, *Affairs of State*, pp. 35, 106, 289, 318.

[82] See Leonard D. White, *The Republican Era* (New York: Macmillan, 1958), pp. 20–21, 48, 84–92.

[83] See Hyman and Wiecek, *Equal Justice Under Law*, p. 487.

[84] Skowronek, *Building A New American State*, p. 24.

[85] See ibid., p. 41; Hyman, *A More Perfect Union*, pp. 227–28.

[86] Keller, *Affairs of State*, p. 343.

[87] See James Willard Hurst, *The Growth of American Law: The Law Makers* (Boston: Little, Brown, 1950), pp. 431–32.

The network of political parties that dominated American politics during the nineteenth century began to form in the 1820s and 1830s around the contestation of presidential elections, the need to fill the many elective offices at the state and local level, and the desire to ensure that all parts of the country received their fair share of government gifts and subsidies. The parties gained what cohesiveness they had from mobilizing the ethnoreligious sentiments of local communities and the practical desire to maintain their power and patronage.[88] They were the primary means by which society organized itself for politics.

The late nineteenth century and the early years of the twentieth century was the period in which the United States came to grips with the need to modernize and increase the administrative capacity of the national state.[89] In the early stages of this adjustment, there was a fundamental mismatch between the rudimentary and nonprogrammatic institutions of government at the federal level and the rapidly developing industrial economy, the growth of large-scale business organizations, and an increasingly urbanized and ethnically pluralistic society.[90] This mismatch strongly influenced the subsequent development of the national state and derived from the two gaps between constitutional powers and institutional means we discussed in the preceding section. Specifically, the Constitution helped create an extremely weak national state with uncertain powers of enforcement and a very limited administrative capacity.

The mismatch between private power and public authority led to a kind of breakdown in the constitutional order. Increasingly, Congress had to deal with complex, ongoing regulatory issues that could not be solved through the distribution of benefits. But Congress found itself unable to resolve these issues through the legislative process. Political parties and elections could not help because they were not oriented toward national policymaking. There was thus a gap between the public authority the electoral process provided and the kind of public authority the elected branches needed to deal with these new issues. The result was a displacement of public authority away from the democratic party-legislative process.

The most characteristic expression of this displacement of public authority was the creation of the independent regulatory agency, a new kind of constitutional entity. The Interstate Commerce Commission, Federal Trade Commission, and Federal Reserve Board were all created during this period. Typically, however, Congress was unable to provide these new agencies with any clear policy direction.[91] The Sherman Act of 1890,

[88] See Richard L. McCormick, *The Party Period and Public Policy* (New York: Oxford University Press, 1986), pp. 3–4, 139, 164, 218–19.

[89] See Skowronek, *Building a New American State*, pp. 10–18.

[90] This is an important theme in Alan Dawley, *Struggles for Justice: Social Responsibility and the Liberal State* (Cambridge: Harvard University Press, 1991).

[91] See Skowronek, *Building A New American State*, pp. 138–50.

which created the nation's antitrust policy, did not provide any clear standards or mechanism for enforcement.[92] As noted above, Congress also delegated authority to the federal judiciary, which it used as a sort of all-purpose government agency.[93]

The creation of independent regulatory agencies is another example of a significant constitutional change that was not initiated by the judiciary, a topic we explored in chapter 1. Given the displacement of public authority that attended their creation, these agencies were delegated substantial legislative power. In addition, they combined the three constitutional powers of legislating, executing the law, and adjudicating specific disputes. The reformers who helped create these agencies knew that this was a departure from previous constitutional norms, but they felt that change was essential. In a well-known address in 1916, Elihu Root, President of the American Bar Association, noted that the "old doctrine" of not delegating legislative power had been abandoned in the creation of these new agencies. He declared, however, that "[t]here will be no withdrawal from these experiments. We shall go on; we shall expand them, *whether we approve theoretically or not*, because such agencies furnish protections to rights and obstacles to wrong doing which under our new social and industrial conditions cannot be practically accomplished by the old and simple procedure of legislatures and courts as in the last generation."[94] Root recognized that constitutional change had to occur even in the absence of a doctrinal rationale. Constitutional change was thus occurring through the political process.

The inability of the elected branches to act more decisively on regulatory issues was partly due to the close competition between the Democratic and Republican parties after the end of Reconstruction. The critical election of 1896 has been seen as important to subsequent efforts to build the national state because it resulted in clear Republican dominance. This enabled leaders like Theodore Roosevelt to articulate a new conception of an empowered presidency and provide for a strengthened bureaucracy. Although Congress found itself creating new regulatory agencies, it by no means relinquished its traditional control over the federal bureaucracy. Jealous of its prerogatives, Congress frustrated the development of a presidentially controlled bureaucracy in favor of a structure in which bureaucracies took the place of party organizations in providing benefits to constituents.[95]

[92] See Friedman, *Crime and Punishment in American History*, pp. 117–18.

[93] On this point, see the discussion in Martin Shapiro, *Courts: A Comparative and Political Analysis* (Chicago: University of Chicago Press, 1981), pp. 30–31.

[94] Elihu Root, "Address of the President," *American Bar Association Journal* 2 (1916): 749–50 (emphasis added).

[95] See Skowronek, *Building A New American State*, pp. 167–76, 287. On the new conception of the presidency established by Theodore Roosevelt and Woodrow Wilson, see the important study by Tulis, *The Rhetorical Presidency*, pp. 95–144.

Since only a limited amount of state-building occurred prior to the Great Depression, the expansion of the state that began after it was largely reactive and crisis-driven.[96] Initially, the federal government, Congress in particular, found itself completely at sea as it attempted to cope with the Depression. It did not possess the expertise to plan a response to the crisis or the bureaucracy necessary to administer any response.[97] During the New Deal, the federal bureaucracy expanded faster than Americans could comprehend, but in an uncoordinated fashion. A relatively strong national state was built during World War II and the Cold War, but scholars generally agree that it continued to be characterized by the fragmentation and dispersion of authority.[98]

To cope with these new challenges, all three constitutional branches underwent important reorganizations that involved changes in the constitutional norms that governed their activities. Although the Reorganization Act of 1939 gave President Franklin Roosevelt much less power than he originally requested, it did provide for badly needed staff and enabled him to submit a reorganization plan which created the Executive Office of the President and transferred the Bureau of the Budget to that office.[99] The Administrative Office Act of 1939 gave the federal courts the ability to cope with the more diverse, expanded caseload that was caused by the expansion in the responsibilities of government.[100] Congress significantly improved its ability to make policy through the Legislative Reorganization Act of 1946, which gave it additional staff and strengthened the committee system by reducing the number of committees and rearranging their jurisdictions.[101] In each instance, the constitutional branches sought to maintain control over the expanding national state through a combination of increased funds, staff, and planning capacity.

As we saw in chapter 1, the presidency experienced the greatest relative increase in power, but the increase in presidential power varied sharply in

[96] See Matthew A. Crenson and Francis E. Rourke, "By Way of Conclusion: American Bureaucracy since World War II," in Louis Galambos, ed., *The New American State: Bureaucracies and Policies since World War II* (Baltimore: Johns Hopkins University Press, 1987), pp. 137, 139.

[97] See Barry D. Karl, *The Uneasy State: The United States from 1915 to 1945* (Chicago: University of Chicago Press, 1983), pp. 116–17, 119–21.

[98] See Stephen D. Krasner, *Defending the National Interest* (Princeton: Princeton University Press, 1978), pp. 61–70.

[99] See Barry Dean Karl, *Executive Reorganization and Reform in the New Deal* (Cambridge: Harvard University Press, 1963), p. 257; Sidney M. Milkis, *The President and the Parties: The Transformation of the American Party System since the New Deal* (New York: Oxford University Press, 1993), pp. 125–34.

[100] See Peter Graham Fish, *The Politics of Federal Judicial Administration* (Princeton: Princeton University Press, 1973), p. 228.

[101] See Richard Franklin Bensel, *Sectionalism and American Political Development 1880–1980* (Madison: University of Wisconsin Press, 1984), pp. 351–53.

different areas of policy. The most significant increase in power was in
foreign policy, as Roosevelt and his successors traded on their power as
Commander in Chief to assume exclusive control over matters of war-
fighting. During the Cold War, "war-fighting" could include any aspect
of policy which affected foreign affairs. The advent of nuclear weapons,
for example, dramatically increased the stakes of any foreign crisis and
presidential control of nuclear weapons implied that the president must
also control all aspects of foreign policy.[102]

This increase in presidential power could not have occurred without
the cooperation of Congress and the Supreme Court. An important reason for Congress's cooperation was that the public did not perceive any
direct benefits from the normal operation of foreign policy and thus members of Congress could not improve their reelection prospects by claiming
credit for oversight or policy initiatives.[103] Congress increased presidential
power by acquiescing to dramatic exercises of power, such as President
Truman's decision to commit U.S. forces to defend Korea in 1950, and by
passing numerous statutes that expanded presidential discretion in foreign
affairs.[104] The Constitution was reinterpreted to allow presidents to exercise routinely what had once been perceived as emergency power and the
Supreme Court, as we noted in chapter 1, almost always deferred to presidential authority in foreign policy.

Increased presidential power in time of war seems natural enough because of the president's military duties, ability to react quickly to any perceived problem, and the public understanding of the president as national
leader in a time of crisis. But the new power of the president in foreign
policy was also an artifact of the lack of a national party system and the
complex relationship between the separately elected political branches. It
is possible for Congress to act as swiftly as the president if the institutional
means are in place to ensure that such collective action is feasible. Since
the public did not normally care about foreign policy, however, there was
no incentive for Congress to establish such institutional means or to
closely scrutinize executive action. Presidential control of foreign affairs
meant that Congress could avoid responsibility for policy blunders while
claiming credit for cleaning up the mess.[105]

---

[102] See Anthony G. McGrew, "Foreign Policy and the Constitution: 'Invitation to a
Perpetual Institutional Struggle'?" in Richard Maidment and John Zvesper, eds., *Reflections on the Constitution: The American Constitution After Two Hundred Years* (Manchester: Manchester University Press, 1989), pp. 172, 178–79, 181–82.

[103] See David R. Mayhew, *Congress: The Electoral Connection* (New Haven: Yale University Press, 1974), pp. 122–23.

[104] See James L. Sundquist, *The Decline and Resurgence of Congress* (Washington:
Brookings Institution, 1981), pp. 92–93, 118–19, 155; Jules Lobel, "Emergency Power
and the Decline of Liberalism," *Yale Law Journal* 98 (1989): 1408.

[105] See Sundquist, *The Decline and Resurgence of Congress*, p. 457.

While the policy of limited legislative responsibility may be appropriate for a specific period of total war, it creates serious problems if it has to be sustained for a long period of time. The Cold War posed precisely this difficulty, as it became apparent that a government war-fighting posture would have to be maintained for an indefinite period.[106] If Congress did not adopt an active role, this meant that a significant amount of "legislating" would have to be performed by the executive branch. The circumstances under which this was done were to prove extremely questionable in later years. Under J. Edgar Hoover, the Federal Bureau of Investigation built an extensive investigative and surveillance operation of all groups which might be engaged in domestic subversion on the basis of a vague 1936 directive from President Roosevelt and a series of informal understandings over the years.[107] The Central Intelligence Agency acquired its authority to conduct covert operations abroad from National Security Council directives approved in 1947–48, rather than from legislation.[108] The most significant exercise of presidential "legislative" power was probably President Truman's secret creation of the National Security Agency in 1952. The NSA became the most influential and expensive intelligence arm of the national security state.[109]

In domestic policy, by contrast, presidents only gained parity with Congress. The reality of limited presidential power in domestic policy in the transformed national state was initially obscured by Roosevelt's sustained legislative leadership during the Depression. But the course of policymaking in the New Deal also indicated the likelihood of a sustained stalemate between Congress and the president. Without a national party structure that would give elections a policymaking role, presidents were forced to base their public authority on charismatic leadership.[110] It became apparent that this kind of authority could be wielded effectively only in the context of a crisis such as a war. Thus, to mobilize the people to support the expansion of the federal bureaucracy and such measures as

[106] See McGrew, "Foreign Policy and the Constitution," pp. 180–81.

[107] See Frank J. Donner, *The Age of Surveillance* (New York: Random House, 1980), pp. 53–54, 77; Richard Gid Powers, *Secrecy and Power: The Life of J. Edgar Hoover* (New York: Free Press, 1987), pp. 228–34, 274.

[108] See John Ranelagh, *The Agency: The Rise and Decline of the CIA* (New York: Simon and Schuster, 1987), pp. 115–17, 133–34.

[109] See James Bamford, *The Puzzle Palace* (New York: Penguin Books, 1983), p. 15. The NSA is nominally a part of the Department of Defense, but in reality it is an independent intelligence agency. Ibid., pp. 16–17, 105.

[110] See Paul K. Conkin, *FDR and the Origins of the Welfare State* (New York: Thomas Y. Crowell, 1967), p. 84; Robert J. McKeever, "Obituary for the 'Living' Constitution? Policy Making and the Constitutional Framework Two Hundred Years On," in Maidment and Zvesper, eds., *Reflections on the Constitution*, pp. 198, 208. See also the discussion in Tulis, *The Rhetorical Presidency*, pp. 189–202.

the National Recovery Administration, Roosevelt had to maintain a sense of emergency and appealed to a wartime analogy to justify what seemed to be an extraordinary increase in state power.[111] President Truman was told he could not rely on self-interest alone to sell the Truman Doctrine; instead he had to " 'scare hell' " out of the American public by convincing them of the need to wage a worldwide war against Soviet communism.[112] The need to create a crisis to move the constitutional machinery meant that policies presidents thought important would be chronically over-sold—thus, the "wars" on poverty in the Johnson Administration, the energy problem in the Carter Administration, and drugs in the Bush Administration.[113]

This need to oversell domestic policies by employing foreign policy metaphors reveals that a lack of public authority continued to plague the transformed national state. Presidents could obtain decisive action from Congress only by invoking the kind of authority that was appropriate in an emergency where the survival of the country was at stake. This kind of authority could not be sustained. The wartime metaphor implied that presidential authority and the measures taken under it would always be temporary.[114] The effective end of the New Deal in 1938 came from an exhaustion of the use of charismatic leadership by Roosevelt and a reassertion of traditional conservative elements in Congress.[115] This foreshadowed the stalemate between Congress and the president that has characterized all subsequent administrations.[116] Presidents have the opportunity to obtain serious consideration of their policies only during the first two years of their term, and they have not been able to pass comprehensive legislative programs except in a few instances.[117]

The lack of public authority and the imbalance between the authority of the president in foreign policy as opposed to domestic policy encouraged a situation in which presidents became frustrated with the unreason-

[111] See Karl, *The Uneasy State*, pp. 119–21.

[112] See William H. Chafe, *The Unfinished Journey: America Since World War II* (New York: Oxford University Press, 1986), p. 67.

[113] For commentary on the wars on poverty and the energy problem, including the use of military metaphors in the war on poverty, see David McKay, *Domestic Policy and Ideology: Presidents and the American State 1964–1987* (Cambridge: Cambridge University Press, 1989), pp. 49, 110; Tulis, *The Rhetorical Presidency*, pp. 161–72. For the war on drugs in the Bush Administration, see Philip Shenon, "War on Drugs Remains Top Priority, Bush Says," *New York Times*, Sept. 6, 1990, at A12.

[114] See Karl, *The Uneasy State*, pp. 119–21.

[115] See Conkin, *FDR and the Origins of the Welfare State*, pp. 101–2.

[116] See Karl, *The Uneasy State*, pp. 154, 160.

[117] "Textbooks tend to emphasize the legislative triumphs of Wilson, Roosevelt, and Lyndon Johnson. But a closer examination of these presidential efforts suggests that they occurred usually during very brief periods (1913–1915, 1933–1935, 1964–1965)." Thomas E. Cronin, *The State of the Presidency* (Boston: Little, Brown, 1975), p. 88.

able (as they saw it) limits on their ability to act. After Roosevelt, presidents reasonably believed that they had been elected to serve as national leader and knew they would be held accountable for their performance, yet the gap in public authority ensured that they would not have the necessary power to carry out their plans. Under these circumstances, it was foreseeable that presidents would be tempted to circumvent the other branches of government and use questionable means to make sure their plans were carried out (and their reelection assured), especially in foreign policy where their authority was greatest.

The lack of sufficient public authority took its toll on other institutions in the transformed national state. The executive branch could have benefited from the existence of a planning agency to bring some coherence to national policy, but Roosevelt's National Resources Planning Board, the prototype for such an agency, was abolished by Congress in 1943.[118] The lack of experience in the federal bureaucracy meant that there was extensive reliance on business to implement New Deal programs and run the agencies created during World War II.[119] This same reliance had occurred in World War I, and it facilitated the integration of state agencies and interest groups.[120] Although the federal bureaucracy increased in size, the rate of increase after the Korean War did not keep pace with the increase in population or the addition of new programs.[121] The failure to create a bureaucracy adequate to administer the tasks it was assigned, along with the failure to create a truly neutral, expert civil service meant that the national state was forced to rely on private agencies and state and local governments to implement national programs.[122]

The displacement of public authority away from the party-legislative process accelerated as the national agenda expanded after the New Deal. As in the early period of state-building in the late nineteenth century, the most characteristic way the elected branches dealt with an important pol-

[118] See G. John Ikenberry, *Reasons of State: Oil Politics and the Capacities of American Government* (Ithaca: Cornell University Press, 1988), pp. 75–76; Milkis, *The President and the Parties*, pp. 129–30.

[119] See the discussion in Alan Brinkley, *The End of Reform: New Deal Liberalism in Recession and War* (New York: Alfred A. Knopf, 1995), pp. 175–200.

[120] See Otis L. Graham, Jr., *Toward A Planned Society: From Roosevelt to Nixon* (New York: Oxford University Press, 1976), pp. 67, 73–75.

[121] Paul P. Van Riper, "The American Administrative State: Wilson and the Founders," in Ralph Clark Chandler, ed., *A Centennial History of the American Administrative State* (New York: Free Press, 1987), p. 28.

[122] See John E. Chubb and Paul E. Peterson, "American Political Institutions and the Problem of Governance," in John E. Chubb and Paul E. Peterson, eds., *Can The Government Govern?* (Washington, D.C.: Brookings Institution, 1989) pp. 15–16; William M. Lunch, *The Nationalization of American Politics* (Berkeley: University of California Press, 1987), p. 166.

icy problem was to shift responsibility to an independent agency.[123] Congress also continued to use the federal courts as a way to fill in the policy gaps left in regulatory statutes.[124] The increased responsibilities of government led to the new form of displacement just mentioned, which involved using private agencies and state and local governments as extensions of the federal bureaucracy.[125]

The continuing problem of displacement might have been mitigated if constitutional amendments had been adopted to render the New Deal reforms legitimate. The elected branches would have been able to use the amending process as a firm basis for the exercise of their new public authority. As we saw in chapter 1, however, reverence for the Constitution and the difficulty of the amending process made reasonable constitutional reform extremely difficult. The text of the Constitution remained frozen in place, like an iceberg around which an ocean of change flowed unimpeded.

Legal scholars often observe that the Supreme Court is the most powerful court in the world. Political scientists add a corollary—that Congress is the world's most powerful legislative body. To the extent that these observations are correct, they demonstrate an important element of continuity in the constitutional order. The main reason these two branches of government are powerful compared with similar institutions in other advanced democracies is that the United States is almost alone in its commitment to a separation of the executive and legislative branches. Twentieth-century constitutions in other advanced democracies were written in the context of strong party systems and a belief that election results should be easily translated into policy changes.[126]

One point our brief review of American efforts at state-building should make clear is that the choice of the founding generation for a more equal distribution of power among the branches has had important implications for these efforts. The federal courts were available as a stand-in for a modernized bureaucracy. Congress was accustomed to running the departments of the executive branch. As the modern national state began to

---

[123] See Thomas K. McGraw, *Prophets of Regulation* (Cambridge: Harvard University Press, 1984), p. 210.

[124] See Lunch, *The Nationalization of American Politics*, p. 133.

[125] See Harold Seidman and Robert Gilmour, *Politics, Position, and Power* (New York: Oxford University Press, 1986), pp. 120–22. Seidman and Gilmour note that the trend toward using nonfederal personnel to implement national programs "reflects political expediency because third-party arrangements permit the president and the Congress to take credit for acting without assuming responsibility for program design, administration, and results." Ibid., pp. 121–22.

[126] See Kenneth Janda, "The American Constitutional Framework and the Structure of American Political Parties," in Nardulli, ed., *The Constitution and American Political Development*, pp. 179–206.

develop in the late nineteenth century, the relative imbalance between these branches and the presidency guaranteed a constitutional conflict that continues today.[127] This imbalance is partly the result of the inadequacy of the Constitution's arrangements concerning public administration. Scholars continue to argue over whether the presidency was intended to be "unitary," that is, whether the president should have primary authority over the departments and agencies of the executive branch.[128] But the practical reality is that presidential authority over the executive branch is significantly limited by the constitutionally rooted powers of Congress and the federal judiciary.

At the beginning of this chapter we noted the difference between providing constitutional power and creating institutions that can wield that power effectively. The slow development of the national state in the United States shows that building effective constitutional institutions was by no means easy or automatic. Indeed, the course of American state-building has been a meandering one. Critical elections such as those in 1860, 1896, and 1932 can lead to relatively quick changes in policy. The process of state-building, however, is far more difficult and requires decades of steady progress to show a clear result.

In their search for the key period that created the national state as it exists today, scholars are continually finding their attention shifting closer to the present. For a time, what is called the Progressive Era looked decisive. Most scholars have emphasized the significance of the New Deal in building the modern national state, but they have also conceded the importance of the state-building that occurred during America's participation in the major wars of the twentieth century. Then again, the advent of many of the programs that now occupy the federal government occurred during the Great Society period of the 1960s. More recently, scholars have focused on the major changes to policy executed in the early years of the Nixon Administration. Perhaps the efforts of the Reagan Administration will one day seem as significant to establishing the contemporary national state as do these earlier efforts. Building the American state has been a halting, patchwork process, as new efforts overlay past accomplishments.

[127] See the discussion of Franklin Roosevelt's efforts to increase presidential power over the executive branch in Skowronek, *The Politics Presidents Make*, pp. 317–24.

[128] For recent contributions to the debate, see Frank B. Cross, "The Surviving Significance of the Unitary Executive," *Houston Law Review* 27 (1990): 599; Steven G. Calabresi and Kevin H. Rhodes, "The Structural Constitution: Unitary Executive, Plural Judiciary," *Harvard Law Review* 105 (1992): 1153; Lawrence Lessig and Cass R. Sunstein, "The President and the Administration," *Columbia Law Review* 94 (1994): 1.

Three

Judicial Review and American Democracy

ON September 1, 1916, President Woodrow Wilson signed a law to prohibit the use of child labor to manufacture products in interstate commerce. The enactment of the law was the culmination of more than a decade of advocacy led by the National Child Labor Committee. The new law underwent exhaustive constitutional analysis before it passed Congress. The interstate commerce power was carefully selected as the most appropriate way to ensure the constitutionality of the legislation. Leaders of the reform effort had been encouraged by a number of rulings by the Supreme Court that suggested Congress had broad power to regulate interstate commerce under the Constitution.[1]

The child labor law was broadly popular. Both political parties supported the law and it passed by overwhelming margins in the House of Representatives and the Senate. The law followed similar reform efforts in the states and public opinion was very favorable.[2] Nevertheless, the law was immediately challenged by a committee of southern mill owners, whose plants relied on child labor. In *Hammer v. Dagenhart*, the Supreme Court ruled by a vote of 5–4 that the child labor law was unconstitutional.[3] The Court held that the law was outside the boundaries of the interstate commerce power and also infringed the rights of states under the Tenth Amendment.

The Supreme Court's decision provoked wide criticism in the press and among supporters of the law, who were surprised by the unfavorable ruling. But criticism of the Court did not extend to the institution of judicial review. In the original debate over passage of the law, members of Congress had agreed that the Court was the ultimate authority on matters of constitutional interpretation. After further consultation of the relevant precedents, supporters of child labor legislation agreed to base their efforts on the taxing power. The idea was to levy an excise tax on items produced by child labor. Such a tax was quickly approved by Congress in 1919.[4] Once again, southern mill owners challenged the new child labor

---

[1] See Stephen B. Wood, *Constitutional Politics in the Progressive Era: Child Labor and the Law* (Chicago: University of Chicago Press, 1968), pp. 1–78.

[2] Ibid., pp. 78–80.

[3] 247 U.S. 251 (1918).

[4] Wood, *Constitutional Politics in the Progressive Era*, pp. 70, 74, 169–219.

tax in federal court. The Supreme Court obliged them by ruling the tax unconstitutional by a vote of 8–1 in *Bailey v. Drexel Furniture Co.*[5] The Court held that the tax violated the Tenth Amendment because it was beyond the power of Congress to use a tax to accomplish what it could not do through direct regulation.

Frustrated twice by the Supreme Court, reformers now turned to amending the Constitution. An amendment to give Congress the power to regulate child labor was sent to the states in June 1924. Although twenty-eight states ratified the Child Labor Amendment, thirteen did not and this ensured the Amendment's defeat. Another effort to prohibit child labor did not occur until well into the New Deal, when Congress adopted the Fair Labor Standards Act of 1938. As part of its general reversal of course after 1937, the Court ruled in *United States v. Darby Lumber Co.* that this law was constitutional, finally bringing to a close a reform effort that had taken nearly four decades.[6]

The story of child labor legislation contains a number of important lessons about the relationship between the Supreme Court and the political system in which it is embedded. The story powerfully suggests how the Court can for decades stifle a reform on which there is widespread agreement. The case of child labor has been cited by scholars who argue that the Court has often unjustifiably overruled legislative majorities.[7] It further suggests the difficulty of the amendment process, which we noticed in chapter 1. Nevertheless, an amendment was not necessary in the end. The Court itself changed its mind in the context of a fundamentally changed political universe. To many scholars, this suggests a relationship of cause and effect—the Court altered the meaning of the Constitution because of the influence of public opinion. This further suggests that the Court is not outside the political system, immune to majoritarian pressure. Nonetheless, the story also suggests the resilience of the institution of judicial review even as the Court acted against an overwhelming lawmaking majority and in the face of strong criticism.

It may seem strange that the Child Labor Amendment was opposed at all. The nature of the opposition provides another important lesson about this period in American history. The opposition included mill owners in the South to be sure, but also the leadership of the Catholic Church and many other Americans concerned about interference with the family and states rights. That their efforts were sufficient to frustrate such a worthy

---

[5] 259 U.S. 20 (1922).

[6] 312 U.S. 100 (1941). This paragraph follows the account in Richard Bernstein with Jerome Agel, *Amending America* (New York: Times Books, 1993), pp. 179–81.

[7] See John Agresto, *The Supreme Court and Constitutional Democracy* (Ithaca: Cornell University Press, 1984), pp. 28–29; John Hart Ely, *Democracy and Distrust: A Theory of Judicial Review* (Cambridge: Harvard University Press, 1980), p. 45.

cause suggests that in many ways, the America of the early twentieth century was a much different place than the America of today. Before the New Deal, Americans placed greater emphasis on the traditional division of responsibility between the states and the federal government, on states rights in general, on individual autonomy understood in a libertarian sense, and they were far more suspicious of the power of the state.[8] In this America the defeat of the Child Labor Amendment was to be regretted, but it did not indicate that the constitutional system was fundamentally unjust.

The modern debate over the role of the federal judiciary in American democracy originated with the slow rise of the national state in the late nineteenth century. We will examine this old debate in three stages. We will first explore briefly the establishment of the independence of the Supreme Court from the other branches of government during the founding era. Then we will review the origins of activist judicial review and the modern debate over the Supreme Court's role in the Populist-Progressive period. Finally, we will examine the contemporary debate over judicial review by identifying the different legal, prudential, and moral arguments used in the debate, placing judicial review in its political context, and considering the institutional aspects of judicial review in the light of international comparisons.

It should be said at the outset that the conclusions of this chapter are largely negative. The discussion will show that the standard arguments used by both sides in the contemporary debate on judicial review have serious flaws that hinder further argumentative progress. Thus this chapter offers no knockdown arguments either for or against the modern institution of judicial review and the doctrine of judicial supremacy. The purposes of this chapter are rather to clarify what the debate is about, clear away a great deal of argumentative deadwood, and indicate how further progress might be made.

The Establishment of Judicial Independence

Article III of the Constitution states that the "judicial power of the United States, shall be vested in one supreme court, and in such inferior courts as the Congress may from time to time ordain and establish."[9] As

---

[8] See the accounts of the conflict over child labor legislation in Alan Dawley, *Struggles for Justice: Social Responsibility and the Liberal State* (Cambridge: Harvard University Press, 1991), pp. 282–83; Morton Keller, *Regulating a New Society: Public Policy and Social Change in America, 1900–1933* (Cambridge: Harvard University Press, 1994), pp. 205–9; William F. Swindler, *Court and Constitution in the Twentieth Century: The Old Legality, 1889–1932* (Indianapolis: Bobbs-Merrill, 1969), pp. 236–39.

[9] U.S. Const., article III, sec. 1.

has so often been noted, Article III says nothing about the power of judicial review. Yet the version of judicial review that is the focus of the contemporary debate over the role of the Supreme Court is more a creation of the modern state than an accepted idea of the late eighteenth century. The modern version of judicial review is not simply a discrete judicial power, but a complex institution that includes important jurisdictional grants not made until after the Civil War and a series of understandings built up over the years among the branches of government. A key element of the modern institution of judicial review that only developed over time is the doctrine of judicial supremacy, the idea that the Supreme Court is the final authority in matters of constitutional interpretation. While the discussion below will elaborate these points further, it is important to note them at the outset, since they are often ignored in the contemporary debate.

Indeed, the ambiguities of the term "judicial review" are a chief source of the conceptual problems of the contemporary debate. To understand the importance of these ambiguities, it is useful to begin with the question of whether the founding generation endorsed judicial review.

The thought of the founding generation has been scrutinized closely to see whether it shows support for judicial review.[10] This inquiry is anachronistic, however, if its purpose is to discover whether the founding generation would have approved of the modern institution of judicial review and the doctrine of judicial supremacy. This commits the error of asking questions of history that history cannot answer.[11] The modern institution of judicial review and the doctrine of judicial supremacy did not exist in the late eighteenth century and the founding generation thus had no opportunity to pass judgment one way or the other.

In creating the judicial branch, the Framers were primarily concerned with the establishment of judicial independence; that is, how the judiciary would fit into the scheme of separated institutions, shared powers, and checks and balances embodied in the Constitution.[12] What was the nature of the judicial power? What specific powers would be necessary to make the judiciary independent of the elected branches of government? These

[10] See, e.g., Raoul Berger, *Congress v. The Supreme Court* (Cambridge: Harvard University Press, 1969).

[11] For a description of the fallacy of anachronism, see David Hackett Fischer, *Historians' Fallacies: Toward a Logic of Historical Thought* (New York: Harper and Row, 1970), pp. 132–33. See also William E. Nelson, "1966: Constitutional History," in William E. Nelson and John Phillip Reid, eds., *The Literature of American Legal History* (New York: Oceana, 1985), p. 121.

[12] See Gordon S. Wood, "Judicial Review in the Era of the Founding," in Robert A. Licht, ed., *Is the Supreme Court the Guardian of the Constitution?* (Washington, D.C.: AEI Press, 1993), pp. 153–63; Robert G. McCloskey and Sanford Levinson, *The American Supreme Court*, 2d ed. (Chicago: University of Chicago Press, 1994), p. 18.

were some of the questions that concerned the Framers. The historical record is somewhat unclear because distinctions were not often made between the different kinds of powers the judiciary could have. This is not because the Framers were confused, but because a national judicial system was a new institution and they were not necessarily concerned with the issues that trouble us today.

To evaluate the historical record, we must distinguish the analytically different constitutional powers or functions the judiciary can be given. Making these distinctions is useful also in analyzing why the form of judicial independence that existed in the antebellum United States developed as it did and how it contributed to the emergence of the modern institution of judicial review and the doctrine of judicial supremacy.

We must first distinguish between the power to hold state and local acts of government unconstitutional and the power to hold acts of the executive and legislative branches unconstitutional. The Supremacy Clause in Article VI of the Constitution suggests that the federal judiciary may have the former power, but nothing in the Constitution helps with respect to the latter power.[13] With regard to the power to hold acts of the executive and legislative branches unconstitutional, the doctrine of separation of powers and the separation of institutions mandated by the Constitution create further variations. These variations arise along two dimensions: the *scope* of the power, that is, to which acts it applies and the *enforcement* of the power, that is, to what extent the elected branches are bound by the rulings of the judiciary.[14]

The first variation is that the Supreme Court may hold acts unconstitutional only when it is necessary to defend itself from encroachments by the other branches. On this understanding, the Court may refuse to issue advisory opinions or allow members of the Court to serve in a legislative or executive capacity if the Court decides that such action is necessary to preserve the independence of the judiciary. Such actions by the Court are fully enforceable on the other branches of government. The Court would not have the power to hold any other actions of the elected branches unconstitutional.

The second variation is that the Court has the power to hold unconstitutional any action of the elected branches, but its holdings are considered advisory and unenforceable unless the other branches concur. A sub-vari-

---

[13] See Dean Alfange, Jr., "Marbury v. Madison and Original Understandings of Judicial Review: In Defense of Traditional Wisdom," in Dennis J. Hutchinson, David A. Strauss, and Geoffrey R. Stone, eds., *The Supreme Court Review 1993* (Chicago: University of Chicago Press, 1994), pp. 416–19.

[14] This list of four variations is by no means exhaustive. In particular, many different schemes of limiting the acts of government that are subject to judicial review can be imagined.

ation is also possible where the other branches agree to obey the ruling of the Court with respect to the specific parties in the case, but not treat the ruling as having general applicability. This is sometimes called the departmental or three-branch theory of constitutional interpretation.[15]

It is important to distinguish the departmental theory from the practical necessity of having the elected branches interpret the Constitution. The President and Congress are bound by oath to support the Constitution under the provisions of Article VI, and must determine its meaning in the ordinary course of their duties, whether or not the Court has ruled on the issue in question.[16] The departmental theory properly understood is an account of what should occur when at least two of the three branches have differing opinions on a question of constitutional law.

The third variation is that the Court has the power to hold unconstitutional any act of the elected branches, but only in a clear case where everyone concedes that a violation of the Constitution has occurred. The decision of the Court would be fully enforceable on the other branches. This variation is suggested by political scientist Sylvia Snowiss's concept of the "concededly unconstitutional act" and its role in debates over the power of the judiciary in the late eighteenth century.[17] This variation does not necessarily make the judicial power trivial. For example, it is possible for Congress to inadvertently violate the Constitution in the sometimes chaotic process of legislation. The power to hold such acts unconstitutional would enable the judiciary to remedy this problem without waiting for corrective legislative action.

[15] For discussion, see Louis Fisher, *Constitutional Dialogues: Interpretation as Political Process* (Princeton: Princeton University Press, 1988), pp. 231–74; Walter F. Murphy, James E. Fleming, William F. Harris II, *American Constitutional Interpretation* (Mineola, N.Y.: Foundation Press, 1986), pp. 184–254.

For contemporary presentations of a three-branch theory of interpretation, see Robert A. Burt, *The Constitution in Conflict* (Cambridge: Harvard University Press, 1992); Stephen Macedo, *Liberal Virtues: Citizenship, Virtue, and Community in Liberal Constitutionalism* (New York: Oxford University Press, 1990), pp. 142–62.

[16] See Fisher, *Constitutional Dialogues*, pp. 233–36. For a recent historical discussion that illustrates this point, see David P. Currie, "The Constitution in Congress: Substantive Issues in the First Congress, 1789–1791," *University of Chicago Law Review* 61 (1994): 775.

[17] See Sylvia Snowiss, *Judicial Review and the Law of the Constitution* (New Haven: Yale University Press, 1990), pp. 34–38. For a critique of Snowiss's account of the origins of judicial review (although not with respect to the idea of the concededly unconstitutional act), see Alfange, "Marbury v. Madison and Original Understandings of Judicial Review," in Hutchinson, Strauss, and Stone, eds., *The Supreme Court Review*, pp. 333–49.

As Snowiss notes, in a famous article James Bradley Thayer attempted to revive the idea of the concededly unconstitutional act and make it the foundation of judicial restraint. Snowiss, *Judicial Review and the Law of the Constitution*, pp. 188–94. See James B. Thayer, "The Origin and Scope of the American Doctrine of Constitutional Law," *Harvard Law Review* 7 (1893): 129.

The fourth variation is that the Court has the power to rule any act of the elected branches unconstitutional and have them comply, both with respect to the parties in the action and as a general matter. This essentially leaves the legal boundaries of the Court's power in its own hands. It is the doctrine of judicial supremacy with which we are familiar. Nevertheless, the Supreme Court committed itself explicitly to this variation only relatively recently. In *Cooper v. Aaron*, for example, the Court stated that the "federal judiciary is supreme in the exposition of the law of the Constitution."[18]

Each variation on the scope and enforcement of the judicial power poses a different problem of justification. The task of understanding the debates concerning the judiciary that took place during the founding era is complicated by the fact that these variations were not sorted out and discussed separately. The founding generation did not focus on or resolve the problems of justification posed by the possible variations on the judicial power. This is why evidence from the founding period is ultimately inconclusive with respect to the justification of the modern institution of judicial review and the doctrine of judicial supremacy. The various statements made in the Federal Convention on the judicial power, for example, do not distinguish between the power to review state and federal legislation and do not specify the scope or enforcement of that power. These statements are thus not relevant to the question of whether the contemporary exercise of judicial review is justified.[19]

We can see this point more clearly by examining Alexander Hamilton's famous essay on the judicial power in *The Federalist* No. 78 and Chief Justice John Marshall's opinion in *Marbury v. Madison*.[20] In *The Federalist* No. 78, Hamilton is clearly discussing judicial independence, not judicial review in the modern sense.[21] Hamilton begins his discussion of "the right of the courts to pronounce legislative acts void" by noting that the Constitution is a "limited constitution" in that it "contains certain specified exceptions to the legislative authority; such for instance as that it shall pass no bills of attainder, no *ex post facto* laws, and the like." Hamilton then declares that it is the duty of the courts "to declare all acts contrary to the manifest tenor of the constitution void."[22] As Snowiss points out, Hamilton's statement of the necessity of judicial independence in this respect relies on the idea of the concededly unconstitutional act. That is, the

---

[18] 358 U.S. 1, 18 (1958).

[19] These statements are reviewed in Berger, *Congress v. The Supreme Court*, pp. 49–81.

[20] See Alexander Hamilton, The Federalist No. 78, in Jacob E. Cooke, ed., *The Federalist* (Middletown, Conn.: Wesleyan University Press, 1961), p. 521; *Marbury v. Madison*, 5 U.S. (1 Cranch) 137 (1803).

[21] See Hamilton, The Federalist No. 78, in Cooke, ed., pp. 524, 527–28.

[22] Ibid., p. 524.

courts have the right to declare acts of the legislature void when an absolutely clear or "manifest" violation of the Constitution occurs.[23]

Hamilton then responds to the charge that this kind of judicial independence makes the judiciary superior to the legislature. Hamilton's
denial rests on the character of the Constitution as a fundamental or supreme law and the doctrine of popular sovereignty. The power of the
people in establishing the Constitution is superior to both the legislative
and judicial powers. If a legislative act is contrary to the Constitution,
it must therefore be invalid.[24] The courts are in a good position to enforce the will of the people as "an intermediate body between the people
and the legislature, in order, among other things, to keep the latter within the limits assigned to their authority." This is confirmed by the idea
that the "interpretation of the laws is the proper and peculiar province of
the courts."[25]

Marshall's argument in *Marbury* concerning the judicial power in constitutional cases is similar in some respects to Hamilton's. Marshall starts
with the general "question, whether an act, repugnant to the constitution,
can become the law of the land," and, like Hamilton, appeals to popular
sovereignty to justify the supremacy of the Constitution as "a superior,
paramount law" over ordinary legislation.[26] But Marshall's argument concerning the role of the courts is not organized as a reply to the objection
that the power to hold legislation unconstitutional implies that the judiciary is superior to the legislature. Marshall argues that the judicial power to
hold legislation void is a necessary implication of the Constitution's status
as supreme law. Since "[i]t is emphatically the province and duty of the
judicial department to say what the law is," a statute conflicting with the
Constitution must be held invalid.[27] Marshall notes that any other result
would allow the legislature to do "what is expressly forbidden."[28]
Marshall then produces some examples that involve the legislature expressly violating a clear provision of the Constitution. He concludes "that
a law repugnant to the constitution is void; and that *courts*, as well as other
departments, are bound by that instrument."[29]

The possible variations on the judicial power that we identified earlier
make it easy to see that the Hamilton-Marshall argument does not come
to grips with many of the important issues posed by the idea of judicial
independence. Neither Hamilton or Marshall explicitly confront the

---

[23] See Snowiss, *Judicial Review and the Law of the Constitution*, pp. 77–82.
[24] See Hamilton, The Federalist No. 78, in Cooke, ed., pp. 524–25.
[25] Ibid., p. 525.
[26] *Marbury*, 5 U.S. at 176–77.
[27] Ibid., p. 177.
[28] Ibid., p. 178.
[29] Ibid., p. 180 (emphasis in original).

problems of specifying the scope and enforcement of the judicial power.
The Hamilton-Marshall argument is directed primarily at a more abstract
proposition—that the judiciary must side with the Constitution in the
case of a direct conflict between it and an ordinary legislative act. If the
Hamilton-Marshall argument supports any particular variation, it is the
third. Both Hamilton and Marshall appeal to absolutely clear cases of constitutional violation to support their argument.[30] Since *Marbury* held unconstitutional a provision of the Judiciary Act of 1789, some commentators have used it to support the first variation, which gives the judiciary the
power to defend itself from encroachments by the other branches.[31] In
any event, the modern institution of judicial review and the doctrine of
judicial supremacy were not established by Hamilton or Marshall.[32]

This poses the interesting problem of determining when the modern
institution of judicial review and the doctrine of judicial supremacy were
established.[33] It is unlikely there was a single point in time at which government institutions and the public agreed that judicial review in the
modern sense was legitimate. There is evidence of respect for the Supreme
Court and deference to its interpretation of the Constitution before the
Civil War.[34] Alexis de Tocqueville noted the prestige of lawyers and judges
in antebellum America in a section of *Democracy in America* titled "The
Temper of the American Legal Profession and How It Serves to Counter-
balance Democracy."[35] He commented that "[a]n American judge,

---

[30] See Snowiss, *Judicial Review and the Law of the Constitution*, pp. 77–82, 109–13.

[31] This is essentially the argument in Robert Lowry Clinton, *Marbury v. Madison and
Judicial Review* (Lawrence: University Press of Kansas, 1989). For a severe critique of Clin-
ton's argument, including the idea that *Marbury* supports the first variation, see Alfange,
"Marbury v. Madison and Original Understandings of Judicial Review," in Hutchinson,
Strauss, and Stone, eds., *The Supreme Court Review*, pp. 368–69, 385–413.

For an influential critique of Marshall's reasoning in *Marbury*, see Alexander M.
Bickel, *The Least Dangerous Branch* (New York: Bobbs-Merrill, 1962), pp. 1–12. See also
Alfange, "Marbury v. Madison and Original Understandings of Judicial Review," pp.
413–44.

[32] At the time, *Marbury* was not perceived as a claim of the supreme authority of the
judiciary in matters of constitutional interpretation. See Richard E. Ellis, *The Jeffersonian
Crisis: Courts and Politics in the Young Republic* (New York: W. W. Norton, 1971), pp.
65–66. See also the discussion in Mark A. Graber, "The Passive-Aggressive Virtues: *Cohens
v. Virginia* and the Problematic Establishment of Judicial Power," *Constitutional Commentary* 12 (1995): 67.

[33] See the discussion in Jennifer Nedelsky, *Private Property and the Limits of American
Constitutionalism: The Madisonian Framework and Its Legacy* (Chicago: University of Chicago Press, 1990), pp. 187–99.

[34] See G. Edward White, *The Marshall Court and Cultural Change, 1815–1835* (New
York: Macmillan, 1988), pp. 935, 963.

[35] Alexis de Tocqueville, *Democracy in America* (Garden City, N.Y.: Doubleday, 1969),
p. 263.

armed with the right to declare laws unconstitutional, is constantly intervening in political affairs" and famously concluded that "[t]here is hardly a political question in the United States which does not sooner or later turn into a judicial one."[36] Tocqueville claimed that the power of state and federal judges to declare legislation unconstitutional "is recognized by all the authorities; one finds neither party nor individual who contests it."[37] With regard to the doctrine of judicial supremacy, historian Phillip Paludan contends that before the Civil War, "the idea that only Supreme Court justices could declare the meaning of the Constitution had not yet been established."[38]

An institutional analysis may prove useful here.[39] The power and activity of the Supreme Court as an institution assumed modern proportions only after the Civil War. This is true both in terms of the number of state and federal laws ruled unconstitutional and the increase in institutional capacity provided to the federal judiciary through various jurisdictional grants from Congress. Prior to 1860, only two federal laws were held unconstitutional, along with thirty-five provisions of state and local law. After 1860, the pace at which state and local laws were held unconstitutional picked up considerably and invalidation of federal laws became common.[40] The ratification of the Civil War Amendments, especially the Fourteenth Amendment, was one important reason for the increase in the activity of the Court. Also important, however, were the Jurisdiction and Removal Act of 1875 and the Judiciary Acts of 1891 and 1925. These acts increased the jurisdiction of the Court under Article III and gave it greater institutional capacity to control its caseload and direct its attention to constitutional cases.[41]

To understand the development of judicial review and acceptance of judicial supremacy, we should place our list of variations on the judicial power in an institutional context. We initially made a distinction between holding acts of state governments unconstitutional and holding acts of

---

[36] Ibid., pp. 269–70.

[37] Ibid., p. 101.

[38] Phillip Shaw Paludan, *The Presidency of Abraham Lincoln* (Lawrence: University Press of Kansas, 1994), p. 13.

[39] See the interesting analysis in Graber, "The Passive-Aggressive Virtues," pp. 88–92.

[40] See Lawrence Baum, *The Supreme Court*, 5th ed. (Washington, D.C.: Congressional Quarterly Press, 1995), pp. 200–205. The cases in which federal laws were held unconstitutional before 1860 were *Marbury* and *Dred Scott v. Sandford*, 60 U.S. 393 (1856).

[41] See Stanley I. Kutler, *Judicial Power and Reconstruction Politics* (Chicago: University of Chicago Press, 1968), pp. 143–60. See also the articles on the various judiciary acts in Kermit Hall, ed., *The Oxford Companion to the Supreme Court of the United States* (New York: Oxford University Press, 1992), pp. 475–77.

the federal government unconstitutional. With regard to the former power, the elected branches are likely to back the Supreme Court if the effect of most decisions is to uphold federal power. This guarantees the existence of the power to review acts of state and local governments and places it on an especially firm footing.[42]

Matters are considerably more complex in the case of holding acts of the elected branches unconstitutional. Of course, the Supreme Court can build goodwill among the branches by ruling that their actions are constitutional. In addition, holding actions unconstitutional may not provoke the other branches if the decision is perceived as a narrow or technical one that does not have important policy implications. Further, even if there are important policy implications, the Court can still escape damage if it is allied with political forces or one of the branches that objected to the legislation. These allies can protect the Court by using the checks and balances the Constitution provides. The legislation may have passed over a presidential veto or may have become unpopular over time. However, it is also possible that the Court may rule legislation unconstitutional when the elected branches and the public have agreed that the law in question is desirable. In this situation, the Court may be overruled by a constitutional amendment (as in the case of the Eleventh and Sixteenth Amendments) or it may back down in a subsequent ruling.

The effects of a fragmented political system filled with checks and balances thus work to the Court's advantage, along with its ability to move quickly if need be to reverse itself. The Court can maneuver to avoid becoming a permanent obstacle to powerful political forces. But we must also take account of a positive source of the Court's power. The Court can take advantage of the legalistic aspects of American ideology and identify itself closely with the Constitution in a patriotic sense.[43] As we noted in chapter 1, the Federalist conception of politics still has a certain appeal in the judicial context. While this conception of politics cannot serve for the political system as a whole, it works very well for the Court and provides a basis for judicial review.

In this regard, we should keep in mind that after the Civil War the Supreme Court did not stand in an unmediated relationship to the public and the elected branches. As the status of lawyers increased and they grew more self-conscious as a profession, they saw the Court as a strong ally and as an expression of their highest sentiments. Any hostility toward the Court during the formative period of judicial supremacy in the late nine-

[42] See William Lasser, *The Limits of Judicial Power: The Supreme Court in American Politics* (Chapel Hill: University of North Carolina Press, 1988), p. 258.

[43] See Michael Kammen, *A Machine That Would Go Of Itself: The Constitution in American Culture* (New York: Alfred A. Knopf, 1986), pp. 8–10.

teenth century was thus mediated by the legal profession.[44] There is a strong relationship between the growing importance of lawyers to American life and the doctrine of judicial supremacy. Support, respect, and reverence for the Supreme Court remain strong today among American lawyers and constitutes one of the main pillars of the Court's power.

Judicial Review and Democracy in the Modern State

The controversy over judicial review took its modern form during the period when the national state began assuming new powers and responsibilities in the last three decades of the nineteenth century and the first three decades of the twentieth. Whether the national state should be activist or restrained in the face of new policy problems was a key question of this period and this phrasing was also applied to the Supreme Court. Our contemporary concern with activist or restrained judicial review thus dates from this period.[45]

As we saw in chapter 2, the federal courts were one of the two integrative institutions in the nineteenth century American state. As discussed above, the federal courts increased their institutional capacity to handle their caseload and decide constitutional questions in the years after the Civil War. Through a series of important statutes, the Court acquired full federal question jurisdiction, justices were removed from the onerous duty of riding circuit, and the Court acquired near-complete power over its own docket. Equally important, the Civil War Amendments gave the Court the opportunity to exercise broad review of state and local government activities.

These new grants of power marked the beginning of the modern period of Supreme Court activism. As noted in the first section, the rate at which state and local laws were struck down first reached significant levels after 1860, and the rate increased after the turn of the century. Roughly the same pattern existed with respect to federal legislation, although the Court did not become wholeheartedly activist until the 1920s. When the Court confronted the New Deal in the mid-1930s, it had been pursuing its activist course for several decades.

---

[44] See Edward A. Purcell, Jr., *Litigation and Inequality: Federal Diversity Jurisdiction in Industrial America, 1870–1958* (New York: Oxford University Press, 1992), pp. 289–91; William G. Ross, *A Muted Fury: Populists, Progressives, and Labor Unions Confront the Courts, 1890–1937* (Princeton: Princeton University Press, 1994), pp. 60–61, 242–44.

[45] Some of the discussion in this section and the next is taken from Rex Martin and Stephen M. Griffin, "Constitutional Rights and Democracy in the U.S.A.: The Issue of Judicial Review," *Ratio Juris* 8 (1995): 180.

The Court's new activism raised the question of its appropriate role in the political system. In famous cases the Court ruled that a federal income tax was unconstitutional, severely limited the reach of antitrust laws, ruled a variety of state and local legislation unconstitutional as violations of legislative power under the Fourteenth Amendment, and acted to restrict the growth of labor unions.[46] Although the Court upheld most of the social-economic regulatory legislation it considered, it rendered numerous decisions that were contrary to the interests of labor and those who sought social and economic reform. These decisions initiated the modern debate over judicial review.[47]

This period, often called the *Lochner* era after *Lochner v. New York*,[48] is perhaps the least understood period in American constitutional history. The shadow of the rejection of the precedents established during this period after 1937 has prevented lawyers and legal scholars from achieving a historical perspective on the *Lochner* era Court. Moreover, the historiography of this period has not been easy to understand or reconcile. Historians, political scientists, and legal scholars have engaged in spirited debate over the impact of the Court's rulings and the characterization of the ideology that influenced the Court.

This debate can be difficult to follow because careful distinctions are not often made between the different kinds and levels of judicial activity during this period. Most scholars examine the record of the Supreme Court, but some cast their net more widely to include the federal judiciary as a whole, as well as state supreme courts. The problem is that the decisions of each set of courts presents a somewhat different picture. In addition, judicial review did not have the same impact in all areas of social and economic policy. Legislation that promoted economic activity and regulated business was often upheld by the courts, while reform legislation designed to benefit workers and labor unions was often struck down. Finally, scholars have not often focused on the jurisprudence of the Gilded Age and the *Lochner* era as a whole. The activism of the Court was not uniform across this entire period, and scholars have painted different pictures depending on the particular segment of time that draws their interest.[49]

---

[46] See *Pollock v. Farmer's Loan and Trust Co.*, 157 U.S. 429 (1895); *Pollock v. Farmer's Loan and Trust Co.*, 158 U.S. 601 (1895)(income tax); *United States v. E.C. Knight Co.*, 156 U.S. 1 (1895)(Sherman Antitrust Act); *In re Debs*, 158 U.S. 564 (1895)(imprisonment of Eugene V. Debs); *Allgeyer v. Louisiana*, 165 U.S. 578 (1897)(use of Fourteenth Amendment to strike down state legislation); *Lochner v. New York*, 198 U.S. 45 (1905)(same); *Coppage v. Kansas*, 236 U.S. 1 (1915)(labor legislation ruled unconstitutional). The child labor cases discussed earlier are also examples of this new activism.

[47] See Ross, *A Muted Fury*, pp. 49–69.

[48] 198 U.S. 45 (1905).

[49] For the view that the activism of state and federal courts in striking down reform legislation was overstated by Progressive critics, see William R. Brock, *Investigation and*

For our purposes, the most important insight to emerge from the recent historiography of the *Lochner* era is that it was neither an aberrant period of activism that represented a fundamental break with the past nor a period in which the Supreme Court suddenly adopted a laissez-faire or pro-business ideology that led to an unjustified departure from precedent. Increasingly, scholars are finding strong links between the judicial philosophy of the *Lochner* era and the thought of the founding generation as filtered through the politics of the Jacksonian period. The judicial philosophy of the Gilded Age was a legitimate descendant of the Madisonian political philosophy expressed in *The Federalist* No. 10. The eighteenth-century republican animus against the politics of faction was modified by Jacksonian democracy into a conviction that the judiciary was responsible for closely scrutinizing legislation that appeared to benefit a particular class of citizens. During the *Lochner* era, the Court applied this standard in good faith to strike down measures that were understood to be beyond the power of the legislature to enact.[50]

It is thus a serious mistake to regard the judicial thought of this period as a deviation from the American constitutional tradition. We should keep in mind that when judges confronted the unprecedented events set in

---

Responsibility: Public Responsibility in the United States, 1865–1900 (Cambridge: Cambridge University Press, 1984), pp. 77–87; John E. Semonche, *Charting the Future: The Supreme Court Responds to a Changing Society, 1890–1920* (Westport, Conn.: Greenwood Press, 1978); Melvin I. Urofsky, "State Courts and Protective Legislation During the Progressive Era: A Reevaluation," *Journal of American History* 72 (1985): 63.

For the view that the courts did constitute an important obstacle to reform, particularly in the area of labor policy, see William E. Forbath, *Law and the Shaping of the American Labor Movement* (Cambridge: Harvard University Press, 1991); Theda Skocpol, *Protecting Soldiers and Mothers: The Political Origins of Social Policy in the United States* (Cambridge: Harvard University Press, 1992), pp. 226–29, 254–61.

[50] See James W. Ely, Jr., *The Chief Justiceship of Melville W. Fuller, 1888–1910* (Columbia: University of South Carolina Press, 1995); Owen M. Fiss, *Troubled Beginnings of the Modern State, 1888–1910* (New York: Macmillan, 1993); Howard Gillman, *The Constitution Besieged: The Rise and Demise of Lochner Era Police Powers Jurisprudence* (Durham: Duke University Press, 1993); Morton Horwitz, *The Transformation of American Law, 1870–1960* (New York: Oxford University Press, 1992); Herbert Hovenkamp, *Enterprise and American Law, 1836–1937* (Cambridge: Harvard University Press, 1991); William E. Nelson, *The Roots of American Bureaucracy, 1830–1900* (Cambridge: Harvard University Press, 1982); Michael Les Benedict, "Laissez-Faire and Liberty: A Re-Evaluation of the Meaning and Origins of Laissez-Faire Constitutionalism," *Law and History Review* 3 (1985): 293; Stephen A. Siegel, "*Lochner* Era Jurisprudence and the American Constitutional Tradition," *North Carolina Law Review* 70 (1991): 1. See also the sources cited in Purcell, *Litigation and Inequality*, pp. 401–2 n. 50.

For the traditional view that the Supreme Court was in the grip of a social contract or pro-business ideology, see Paul Kens, *Judicial Power and Reform Politics: The Anatomy of Lochner v. New York* (Lawrence: University Press of Kansas, 1990); Arnold M. Paul, *Conservative Crisis and the Rule of Law* (Ithaca: Cornell University Press, 1960).

motion by the industrialization and urbanization of late nineteenth-century America and the social consequences of economic upheavals and immigration, their ideological resources remained rooted in antebellum America. There was no other constitutional philosophy on which the judges of this period could draw. This remained true when the Court reversed course after 1937. After 1937, there was a sense in which the Court was cut off from the thought of the founding generation and would have to find its own way.[51]

The first modern debate over the legitimacy of judicial review in American democracy was a sham in a certain sense. The elite Mugwump reformers of the late nineteenth century and those who sought reforms of various kinds in the early twentieth century were not interested in establishing a democracy in the United States in a contemporary sense. The U.S. may have been a democracy by the standards of the time, particularly in relation to other countries.[52] But the U.S. of the turn of the century was not democratic by our standards, nor did it embrace many of the political values we now take for granted.[53]

On balance, despite such improvements as the direct election of senators and the extension of suffrage to (white) women, the American state moved toward a less democratic politics during the *Lochner* era. The political aspirations of African-Americans, poor whites, and Populists were suppressed by force and fraud.[54] Attempts by workers to organize unions were met by a devastating combination of court decisions and unrestrained violence. Business used omnibus labor injunctions to throw a net over all political activity in working-class communities and used the state to suppress civil liberties.[55]

The status of democracy in the founding and Progressive eras is impor-

[51] See Nedelsky, *Private Property and the Limits of American Constitutionalism*, pp. 229–30. See also the suggestive article by George D. Braden, "The Search for Objectivity in Constitutional Law," *Yale Law Journal* 57 (1948): 571.

[52] For doubts even on this score, see Robert A. Dahl, *Polyarchy: Participation and Opposition* (New Haven: Yale University Press, 1971), p. 29.

[53] For comments on antidemocratic thought in the *Lochner* era, see Kammen, *A Machine That Would Go Of Itself*, pp. 228–29; Nelson, *The Roots of American Bureaucracy*, pp. 87–89; Paul, *Conservative Crisis*, pp. 229–30, 233. See also the description of the United States as a *Herrenvolk* democracy in George M. Fredrickson, *White Supremacy: A Comparative Study in American and South African History* (New York: Oxford University Press, 1981), pp. xi–xii, 154–55, 166–67.

[54] See Eric Foner, *Reconstruction: America's Unfinished Revolution, 1863–1877* (New York: Harper and Row, 1988), p. 598; Lawrence Goodwyn, *Democratic Promise: The Populist Movement in America* (New York: Oxford University Press, 1976), pp. 299–300, 304–5, 535.

[55] See Forbath, *Law and the Shaping of the American Labor Movement*, pp. 59–97; Harold G. Vatter, *The Drive to Industrial Maturity: The U.S. Economy, 1860–1914* (Westport, Conn.: Greenwood Press, 1975), pp. 280–81, 296.

tant because it relates to the contemporary debate over judicial review. One common response to the charge that judicial review is undemocratic, for example, is that the United States was not established as a pure or majoritarian democracy, but as a representative or constitutional democracy. The very existence of the Constitution establishes that Americans have traditionally regarded restraints on the will of a democratic majority as legitimate.[56] The trouble with this response is that it flattens the historical record and directs our attention away from how democracy in the United States has evolved through time and how democratic principles have provided the basis for an ongoing critique of the relatively undemocratic (by contemporary standards) order established by the Constitution of 1787.[57]

Democracy as it presently exists in the United States and other western nations is largely a product of the last one hundred years.[58] It is only in this period that women's suffrage was achieved, that political rights, including the right to vote, were effectively guaranteed to all citizens, and that issues affecting all groups and classes of citizens began to be discussed and resolved at the national level of government. These achievements can guide us in specifying how contemporary American democracy differs from the democracy of the Framers and Progressive reformers.

First, contemporary American democracy recognizes the importance of a national guarantee of civil rights and civil liberties, backed by appropriate enforcement agencies. These civil rights and liberties apply to all citizens and include full political rights, including the right to vote, to run for office, and to participate in politics generally. There are no property, class, race, or sex-based restrictions on the right to vote.[59] Second, contemporary democracy accepts the institutions of political parties and interest groups as legitimate means of organizing citizens for politics. Third, it accepts to a certain extent a populist form of democracy in which all of the elected branches are understood to be elected directly by the people on a state-by-state basis (the Electoral College notwithstanding), and it accepts a more direct role for public opinion in the policy process in the form of polls, initiatives, and referenda. Fourth, contemporary democracy involves the rejection of white supremacy and the structure of federalism and states rights that supported that system of oppression. Fifth, contem-

---

[56] See, e.g., H. N. Hirsch, *A Theory of Liberty: The Constitution and Minorities* (New York: Routledge, 1992), pp. 4–5.

[57] For useful commentary, see Morton J. Horwitz, "Foreword: The Constitution of Change: Legal Fundamentality Without Fundamentalism," *Harvard Law Review* 107 (1993): 57–65.

[58] See Arend Lijphart, *Democracies: Patterns of Majoritarian and Consensus Government in Twenty-One Countries* (New Haven: Yale University Press, 1984), p. 37.

[59] See Rex Martin, *A System of Rights* (New York: Oxford University Press, 1993), pp. 98–126.

porary democracy does not accept any constitutional limit on the national political agenda. If the public demands action on a given policy issue, no matter how local the response of government has been traditionally, the national state must take action.

This specification of contemporary American democracy will assist us in making two points in the discussion below. First, the appropriate question with respect to judicial review is whether it can be justified under these contemporary principles, not how it fares under the principles of the late eighteenth century. Second, it is apparent that the United States began to become a contemporary democracy only after World War II.[60] As we shall see, this affects how we assess the ability of the different branches of government to protect civil rights and civil liberties.

The Contemporary Debate and the Role of the Supreme Court

The criticism directed at the Supreme Court during the *Lochner* era was greatly reinforced by the conflict between President Roosevelt and the Court during the New Deal. In 1935–36 the Court decided eight major cases against the New Deal and so provoked the "Court-packing" crisis of 1937, in which Roosevelt tried to force the appointment of new justices to the Court. Roosevelt's plan was defeated, but he was shortly able to place a number of supporters of the New Deal on the Court. Even before Roosevelt secured these appointments, however, the Court shifted direction and began holding New Deal social and economic legislation constitutional on a regular basis.[61]

The "Court-packing" crisis was important to the development of American constitutional theory because of the lessons scholars drew from the crisis. In its aftermath, it appeared that the effect of the Supreme Court's exercise of judicial review during the previous decades was to obstruct the inevitable development of a greater role for government in regulating the economy. Moreover, the Court had obstructed the regulatory-welfare state by using (it was argued) dubious reasoning and focusing on some of the most ambiguous clauses in the Constitution. Scholars drew the conclusion that it was a mistake for the Court to oppose a determined national majority based on nothing more than a desire to protect property rights. The New Deal debate thus showed that there was a tension between the exercise of judicial review and democratic government, a tension that many felt should be resolved in favor of democracy.

[60] See Lijphart, *Democracies*, p. 39.

[61] See generally William E. Leuchtenburg, *The Supreme Court Reborn: The Constitutional Revolution in the Age of Roosevelt* (New York: Oxford University Press, 1995).

At the very time the Supreme Court was declaring that reviewing regulatory legislation was not part of its constitutional role, it was developing a new role for itself as a defender of individual rights, especially rights related to the political process, such as the First Amendment's protection of freedom of speech. Judicial review to protect individual rights was justified on the ground that the exercise of such rights by minorities was least likely to be protected by the democratic process. Majorities have an incentive to deprive their opponents of their political rights because this helps the majority retain power. The Court could play a legitimate role to defend the Bill of Rights against majoritarian incursions.

This reasoning emerged clearly in the famous footnote four of *United States v. Carolene Products Co.* In this footnote, the Court reflected on its role in an unusually self-conscious fashion. Essentially the Court stated that it should strictly enforce the Constitution when the legislation in question (1) clearly infringed a specific right identified in the text of the Constitution, (2) had the effect of excluding citizens from the political process, or (3) was the result of prejudice against discrete and insular minorities.[62] The second and third provisos of the footnote suggested that there was a special need for the Court to intervene when the democratic process breaks down, even when no specific provision of the Constitution was violated.[63]

Another important theme sounded by the Court in its search for a new role emphasized the special or fundamental character of constitutional rights. Justice Robert Jackson stated that the purpose of attaching the Bill of Rights to the Constitution was to place its guarantees "beyond the reach of majorities and officials and to establish them as legal principles to be applied by the courts." Jackson argued that these "fundamental rights may not be submitted to vote; they depend on the outcome of no elections."[64]

The contemporary debate concerning democracy and judicial review must be understood against this historical background. When Alexander Bickel argued that "judicial review is a deviant institution in the American democracy," he was not announcing a self-evident truth.[65] It seemed just as obvious to other scholars that the United States was a *constitutional* democracy, the word denoting the legitimacy of placing restraints on the

---

[62] 304 U.S. 144, 152–53 n. 4 (1938).

[63] For commentary on the *Carolene Products* footnote, see Robert M. Cover, "The Origins of Judicial Activism in the Protection of Minorities," *Yale Law Journal* 91 (1982): 1287; Louis Lusky, "Footnote Redux: A *Carolene Products* Reminiscence," *Columbia Law Review* 82 (1982): 1093; Bruce A. Ackerman, "Beyond *Carolene Products*," *Harvard Law Review* 98 (1985): 713.

[64] *West Virginia Board of Education v. Barnette,* 319 U.S. 624, 638 (1943).

[65] Bickel, *The Least Dangerous Branch,* p. 18.

representatives of the people.[66] But scholars like Bickel had the edge in the post–New Deal debate because of the impact of the confrontation between President Roosevelt and the Supreme Court. The New Deal experience appeared to show the folly of the Court trying to stand against the considered judgment of a massive and persistent electoral majority and the wisdom of judicial self-restraint. This was the lesson Justice Felix Frankfurter, his clerk Bickel, and subsequent generations of constitutional scholars drew from the New Deal.[67] The Court was perceived to be "deviant" because of the new power and legitimacy of the elected branches of government. The Court was different and thus deviant because it was not an elected body.

It is important to understand that scholars like Bickel were not interested in using this argument as a tool to abolish judicial review or even to significantly restrict its scope. Bickel's concern was ultimately to specify the proper function or role for the Supreme Court in American democracy.[68] The idea that judicial review was a suspect institution because it was countermajoritarian was only one element in Bickel's analysis. The thought that guided such scholarly efforts was that the undemocratic character of judicial review meant that the Court had to behave in a certain way to avoid repeating the mistakes of the pre–New Deal Court. Thus the debate is better characterized as one over the proper role of the Supreme Court in American democracy. We will explore this debate by distinguishing among legal, prudential, and moral arguments concerning judicial review, examining the political context in which judicial review is exercised, and analyzing judicial review in the light of institutional considerations and comparisons with similar institutions in other countries.[69]

Legal, Prudential, and Moral Justifications for Judicial Review

It will be useful to distinguish among three kinds of arguments that are used in the debate over the role of the Supreme Court: legal, prudential, and moral. Legal arguments rely on legal materials such as the text of the Constitution, precedent, and the intent of the Framers. Prudential arguments assess judicial review in the same way that other political practices,

---

[66] See, e.g., Erwin Chemerinsky, "The Price of Asking the Wrong Question: An Essay on Constitutional Scholarship and Judicial Review," *Texas Law Review* 62 (1984): 1232–33.

[67] On Frankfurter's views, see H. N. Hirsch, *The Enigma of Felix Frankfurter* (New York: Basic Books, 1981), p. 132.

[68] See Bickel, *The Least Dangerous Branch*, pp. 23–24.

[69] Theories that use democratic principles or appeals to the *Carolene Products* footnote to ground a particular interpretation of the Constitution will be considered in chapter 5. See, e.g., Ely, *Democracy and Distrust*.

broadly understood, are assessed—whether they make sense, on-balance, in light of contemporary political values, beliefs, and circumstances, and taking practical considerations into account. Moral or abstract normative arguments consider judicial review in light of fundamental ideals and principles and abstracted from actual institutions and considerations of practical politics.

When the modern debate over judicial review began in the Progressive era, it was conducted largely through legal arguments. Scholars such as the famous historian Charles Beard studied the historical record left by the founding generation to see whether it supported the establishment of judicial review.[70] Although legal arguments for and against judicial review are still made, we will not examine them here. Earlier in this chapter, we established that the precedents concerning judicial review are ambiguous because the founding generation did not distinguish among the different variations on the judicial power. Perhaps more important, legal arguments are limited in what they can justify. They can establish what we have done, but not necessarily what we should do. The predominance of prudential and moral arguments in the contemporary debate derives from the thought, well expressed by Alexander Bickel, that "[j]udicial review is . . . a choice that [we] have made, and ultimately we must justify it as a choice in our own time."[71]

Bickel's argument concerning the "counter-majoritarian difficulty" and role of the Supreme Court set the terms of the contemporary debate over the justification of judicial review, a debate that tended to remain static in the ensuing years.[72] Bickel argued that the central characteristic of American democracy is popular representation through election and that judicial review runs counter to this characteristic. While he was aware that American government is one of checks and balances and that judicial review can be understood as a check against the elected branches, he argued that judicial review is unique because it is final. Bickel argued, in effect, that there is no other national government institution that makes decisions that cannot be overturned by an ordinary legislative majority. Presumably even the decisions of the Federal Reserve Board can be altered by a legislative majority, but not the rulings of the Supreme Court. To further heighten the insult to democratic institutions, the members of the

[70] See, e.g., Charles A. Beard, *The Supreme Court and the Constitution* (Englewood Cliffs, N.J.: Prentice Hall, 1962 [1938]); Louis B. Boudin, *Government by Judiciary* (New York: William Godwin, 1932). For commentary, see Ross, *A Muted Fury*, pp. 49–56.

[71] Bickel, *The Least Dangerous Branch*, p. 16. See also McCloskey and Levinson, *The American Supreme Court*, p. 207.

[72] For examples and commentary on Bickel's influence, see Jesse H. Choper, *Judicial Review and the National Political Process* (Chicago: University of Chicago Press, 1980), pp. 4–10; Ely, *Democracy and Distrust*, pp. 4–9; Bruce Ackerman, "The Storrs Lectures: Discovering the Constitution," *Yale Law Journal* 93 (1984): 1014.

Court have life terms and are not subject to any periodic review or, of course, to elections.[73]

There were a number of important elements to Bickel's analysis that were often overlooked in the debate that followed. First, Bickel offered prudential rather than moral arguments to evaluate judicial review. He appealed to common values and practical considerations, and urged that judicial review should be judged as an institution in an on-balance sense.[74] Second, a key assumption in Bickel's argument was that the determinations the Supreme Court necessarily had to make in the exercise of judicial review had the character of policy judgments rather than legal judgments.[75] Third, Bickel's argument was built on an appeal to democratic principles understood as a complex set, not an assumption that majoritarianism was the supreme principle of American democracy (despite the phrase "countermajoritarian difficulty").[76]

In contrast to Bickel's nuanced analysis, the contemporary debate tended to focus on two of his arguments—that American government is essentially majoritarian and that there is no effective appeal from a Supreme Court decision.[77] Although the assumption that judicial review is final appears at the end of the standard argument against judicial review, it is actually the key to the entire argument. The standard argument is better understood if we use the finality assumption as the starting point. The argument proceeds as follows. Supreme Court decisions are final and unreviewable by ordinary legislative majorities. This unique power of the Court stands in need of justification, given that our system emphasizes electoral accountability.

Once this assumption is highlighted, however, it becomes clear that the idea of finality is a legal concept. Supreme Court decisions are final because the only legal way to overturn them is by passing a constitutional amendment. The finality assumption thus evades the question of the actual impact of Court decisions on the political system. Are Court decisions effectively final in the political system? Many studies of judicial impact have emphasized that the Court has only one move in what is always a larger political struggle, particularly in the context of controversial decisions that other political actors care about.[78]

On the other hand, the opposing point of view, which we may label

---

[73] Bickel, *The Least Dangerous Branch*, pp. 16–20.

[74] Ibid., p. 24. For relevant commentary, see Anthony T. Kronman, "Alexander Bickel's Philosophy of Prudence," *Yale Law Journal* 94 (1985): 1573–79.

[75] Bickel, *The Least Dangerous Branch*, p. 3.

[76] Ibid., pp. 24–28.

[77] See the arguments of Choper and Ely cited in note 72.

[78] See, e.g., David M. O'Brien, *Storm Center: The Supreme Court in American Politics*, 3d ed. (New York: W. W. Norton, 1993), pp. 357–409.

constitutionalist, does not fare much better. On this view, it is clear that we live in a constitutional democracy where the Constitution specifies limits on majority rule and the normal operation of electoral democracy, limits that are widely accepted. If judicial review is used to enforce these limits, it simply operates as a further check on majority will. The limits the Supreme Court enforces are those having to do with individual rights. These rights are thought to be especially vulnerable to majoritarian violations. So judicial review only differs in degree, not in kind, from other countermajoritarian restraints such as bicameralism, the congressional committee system, and the presidential veto. Furthermore, the justices do have an electoral pedigree to the extent that they are nominated by the President and confirmed by the Senate.[79]

This constitutionalist position has the same problem as the countermajoritarian position. It reflects a legal point of view in assuming Supreme Court decisions are final.[80] The Court can be an effective check on the elected branches only if its mandates cannot be frustrated by the political system. If the elected branches have an effective response to Court decisions, the Court cannot meaningfully protect individual rights.[81]

The underlying difficulty with contemporary prudential arguments is that they are focused around contesting the idea that the American system of government is majoritarian. Centering arguments around the "countermajoritarian difficulty" is a false trail that should have been avoided. Although American democracy could not work without the use of majority rule in elections and the lawmaking process, it also quite clearly includes significant values, rules, and institutions that work against majority rule.[82] More important, there is no reason to focus on any particular decision procedure in trying to understand American democracy. As we have seen, historical considerations show that American democracy is best understood in terms of a complex set of normative principles.[83]

[79] See Erwin Chemerinsky, "Foreword: The Vanishing Constitution," *Harvard Law Review* 103 (1989): 43, 74–83; Barry Friedman, "Dialogue and Judicial Review," *Michigan Law Review* 91 (1993): 617–27.

[80] Friedman does criticize the assumption that Supreme Court decisions are final, but he does so from a legalistic perspective. See Friedman, "Dialogue and Judicial Review," pp. 643–53.

[81] See Gerald N. Rosenberg, "Judicial Independence and the Reality of Political Power," *Review of Politics* 54 (1992): 369.

[82] For a review of majoritarian and antimajoritarian elements in American democracy, see Choper, *Judicial Review and the National Political Process*, pp. 12–59.

[83] For an elaboration of democratic theory that makes this point in the context of describing a number of models of democracy, see David Held, *Models of Democracy* (Stanford: Stanford University Press, 1987). See also the discussion in Daniel A. Farber and Philip P. Frickey, *Law and Public Choice: A Critical Introduction* (Chicago: University of Chicago Press, 1991), pp. 55–62.

This illustrates a general problem with prudential arguments—they by-pass too many normative considerations. *Do* we live in a democracy? By what criteria? Do those criteria inevitably condemn judicial review or can they provide some place for it? Bickel, John Hart Ely, and other legal scholars take it for granted that the American system of government is a democracy and that it is obvious that this fact poses a problem for judicial review. But whether the American system of government is a democracy is not a fact but only the possible conclusion of a complex normative argument grounded in democratic theory. The legal scholars that have contributed to the judicial review and democracy debate have generally not undertaken the difficult task of building such an argument.

This problem with prudential arguments suggests the need to examine justifications of judicial review based on moral theory and abstract normative arguments. Recent scholarship provides a number of different rationales for judicial review. Whether scholars start from rational choice theory,[84] Madisonian political theory,[85] or John Rawls's theory of justice,[86] they are able to make straightforward arguments to justify the idea of having the judiciary serve as an extra check on government action, particularly in the area of individual rights.[87]

The arguments of Freeman and Riley are illustrative. Their arguments are similar, although Freeman operates within the framework of Rawls's theory of justice and Riley appeals to the American political tradition. Freeman presents a Rawlsian argument that free and equal persons would seek to further their interests in advancing and protecting their sense of justice and their conception of the good by endorsing a set of equal basic rights and liberties. One equal basic right would be the right to political

---

[84] See Jon Elster, *Ulysses and the Sirens* (Cambridge: Cambridge University Press, 1984), p. 93. See also Jon Elster, "Majority Rule and Individual Rights," in Stephen Shute and Susan Hurley, eds., *On Human Rights: The Oxford Amnesty Lectures 1993* (New York: Basic Books, 1993), pp. 175–216.

[85] See Stephen Holmes, *Passions and Constraint: On the Theory of Liberal Democracy* (Chicago: University of Chicago Press, 1995), pp. 134–77; Jonathan Riley, "American Democracy and Majority Rule," in John W. Chapman and Alan Wertheimer, eds., *Majorities and Minorities* (New York: New York University Press, 1990), pp. 267–307.

[86] See Samuel Freeman, "Constitutional Democracy and the Legitimacy of Judicial Review," *Law and Philosophy* 9 (1990–1991): 327. For another argument that Rawls's theory can justify judicial review, see Stephen M. Griffin, "Reconstructing Rawls's Theory of Justice: Developing a Public Values Philosophy of the Constitution," *New York University Law Review* 62 (1987): 772–75. For Rawls's most recent views on judicial review, see John Rawls, *Political Liberalism* (New York: Columbia University Press, 1993), pp. 233–40.

[87] For an important recent exception and critique of judicial review, see Jeremy Waldron, "A Right-Based Critique of Constitutional Rights," *Oxford Journal of Legal Studies* 13 (1993): 18; Jeremy Waldron, "Freeman's Defense of Judicial Review," *Law and Philosophy* 13 (1994): 27.

participation. Free and equal persons attempting to specify their rights in the original position would also recognize various civil rights, including property rights and rights of legal process. It would then be reasonable for them to protect such rights by placing them in the constitution as a bill of rights. The question then becomes how such rights are to be enforced. Judicial review enters the picture as one of the possible checks and balances that can be used to enforce a bill of rights. Since the protection of equal basic rights is part of our idea of democracy, the use of judicial review to enforce such rights is not undemocratic.[88]

One important idea that Freeman takes from Rawls is that in a just political system, the exercise of judicial review (or the use of any other constitutional check) is an infringement of the right of equal political participation. This infringement may be justified by the necessity of protecting other basic rights, but it is still an infringement. This means that the legitimacy of judicial review is a matter of resolving a conflict of rights, not simply a matter of protecting the rights of the minority against the power of the majority. Democratic rule is also based on a constitutional right, the right of political participation.[89]

Riley is concerned to show that American democracy is a "logically coherent form of just majority rule, where justice connotes protection of equal basic rights."[90] Democracy involves popular majority rule, but that rule is only legitimate to the extent it conforms to standards of justice. Riley argues that in societies with a British common-law heritage, justice consists of protecting fundamental equal rights. In American democracy, such rights are protected by a written constitution that derives its authority from a unique conception of popular sovereignty. This conception of popular sovereignty holds that no government institution can ever possess complete sovereignty, and so the right to rule is divided among various levels and branches of government. American democracy thus involves a commitment to a strong version of separation of powers (or separated branches of government) and an extensive set of checks and balances. Like Freeman, Riley sees judicial review as one of the checks and balances it is appropriate to employ to protect fundamental rights in service of the sovereign Constitution.[91]

---

[88] Freeman, "Constitutional Democracy," pp. 338–39, 343–48, 352–53. For a similar argument from a different perspective, see Martin, *A System of Rights*, pp. 171–73.

[89] Freeman, "Constitutional Democracy," pp. 332–34. For Rawls's view on this point, see John Rawls, *A Theory of Justice* (Cambridge: Harvard University Press, 1971), p. 224. The point is also emphasized in Waldron, "A Right-Based Critique of Constitutional Rights," pp. 36–46.

[90] Riley, "American Democracy and Majority Rule," in Chapman and Wertheimer, eds., *Majorities and Minorities*, p. 270.

[91] Ibid., pp. 274–77, 280.

If the arguments of Freeman and Riley seem familiar, one reason is that they are sophisticated versions of the prudential constitutionalist position. But the constitutionalist position and the arguments that Freeman and Riley derive from political philosophy are not equivalent. The purpose of the constitutionalist position is to justify the exercise of judicial review by the Supreme Court in the here and now. Freeman and Riley show that judicial review is *consistent* with the philosophy underlying American democracy, but they do not purport to show that judicial review is a *necessary* check on government. There are many possible checks on government action, each with its own advantages and disadvantages. In a specific society under a specific set of historical circumstances, it may be wise or unwise to use judicial review as a check. Whether judicial review is appropriate for a particular constitution is a prudential matter, one not admitting of an answer from a theory of justice.[92]

Furthermore, the arguments of Freeman and Riley only justify a role for judicial review in protecting basic rights. While this justification addresses a large fraction of the Supreme Court's business, it does not cover the field. In particular, such arguments do not justify judicial review of the power-granting clauses of the Constitution. The constitutionalist position implies that the Court should have the power to review any government action that violates any part of the Constitution. It is not clear, however, whether the appeal Freeman and Riley make to the protection of basic rights could be extended to cover this kind of judicial review.

This brief review of the legal, prudential, and moral arguments concerning the legitimacy of judicial review gives us a general idea of the terrain of the contemporary debate. If we stay within the framework offered by these arguments, however, we will achieve only a partial understanding of the important questions posed by the modern institution of judicial review. To achieve a better understanding, we must situate judicial review in its political context.

Judicial Review and the Political System

The first analysis of the place of the judiciary in the American political system is still the best known. In *The Federalist* No. 78, Alexander Hamilton argued in favor of giving federal judges life tenure as a necessary element of the independence of the judicial branch. Without life tenure, the judiciary would become dependent on the elected branches since the judicial power was the weakest of the three powers of government.[93]

---

[92] Freeman, "Constitutional Democracy and the Legitimacy of Judicial Review," p. 361.
[93] Hamilton, The Federalist No. 78, in Cooke, ed., pp. 522–24.

Whoever attentively considers the different departments of power must perceive, that in a government in which they are separated from each other, the judiciary, from the nature of its functions, will always be the least dangerous to the political rights of the constitution; because it will be least in a capacity to annoy or injure them. The executive not only dispenses the honors, but holds the sword of the community. The legislature not only commands the purse, but prescribes the rules by which the duties and rights of every citizen are to be regulated. The judiciary on the contrary has no influence over either the sword or the purse, no direction either of the strength or of the wealth of the society, and can take no active resolution whatever. It may truly be said to have neither Force nor Will, but merely judgment; and must ultimately depend upon the aid of the executive arm even for the efficacy of its judgments.[94]

The analysis of constitutional change presented in chapter 1 seems to confirm Hamilton's argument. We saw in that chapter how the Supreme Court cannot serve as the gatekeeper for constitutional change. The Court did not have the option of maintaining its resistance to the new power the federal government acquired during the New Deal or the expanded power of the presidency during the Cold War. As Hamilton anticipated, the executive and legislative branches have more inherent political power than the Court.

The analysis in chapter 1 was based on historical observations of the evolution of American constitutionalism. Modern studies that concentrate on specific aspects of the Supreme Court's interaction with the political system also confirm Hamilton's original insight. In one well-known study, Robert Dahl concluded that "[b]y itself, the Court is almost powerless to affect the course of national policy."[95] Dahl's study proved durable because he situated the Court in American politics in an especially clear fashion. Dahl concentrated on Court rulings holding federal legislation unconstitutional and pointed out that if a lawmaking majority was persistent, it would eventually prevail over the Court. Either the Court would change its mind and reverse the earlier precedent or the lawmaking majority would ensure the reversal by appointing justices favorable to the views of the majority. Since vacancies on the Court are inevitable, the Court does not have the ability to resist a persistent lawmaking majority for very long.[96] Dahl generalized this argument by noting that American politics is dominated by long-lived political coalitions. These coalitions have sufficient staying power to influence the membership of

---

[94] Ibid., pp. 522–23.

[95] Robert A. Dahl, "Decision-Making in a Democracy: The Supreme Court as a National Policy-Maker," *Journal of Public Law* 6 (1957): 293. For the continuing influence of Dahl's study, see Baum, *The Supreme Court*, pp. 219–21.

[96] Dahl, "Decision-Making in a Democracy," pp. 284–91.

the Court and so ensure that the Court upholds those policies that they see as crucial.[97]

While Dahl's study was criticized on the ground that his analysis could not account for the activism of the Warren Court, studies of the relationship between public opinion and the Court's rulings tend to confirm the idea that the Court needs substantial assistance from the rest of the political system in order to initiate fundamental change.[98] As we saw in chapter 1, the activism of the Warren Court was almost entirely directed at state and local legislation. Earlier in this chapter, we observed that the Court does not risk as much when it rules state and local legislation unconstitutional because of the division of power in the nation's federal structure. An unconstitutional state policy may be limited to a few states. It is therefore possible for the Court to be supported by a national majority when it strikes down legislation prevalent in a limited number of states or even in an entire region (as was the case with southern policies of segregation). Several studies of public opinion suggest that this is exactly what occurred during the Warren Court era and after.[99]

Research on the ability of the Supreme Court to enforce its judgments in specific cases also suggests the inherent limits on the power of the Court. Studies of the impact of judicial rulings show that they can be blunted or even rendered irrelevant by public and governmental noncompliance and resistance.[100] Important civil rights decisions made by the Court, for example, were effectively implemented only once all the resources of the executive and legislative branches were brought to bear.[101]

Some of these findings have been employed in the prudential debate over the legitimacy of judicial review. As we have seen, constitutionalists defend the democratic character of the Supreme Court by appealing to the influence the political system has through the appointment process.

[97] Ibid., pp. 293–94. See also the discussion in Martin Shapiro, *Courts: A Comparative and Political Analysis* (Chicago: University of Chicago Press, 1981), p. 34.

[98] For the criticism referred to, see Jonathan D. Casper, "The Supreme Court and National Policy Making," *American Political Science Review* 70 (1976): 50.

[99] See Thomas R. Marshall, *Public Opinion and the Supreme Court* (Boston: Unwin Hyman, 1989); David G. Barnum, "The Supreme Court and Public Opinion: Judicial Decision Making in the Post-New Deal Period," *Journal of Politics* 47 (1985): 652; William Mishler and Reginald S. Sheehan, "The Supreme Court as a Countermajoritarian Institution? The Impact of Public Opinion on Supreme Court Decisions," *American Political Science Review* 97 (1993): 87. See also Stuart S. Nagel, "Court-Curbing Periods in American History," *Vanderbilt Law Review* 18 (1965): 925.

[100] See Baum, *The Supreme Court*, pp. 229–46; Fisher, *Constitutional Dialogues*, pp. 221–30; O'Brien, *Storm Center*, pp. 357–409. See generally Charles A. Johnson and Bradley C. Canon, *Judicial Policies: Implementation and Impact* (Washington, D.C.: Congressional Quarterly Press, 1984).

[101] See Gerald N. Rosenberg, *The Hollow Hope: Can Courts Bring About Social Change?* (Chicago: University of Chicago Press, 1991), pp. 42–106. Rosenberg provides an excellent summary of the research on the limits on the courts in ibid., pp. 10–21.

But Hamilton's influential argument and these studies have disquieting implications for the constitutionalist position. Constitutionalists do not simply defend the Court against charges that it is undemocratic, they also affirm that the Court can play a valuable role in protecting individual rights. Studies of the relationship of the Court to public opinion and the impact of Court rulings suggest that the Court cannot have a strong role defending the rights of minorities. Since the Court's rulings are not final in any strong sense and the Court is influenced over the long run by public opinion, the Court can defend individual and minority rights only to the extent that such a defense is consistent with the beliefs and interests of other political actors. Under these circumstances, the Court can hardly serve as a bulwark of civil rights and liberties.

This sobering conclusion may help explain why the Supreme Court has such a checkered history of protecting constitutional rights. Critics of the affirmative side of the constitutionalist position often point to the Court's failure to protect the rights of African-Americans in any consistent way before the middle of the twentieth century (as in *Dred Scott v. Sandford* and *Plessy v. Ferguson*), and the Court's generally poor record in defending civil liberties against infringement by the executive and legislative branches.[102] The failure of the Court to prevent the internment of citizens of Japanese descent in concentration camps during World War II and its meek response to McCarthyism are usually cited in this regard.[103] In both instances, the Court appeared to be following rather than challenging the dominant assumptions of the day concerning the extent of civil rights and liberties. If this shows that the Court must bow to realistic democratic constraints, it also demonstrates that its ability to defend individual rights is limited to the same extent.[104]

We should not embrace this point of view, however, without noticing some substantial complications. In the first place, the studies just discussed are limited in what they can show. They do not address all Court decisions to rule legislation unconstitutional, and the links between public opinion and Court rulings must be interpreted with special caution.[105] The studies of judicial impact are also open to question. If they show that

---

[102] See *Dred Scott v. Sandford*, 60 U.S. 393 (1856); *Plessy v. Ferguson*, 163 U.S. 537 (1896).

[103] For representative samples of this criticism, see Leonard W. Levy, *Judgments: Essays on American Constitutional History* (Chicago: Quadrangle Books, 1972), pp. 24–63; Louis Fisher, "One of the Guardians Some of the Time," in Licht, ed., *Is the Supreme Court the Guardian of the Constitution?* p. 82.

[104] See Rosenberg, "Judicial Independence and the Reality of Political Power," p. 398.

[105] See Gregory A. Caldeira, "Courts and Public Opinion," in John B. Gates and Charles A. Johnson, eds., *The American Courts: A Critical Assessment* (Washington, D.C.: CQ Press, 1991), p. 303; O'Brien, *Storm Center*, pp. 375–78. For a methodological discussion, see "Controversy: Popular Influence on Supreme Court Decisions," *American Political Science Review* 88 (1994): 711.

some rulings were widely ignored, such as those relating to desegregation and prayer in schools, other Court decisions endured for decades. Our opening story of child labor legislation is an illustration, as well as Warren Court decisions regarding reapportionment of legislative districts and the right of privacy. The child labor decisions were eventually reversed through the influence of election results on the appointment process, but the damage had presumably already been done to thousands of children over the two decades it took to obtain the reversal. If the Court can resist regulatory legislation for decades, perhaps it can be similarly effective in defending the rights of minorities. This is what the *Carolene Products* footnote seemed to imply.

There are yet further complications that deserve mention. The emphasis on majoritarianism as the fundamental principle of American democracy in the debate over judicial review and the constitutionalist position rest on the assumption that only the Supreme Court can play a credible role in defending constitutional rights. This is clearly not the case.[106] Table 3.1 lists significant civil rights and liberties laws enacted after the election of President Ronald Reagan in 1980. Many of these laws, including the Voting Rights Act Amendments of 1982 and the Civil Rights Act of 1991, were passed in response to numerous Court rulings that restricted the scope of laws designed to ensure the enforcement of civil rights. The contemporary debate over judicial review is at a loss with respect to such consistent legislative protection of individual rights. The debate accepts the simplistic view that majorities are always interested in violating the rights of minorities. This makes it difficult to explain why Congress is able to produce consistent majorities in favor of civil rights and liberties legislation.

The climate in which such laws emerged is largely a product of the civil rights movement and the way it highlighted the importance of civil rights and liberties for all Americans. As the United States finally began to move toward full democratic status after World War II, it became easier for African-Americans to win political battles by building coalitions in the same manner as other interest groups. After passage of the Voting Rights Act in 1965, a political logic took hold in which the elected branches were rewarded for approving civil rights and liberties legislation. Certainly the role of the civil rights movement in building coalitions to defend rights was important here, but many other Americans (including most recently religious groups and those with disabilities) perceived the advantages of effective constitutional-legal rights. During the Reagan Administration, this logic was extended to the Supreme Court nomination process, as each

---

[106] See Cass R. Sunstein, *The Partial Constitution* (Cambridge: Harvard University Press, 1993), pp. 145–46.

TABLE 3.1
Significant Civil Rights and Liberties Laws Enacted since 1980

1982
Voting Rights Act Amendments of 1982, Pub. L. No. 97–205, 96 Stat. 131.

1983
United States Commission on Civil Rights Act of 1983, Pub. L. No. 98–183, 97 Stat. 1301.

1984
Equal Access Act, Pub. L. 97–377, Title VIII, 98 Stat. 1302.
Voting Accessibility for the Elderly and Handicapped Act, Pub. L. 98–435, 98 Stat. 1678.

1986
Comprehensive Anti-Apartheid Act of 1986, Pub. L. 99–631, § 1(a), 100 Stat. 3515.

1987
Civil Rights Restoration Act of 1987, Pub. L. 100–259, 102 Stat. 28.

1988
Civil Liberties Act of 1988, Pub. L. No. 100–383, 102 Stat. 903.
Fair Housing Amendments Act of 1988, Pub. L. No. 100–430, 102 Stat. 1619.
Women's Educational Equity Act, Pub. L. 100–297, Title I, § 1001, 102 Stat. 234.

1990
AIDS Housing Opportunity Act, Pub. L. 101–625, Title VIII, §§ 851–863, 104 Stat. 4375.
Americans with Disabilities Act of 1990, Pub. L. 101–336, 104 Stat. 327.

1991
Civil Rights Act of 1991, Pub. L. No. 102–166, 105 Stat. 1071.

1993
Religious Freedom Restoration Act of 1993, Pub. L. No. 103–141, 107 Stat. 1488.

1994
Freedom of Access to Clinic Entrances Act of 1994, Pub. L. 103–259, 108 Stat. 54.

nominee was required to demonstrate his or her support of past Court decisions that various groups saw as fundamental.[107]

It appears that once the United States began to achieve full democratic status during the 1960s, the constitutional logic of separated and divided power began to work for individual rights as well as it does with respect to other policy matters. That is, if state and local governments violate constitutional rights, citizens can turn to the Supreme Court for assistance. If, on the other hand, the *Court* fails to protect constitutional rights, citizens can turn to the elected branches for redress. Past experience is not of much use in understanding this new democratic reality since the United States was not a democracy by contemporary standards for most of its history. Minorities may have needed the Court more in the past, but that is because they were outside the political system. Once minorities were brought into the system, the elected branches began responding to at least some of their political demands.

This conclusion should not be taken to imply that the United States has achieved some sort of democratic utopia. We have established, however, that the contemporary debate over judicial review must be complicated considerably if it is to accurately reflect American political reality.[108] If we want to justify judicial review in a prudential sense, we must first understand it as a complex institutional practice.

Institutional Considerations and
International Comparisons

One advantage of approaching the contemporary debate over judicial review from an institutional standpoint is that it helps clarify what the debate is about. We have already noted that the contemporary debate concerns the role of the Supreme Court in American democracy rather than the question of whether judicial review is justified in the first instance. This distinction is sometimes lost in the tangle of arguments. If the question is stated as one of justification and it is approached through abstract normative arguments, then the case for judicial review is not difficult to make as we have seen. Since the contemporary debate is not

---

[107] See Mark Silverstein, *Judicious Choices: The New Politics of Supreme Court Confirmations* (New York: W. W. Norton, 1994). For commentary on the failed nomination of Judge Robert Bork that is relevant to this point, see Stephen M. Griffin, "Politics and the Supreme Court: The Case of the Bork Nomination," *Journal of Law and Politics* 5 (1989): 551.

[108] For an in-depth presentation of this argument, illustrated by the phenomenon of elected officials inviting the judiciary to resolve difficult political issues, see Mark A. Graber, "The Nonmajoritarian Difficulty: Legislative Deference to the Judiciary," *Studies in American Political Development* 7 (1993): 35.

primarily concerned with the question of justifying judicial review in the abstract, however, this does not take us very far.

If our concern is the appropriate role of the Supreme Court in American democracy, we must take into account the institutional complexity of the Court's power. That power derives not only from the ability to rule legislation unconstitutional, but from institutional features that set the Court apart from the elected branches and help define its mission. A ready example is the life tenure the justices enjoy. If the justices served for a nonrenewable six-year term, the power of judicial review would be affected significantly by the different relationship to the elected branches such a term would imply. Justifying the contemporary role of the Supreme Court thus involves specifying all of the dimensions of the Court's power and showing how they can be supported through prudential arguments.

The historical experience with judicial review in the United States and other democracies suggests that there are a number of dimensions to the institutional power of a national constitutional court in addition to whether it can hold legislation unconstitutional. How is the court selected? What term of office do the justices hold and how can they be removed from office? Is the court part of a larger national judicial system enabling it to hear ordinary cases of law, or is it a special constitutional tribunal? Can the court issue advisory opinions (that is, undertake abstract review without an actual lawsuit)? Are the rights guaranteed by the constitution and enforced by the court written broadly or narrowly? What is the court's conception of its own role in terms of being relatively active or passive in defense of constitutional rights? However these institutional questions are answered, all of the resulting characteristics stand in need of justification.

With reference to these questions, the Supreme Court and the modern institution of judicial review can be defined as follows: the justices are selected by the President with the consent of the Senate to sit for life on a final court of appeal in a federal judicial system. The justices also hear nonconstitutional cases, but cannot issue advisory opinions and can be impeached for misbehavior. The Constitution the Court enforces contains broad normative clauses, and the Court has had an active conception of its role in the post–World War II period. The Court exercises judicial review in accordance with the fourth variation on the judicial power we defined in the first section of this chapter.

Many of these characteristics of American judicial review have been rejected by countries that have adopted judicial or constitutional review since World War II. These countries have had the opportunity to learn from both the positive and the negative aspects of the American experience with judicial review. On the positive side, the American experience has inspired other countries to place a check on government in the hands of a court (in France a Constitutional Council situated in the executive branch) in order to preserve basic rights. On the negative side, the record of the Supreme Court during the *Lochner* and New Deal eras is world famous and the countries that have adopted some form of constitutional review have sought to avoid what they see as an unfortunate American experience with a Court determined to retard social progress.[109]

Among the different types of review adopted by such countries as Germany, France, Canada, Italy, India, and Japan, three differences with the American institution stand out. First, the American commitment to life tenure for justices has been rejected in favor of nonrenewable terms that vary between seven and twelve years and mandatory retirement ages.[110] This is presumably to ensure that each new government will have the opportunity to appoint justices that are familiar with contemporary conditions, and so avoid any repetition of the American experience during the New Deal.[111] Mandatory retirement guards against the danger of justices hanging on to their posts after their legal skills have declined. Second, review has often been established as *constitutional* review, that is, review by a special constitutional tribunal that sits apart from the judicial system and has the power to issue advisory opinions.[112] Third, the definition of rights in post–World War II democratic constitutions is more lengthy and precise than is true of the American Bill of Rights.[113]

The case of Germany is instructive. The Federal Constitutional Court consists of two panels of eight members each. The Court is a specialized tribunal that decides only constitutional questions and has the power to issue advisory opinions to the national and state governments. All judges serve for a nonrenewable twelve-year term and must retire at age sixty-eight. Half the Court's members are elected by a judicial selection committee of the Bundestag (the national parliament) and half by the Bundesrat (the council of constituent states).[114] The process of judicial selection

[109] See, e.g., Alec Stone, *The Birth of Judicial Politics in France* (New York: Oxford University Press, 1992), pp. 39, 79.

[110] See Edward McWhinney, *Supreme Courts and Judicial Law-Making: Constitutional Tribunals and Constitutional Review* (Dordrecht: Martinus Nijhoff Publishers, 1986), pp. 52, 57, 291. The example of Australia is also worth noting. Although judicial review was instituted at the turn of the century, a 1977 constitutional amendment adopted a mandatory retirement age of seventy for judges of the High Court. See Brian Galligan, *Politics of the High Court* (Queensland: University of Queensland Press, 1987), p. 188.

[111] For supporting evidence, see Mary L. Volcansek, "Judicial Review in Italy: A Reflection of the United States?" *Policy Studies Journal* 19 (1990): 136.

[112] Carl J. Friedrich, *The Impact of American Constitutionalism Abroad* (Boston: Boston University Press, 1967), p. 87.

[113] See Mary Ann Glendon, *Rights Talk* (New York: Free Press, 1991), pp. 160–67.

[114] See Donald P. Kommers, *The Constitutional Jurisprudence of the Federal Republic of Germany* (Durham: Duke University Press, 1989), pp. 3–25.

is "highly politicized,"[115] as "formalized negotiations among the major political parties determine which party will fill vacancies on the court."[116] Because the Court is separate from the system of ordinary courts, it does not enforce its decrees by issuing orders to lower courts. The Court must rely on other public officials to carry out its decisions.[117]

Perhaps the reasons that led other democracies to deviate from the American example have no implications for the American institution of judicial review. There are many differences between the political-legal systems of these countries and that of the United States. Many of the countries that have adopted some form of review since World War II are parliamentary democracies with legal systems based on a civil code rather than the common law. But it is not hard to see how it might be otherwise. The underlying logic is straightforward. If other countries can learn from the American experience with judicial review, so can Americans. Other countries have learned from the American experience and ensured that their constitutional courts are responsive to contemporary political conditions. They have accomplished this by using an overtly political selection process, nonrenewable terms, and mandatory retirement. Perhaps the considerations that led these countries to deviate from the American example would also be persuasive for American citizens. That is, in light of the *Lochner* and New Deal eras (among other examples), it would be appropriate to alter our present constitutional arrangements to ensure a greater correspondence between the views of the Court and other political institutions. Nonrenewable terms and a mandatory retirement age for Supreme Court justices would be reasonable means of accomplishing this end.[118]

These international comparisons thus suggest that we should take a fresh look at the American institution of judicial review. The rather complacent acceptance of judicial review that is common among many scholars may not be justified. The standard arguments justifying judicial review do have significant weaknesses that must be overcome before further argumentative progress can occur. In reviewing these arguments, we can reap the rewards of the discussions of American constitutionalism and popular sovereignty in chapter 1.

---

[115] Ibid., p. 25.

[116] Stone, *The Birth of Judicial Politics in France*, p. 234.

[117] Kommers, *The Constitutional Jurisprudence of the Federal Republic of Germany*, p. 57. For a general discussion, see David P. Currie, *The Constitution of the Federal Republic of Germany* (Chicago: University of Chicago Press, 1994), pp. 27–30, 149–72.

[118] For an argument in favor of an eighteen-year term for Supreme Court justices, see Sanford Levinson, "Contempt of Court: The Most Important 'Contemporary Challenge To Judging,'" *Washington and Lee Law Review* 49 (1992): 339. See also Michael J. Perry, *The Constitution in the Courts* (New York: Oxford University Press, 1994), pp. 196–97.

One problem that runs through the contemporary debate derives from the dependence of the Hamilton-Marshall argument on the doctrine of popular sovereignty. Popular sovereignty establishes the status of the Constitution as supreme law and implies that when the judiciary enforces the Constitution, it does so in the name of the people, not in service of its own power. This appeal to popular sovereignty to establish both the supreme status of the Constitution and judicial review continues to attract support today.[119]

Unfortunately, as we saw in chapter 1, the doctrine of popular sovereignty has serious flaws that suggest it should not have any significant role in American constitutional theory. Its operational form, the constitutional convention, cannot be used as an ongoing political agency to settle fundamental disputes over the location of political authority. The doctrine of popular sovereignty is best understood as an expression of an unsatisfiable wish for direct democracy. In the context of the debate over judicial review, the doctrine can be persuasive only if we ignore these criticisms and the fact that the debate arises in the specific context of the Supreme Court making controversial and politically significant judgments about the meaning of the Constitution. This was well understood by Alexander Bickel, who responded to Marshall's argument in *Marbury* by noting that whether a law is unconstitutional "is in most instances not self-evident; it is, rather, an issue of policy that someone must decide."[120] In deciding constitutional cases, the Court cannot simply read the will of the people off the text of the Constitution. It must instead make controversial value judgments, the kind of judgments that are normally left to the political process.

Bickel's comment reveals another fault line running through the contemporary debate over judicial review. The democratic critics of judicial review and its constitutionalist supporters necessarily talk past one another unless they share a common understanding of the nature of the decisions made by the Supreme Court. Bickel appeared to deny that constitutional judgments are legal judgments in any strong sense. They are rather controversial policy judgments of the kind that are normally made by elected officials. On the other hand, constitutionalists tend to accept the Hamilton-Marshall argument that the Constitution is law and that the courts have a special responsibility to enforce it in the same way other laws are enforced. This fault line is the result of the inherent tensions in American constitutionalism we explored in chapter 1. Since there are significant differences between the Constitution and ordinary law, there is

---

[119] For a theory of constitutional change that stresses popular sovereignty, see Bruce Ackerman, *We The People: Foundations*, vol. 1 (Cambridge: Harvard University Press, 1991), pp. 230–65.

[120] Bickel, *The Least Dangerous Branch*, p. 3.

reason to think that the interpretation of ambiguous constitutional provisions involves policy or political judgments rather than legal judgments. This increases the burden of justification on those who take the constitutionalist position.

A third weakness in the contemporary debate is the failure to take into consideration the insight, inspired by the work of Rawls, that justifying the institution of judicial review through moral arguments is inherently a matter of resolving a conflict of basic rights, not simply a decision to protect basic rights against infringement by democratic majorities.[121] Deciding to place the protection of basic rights in the hands of the judiciary is also a decision to remove such issues from the agenda of the elected branches. This restricts the basic right of citizens to participate in important political decisions respecting the content of such rights. While this consideration is by no means decisive, it provides a salutary reminder that the decision to adopt judicial review involves restricting some basic rights in order to promote others. This immediately raises the question of whether the rights to be promoted are of greater importance than the political rights that are restricted.

A final weakness in the contemporary debate is the tendency of constitutionalist supporters of judicial review to fail to take into account the institutional realities of Supreme Court decisionmaking and the limits on the Court's power to enforce constitutional rights. Constitutionalists sometimes compare an ideal Court to the nonideal world of legislative decisionmaking and argue that judicial review is justified because it contributes a desirable element of deliberation, even scholarly wisdom, to the sordid world of interest group politics.[122] This is clearly a non sequitur. To fairly justify judicial review in a prudential sense, we must compare the nonideal legislative process to the nonideal judicial process.[123]

Because of these weaknesses in the contemporary debate, the seminal justification for the present role of the Supreme Court in American democracy remains to be written. Producing such a justification will not be easy, for it must address these weaknesses, employ contemporary democratic principles as normative standards, take into account the evolution of democracy in the United States, and justify judicial review as an institution, including the need for life tenure instead of long terms followed by mandatory retirement, and the unique power granted by ambiguous con-

---

[121] Robert Dahl's work is another important source of this argument. See Robert A. Dahl, *Democracy and Its Critics* (New Haven: Yale University Press, 1989), pp. 169–71. See also the articles by Waldron cited in note 87.

[122] See, e.g., Perry, *The Constitution in the Courts*, pp. 106–10.

[123] For an important discussion relevant to this point, see Einer R. Elhauge, "Does Interest Group Theory Justify More Intrusive Judicial Review?" *Yale Law Journal* 101 (1991): 66–87.

stitutional clauses. Any attempt to justify the role of the Court must also deal with the question of the appropriate scope of judicial review in light of the narrowed field for judicial action in the wake of the New Deal. That is, such a justification must come to grips with the account of constitutional change presented in chapter 1 and its implications for the limits on the judicial sphere of action in contemporary American democracy.

Alexander Bickel's attempt to justify judicial review on the basis that it allows the Supreme Court to serve as the guardian of enduring political and constitutional values remains one of the most influential contributions to the debate over judicial review.[124] Constitutionalist supporters of the Court still appeal to its unique role as conservator of the nation's constitutional heritage. Yet the record of the elected branches since the 1960s shows that the Court is not the only defender of the enduring values advanced by civil rights and liberties laws. It was the elected branches, not the judiciary, that finally moved to correct a great historical wrong by compensating citizens of Japanese descent for their internment in concentration camps in the Civil Liberties Act of 1988.[125] The Court had not protected these citizens during World War II and was incapable of remedying this severe violation of civil liberties on its own. The Civil Liberties Act demonstrates the real influence of the slow tidal forces of democratic self-criticism and public opinion. It also illustrates the fundamentally different character of American democracy in the wake of the civil rights movement. The great challenge for the future debate on judicial review is to take into account this extraordinary change in American democracy.

[124] See Bickel, *The Least Dangerous Branch*, pp. 24–28.

[125] See Fisher, "One of the Guardians Some of the Time," in Licht, ed., *Is the Supreme Court the Guardian of the Constitution?* pp. 93–95.

Four

Problems of Constitutional Adjudication

THE INDEPENDENCE of the Supreme Court as a separate branch of the federal government was not symbolized by a building of its own until 1935. Prior to that time, the Court had occupied different quarters in the Capitol. The architecture and artwork of the Supreme Court building were deliberately designed as a tribute to the majesty of the law. The building is a massive structure of white marble that suggests a temple of justice. The plaza in front of the building is dominated by two large sculptures. One is a male figure representing the "Authority of Law," while the other is a female figure representing the "Contemplation of Justice." The motto above the entrance, "Equal Justice Under Law" is well known.[1]

The courtroom, framed by red curtains and marble columns, is the spiritual center of the building. The friezes that adorn its walls contain figures representing such abstract concepts as the "Majesty of Law," "Power of Government," "Justice," "Wisdom," "Truth," and "Ancient Lawgivers." The overall effect of the building and its ornamentation is to "evoke the feelings of apprehension and awe that laymen tend to associate with the expounders of black-letter law."[2]

An interesting aspect of this design is that one cannot tell from the architecture and most of the artwork whether the building is intended to house a supreme court for the United States or for Planet Earth. The building celebrates law as a timeless universal ideal rather than as a historically evolving human practice. The reality of constitutional amendments, the Civil War, and the struggle against racial discrimination are all missing. Indeed, even the Constitution itself is missing from the building's artwork. Chief Justice John Marshall and other Supreme Court justices are represented, but not James Madison, Alexander Hamilton, Thomas Jefferson, Abraham Lincoln, or others who have contributed to the formation of American constitutionalism.

---

[1] See the interesting articles by Maxwell Bloomfield, "Architecture of the Supreme Court Building," "Buildings, Supreme Court," and "Sculpture in the Supreme Court Building," in Kermit L. Hall, ed., *The Oxford Companion to the Supreme Court of the United States* (New York: Oxford University Press, 1992), pp. 43, 99, 761. See also John Brigham, *The Cult of the Court* (Philadelphia: Temple University Press, 1987), pp. 108–12.

[2] Bloomfield, "Architecture of the Supreme Court Building," in Hall, ed., *The Oxford Companion to the Supreme Court of the United States*, p. 43.

As the building's tenants, the justices can only hope that the image of legitimate power projected by its architecture transfers to them. For how to apply the abstract ideals of justice and law in the context of the Constitution and concrete cases is the focus of many of the most enduring conflicts in American constitutionalism. In this chapter and the next, we discuss what most scholars consider to be the heart of American constitutional theory—the problems posed by the process of adjudicating constitutional cases and theories of constitutional interpretation. These subjects inevitably overlap, but some individual topics are distinct in the literature on the Supreme Court, as in the case of political science research on judicial behavior.

In this chapter, which serves as a sort of preface to chapter 5, we deal with questions raised by how the Supreme Court acts as an institution. The first section places the Court in the account of American constitutionalism offered in chapter 1. The second section is largely concerned with the validity of the model of Supreme Court decisionmaking offered by political scientists working in the behaviorist tradition. We will also discuss the implications of institutional research on the Court for the debate over how the Court should decide constitutional cases.

The Supreme Court and American Constitutionalism

Accounts of constitutional adjudication often proceed on the assumption that it is simply another form of judging. The analysis typically describes the principles of legitimate adjudication in general and then applies those principles to judging in the constitutional context. The preceding chapters should have made us wary of this approach. Constitutional adjudication cannot be understood without first situating it within constitutionalism as a distinctive political practice and the particular institutional framework of the federal judiciary.

As we saw in chapter 1, American constitutionalism is best seen as a unique blend of law and politics. While there are important points of analogy between the Constitution and other forms of law, there are also significant points of disanalogy. As we noted in chapter 1, the Constitution serves as a framework for government and politics, a role that no other law approximates. In the context of Supreme Court adjudication, this means that the constitutional decisions of the Court often have unusual importance compared with the rulings of other appellate courts. Supreme Court decisions can have profound effects on the structure of federal and state governments and the issues that are debated in national politics.

Another difference between constitutional adjudication and adjudication in other courts of law is that the clauses the Supreme Court most often interprets are general and abstract in character. The constitutional provisions the Court has concerned itself with in the latter half of the twentieth century are contained, for the most part, in the Bill of Rights and Civil War Amendments. In the Bill of Rights, the provisions of the First and Fifth Amendments are some of the best examples of this generality. The terms of the First Amendment are well known. Congress and the states (due to the incorporation of the First Amendment into the Fourteenth), can make no law "respecting an establishment of religion, or prohibiting the free exercise thereof; or abridging the freedom of speech, or of the press . . ."[3] The takings clause of the Fifth Amendment is a virtual thesaurus of significant terms from eighteenth-century political philosophy. "Private property" cannot be taken for "public use" without awarding compensation that is "just."[4] The phrasing of the first section of the Fourteenth Amendment is equally abstract. "No state shall make or enforce any law which shall abridge the privileges or immunities of citizens of the United States; nor shall any State deprive any person of life, liberty, or property, without due process of law; nor deny to any person within its jurisdiction the equal protection of the laws."[5]

Such clauses pose unusual challenges for Supreme Court justices.[6] Constitutional clauses that use terms drawn from political and moral ideals seem to lack some of the characteristics of ordinary legal rules. They do not provide the same guidance given by ordinary legal rules, thus creating tensions with the values embodied in the rule of law. The abstract character of these clauses means that it is difficult to tell when judges are following or deviating from the rules contained within them. Even if these clauses provide some direction, their practical effect is to delegate an unusual amount of power to judges.

We also noticed in chapter 1 that the Constitution cannot be enforced in the same manner as other laws. Although the Supreme Court can use the federal district and appellate courts to enforce its judgments, the Court is aware that its rulings can be difficult to enforce and may be ignored. This can influence the willingness of the Court to take on certain cases and may limit the remedies the Court applies in cases it does decide. The limits on what remedies the Court can impose may then affect the practical scope of constitutional rights. The common-law maxim that when a right is violated there must be a remedy cannot always be followed in constitutional adjudication.

[3] U.S. Const., Amend. I.
[4] U.S. Const., Amend. V.
[5] U.S. Const., Amend. XIV.
[6] For an illustrative example, see John C. Jeffries, Jr., *Justice Lewis F. Powell, Jr.: A Biography* (New York: Charles Scribner's Sons, 1994), pp. 409–10.

Just as these points of disanalogy create tensions within constitutionalism, they create tensions within the sphere of constitutional adjudication. On the one hand, the justices of the Supreme Court are members of an appellate court and must act accordingly. That is, they must arguably restrain themselves from employing the broad power created by the points of disanalogy between the Constitution and other forms of law. If their decisions could have enormous implications for the American political system, they must limit the number of such interventions. If the clauses they interpret are abstract and appear to refer to political and moral ideals, they must find a method of interpretation that limits their potential to upset traditional legal and political arrangements in order to preserve some link with the rule of law. If their decisions are difficult to enforce, they must limit the remedies they impose and proceed with caution when addressing new constitutional issues.

On the other hand, the justices are under pressure to fulfill the unique role that American constitutionalism and the legalized Constitution creates for them. They must influence the structure of federal and state governments over time to ensure that these governments stay within constitutional boundaries. The great abstract clauses of the Bill of Rights and Civil War Amendments summon them to implement the ideals of liberty and equality for every citizen and to wield their enforcement and remedial powers to ensure that the rights that follow from these clauses are effectively guaranteed.

These tensions create the unique terrain of constitutional adjudication, a form of judging that resists assimilation to other forms of judging, just as the Constitution resists assimilation to other forms of law. The unique nature of constitutional adjudication is also apparent when we examine the Supreme Court from an institutional perspective. The near-total control the Court has over its docket is a highly significant difference between it and other appellate courts. As mentioned in chapter 3, the Court achieved substantial control over the decision as to which cases it would hear as a result of the Judiciary Act of 1925. This control contributed to the sense of the justices that the Court has a special mission that differentiates it from other courts. Chief Justice Fred Vinson stated that "[t]he Supreme Court is not, and never has been, primarily concerned with the correction of errors in lower court decisions. . . . To remain effective, the Supreme Court must continue to decide only those cases which present questions whose resolution will have immediate importance far beyond the particular facts and parties involved."[7]

---

[7] Quoted in H. W. Perry, Jr., *Deciding to Decide: Agenda Setting in the United States Supreme Court* (Cambridge: Harvard University Press, 1991), p. 36. See also David M. O'Brien, *Storm Center: The Supreme Court in American Politics*, 3d ed. (New York: W. W. Norton, 1993), pp. 248–49, 259–62.

While the idea that the Supreme Court exists to decide cases of national importance is understandable, it has significant implications for the theory of constitutional adjudication.[8] The special mission of the Court means that there is not necessarily a strong analogy between it and any other U.S. appellate court. The standards we normally use to evaluate courts may not be appropriate in the case of the Supreme Court. To a certain extent, the Court's control over its docket gives it the power to act as a roving commission seeking out important constitutional questions. The Court can deliberately avoid cases that are poor vehicles for new constitutional rules and seek out cases that are good vehicles. The ability to select cases also means that the Court can respond relatively quickly to a public demand to resolve an important constitutional issue.[9] If this activity seems questionable, it is worth keeping in mind that the elected branches gave the Court this power.

Another important aspect of the Supreme Court's institutional character is simply that it is the highest court in the land. Given this status and the Court's role in American history, the justices can easily acquire a fateful sense of responsibility toward the task of constitutional adjudication. Certainly the justices appreciate that mistakes can only be corrected by themselves or by the slow forces of history. Such a sense of weighty responsibility can contribute to the individuality that has led to the widely noted increase in dissenting and concurring opinions in recent decades.[10] Justices are typically strong-minded, experienced men and women of affairs and it is not easy to obtain consensus among such individuals even in the best of circumstances.

A third important aspect of the Supreme Court's institutional character is that it is an unusually large appellate court. Panels that hear cases in the federal courts of appeals are composed of three judges in the ordinary course of events. Only six states have supreme courts as large as the U.S. Supreme Court and none are larger.[11] The problems just noted of reaching consensus among strong-minded individuals intensify as the size of the group increases. There is some evidence that as constitutional courts become larger, they take on a distinctly legislative character. This phenomenon can be observed when the larger federal circuits attempt to hold sessions *en banc.*[12] The U.S. Court of Appeals for the Ninth Circuit, for

---

[8] See the discussion in Martin Shapiro, *Courts: A Comparative and Political Analysis* (Chicago: University of Chicago Press, 1981), p. 56.

[9] See Perry, *Deciding to Decide,* pp. 198–215, 253–65.

[10] See O'Brien, *Storm Center,* pp. 329–46.

[11] The six states are Alabama, Iowa, Mississippi, Oklahoma, Texas, and Washington. Most state supreme courts have five or seven members.

[12] See Louis Fisher, *Constitutional Dialogues: Interpretation as Political Process* (Princeton: Princeton University Press, 1988), pp. 193–94.

example, currently has twenty-eight judges, a greater membership than the senates of five states.[13]

These characteristics help form an institution in which the justices tend to work separately to reach their judgments and collective deliberation based on personal contacts plays a minimal role. While justices can change their views in reaction to argument and persuasion in the opinion-writing process, it appears that changes of language in the final opinion are more common than complete changes of view. As one study concludes:

> The trend is now toward less consensus on the Court's rulings. The justices tend to be increasingly divided over their decisions. Individual opinions have become more highly prized than institutional opinions. The Court now functions more like a legislative body relying on a tally of the votes to decide cases than like a collegial body working toward collective decisions and opinions.[14]

It is well known that the difficulties of obtaining a majority on the Supreme Court can lead to opinions that are not coherent. Whether the difficulties inherent in making decisions through voting pose a problem for the Court's legitimacy or should make a difference to the criteria by which we evaluate the Court's conduct is unclear.[15]

What is important for our purposes is what these institutional characteristics imply about the nature of constitutional adjudication. As has been noted so often, the Court's institutional position and control over its docket means that it decides the most problematic cases in American jurisprudence under circumstances that make it hard to reach consensus on the right course of action. The process of deciding complex policy questions with significant political and legal implications produces dissensus and conflict in the elected branches and the Court has no special ability to avoid similar strong and lasting disagreements. The problems inherent in deciding such cases thus take the Court away from the virtues of channeled discretion, stability, and certainty implied by the rule of law. It is not

---

[13] It should be noted that *en banc* courts in the Ninth Circuit consist of eleven judges, not twenty-eight. However, all eligible judges in the Ninth Circuit vote whether to hear a case *en banc*. See Arthur D. Hellman, "Maintaining Consistency in the Law of the Large Circuit," in Arthur D. Hellman, ed., *Restructuring Justice: The Innovations of the Ninth Circuit and the Future of the Federal Courts* (Ithaca: Cornell University Press, 1990), p. 62.

[14] O'Brien, *Storm Center*, p. 284. See also ibid., pp. 164–66.

[15] The debate over the applicability of Arrow's Theorem to the Supreme Court continues with no end in sight. See Frank H. Easterbrook, "Ways of Criticizing the Court," *Harvard Law Review* 95 (1982): 802; Lewis A. Kornhauser and Lawrence G. Sager, "Unpacking the Court," *Yale Law Journal* 96 (1986): 82; Richard H. Pildes and Elizabeth S. Anderson, "Slinging Arrows at Democracy: Social Choice Theory, Value Pluralism, and Democratic Politics," *Columbia Law Review* 90 (1990): 2121; Maxwell L. Stearns, "The Misguided Renaissance of Social Choice," *Yale Law Journal* 103 (1994): 1219.

reasonable to expect the Court to act as other courts and decide cases in the same manner. To some extent, therefore, the criteria we use to evaluate the Court's conduct must differ from the criteria we use to evaluate other courts.

The Process of Judicial Decisionmaking

The most significant difference between how legal scholars and political scientists regard the Supreme Court emerges in the study of judicial decisionmaking. The most common form of legal scholarship on the Supreme Court is exemplified by the annual November issue of the *Harvard Law Review*. This issue summarizes the significant cases from the Court's Term of the previous year and evaluates the Court's reasoning by means of a close doctrinal examination of the majority, concurring, and dissenting opinions. The bread and butter of law review commentary on the Court consists of the same sort of doctrinal exegesis, criticism of the coherence of the Court's reasoning, and suggestions on how the Court should decide future cases. The orientation of this law review scholarship is overwhelmingly normative.

Studies of Supreme Court decisionmaking by political scientists, particularly those influenced by the behavioral tradition, present a sharp contrast. Although political scientists used to produce doctrinal summaries of Court decisions, this practice died out in the 1960s. Contemporary political science studies of Court decisionmaking are overwhelmingly descriptive-explanatory in character. Influenced by legal realism, political scientists proceed on the assumption that the Court can be understood in the same manner as other important government agencies that make policy. As summarized by one respected political scientist, "[T]he dominant conception of the Supreme Court [in political science] is of an institution in which justices' policy preferences are the primary basis for decisions and legal considerations—the desire to follow legal rules correctly—are much less important . . . the primary reason for the dominance of this conception is that it is largely accurate."[16]

While legal scholars recognize that the personal background of the justices influences the attitudes they bring to the Supreme Court and the cases they decide, it is likely that many of them would reject out of hand the idea that the justices' policy preferences are the primary basis for decision.[17] Some legal scholars would surely claim that acceptance of any such

[16] Lawrence Baum, "Selection Effects and Judicial Behavior," paper presented at the 1994 Annual Meeting of the American Political Science Association, pp. 8–9.

[17] For a recent example of this view, see Barry Cushman, "Rethinking the New Deal Court," *Virginia Law Review* 80 (1994): 238–61.

notion would entail abandonment of the rule of law. There is thus some irony in the fact that political scientists take much of their inspiration from the legal scholars known as legal realists and famous justices such as Oliver Wendell Holmes, Jr. The most significant study that advances the "attitudinal model," that is, that justices make decisions based on the political attitudes they bring to the bench, quotes Holmes's definition that " 'the prophecies of what courts will do in fact, and nothing more pretentious, are what I mean by law.' "[18] The object of the attitudinal model is to show how the votes of individual justices are the product of liberal or conservative political attitudes, thus enabling predictions as to how future cases will be resolved.[19]

The reasoning behind the attitudinal model is based largely on two observations about the votes of justices in specific cases. One observation is that justices over roughly the last half century do not seem to adhere to a strictly legalistic conception of their role. The justices frequently overturn important precedents and thus do not accept a strong version of *stare decisis*. The often strained reasoning in Court opinions leads to the suspicion that justices manipulate legal doctrines to produce results that accord with their policy preferences. The second observation is that when justices are classified as liberal or conservative (on the basis of definitions developed by political scientists), their patterns of decision in broad constitutional areas such as criminal procedure and civil liberties are consistent with those classifications.[20]

Segal and Spaeth's study goes beyond these observations to produce statistical evidence that the justices' political attitudes predict their votes in specific cases with a high degree of accuracy.[21] Their evidence of the political attitudes justices bring to the bench, however, is somewhat weak. They use justices' votes in past cases to predict their votes in future cases and assess the justices' attitudes prior to appointment by consulting newspaper editorials speculating on the justices' political orientation. While studying past votes as a guide to future votes can establish that a particular justice reaches consistent judgments in a given case area, it does not show what the justice's political attitudes were prior to appointment. Newspaper editorials reflect rather general opinions about the political orientation

---

[18] Quoted in Jeffrey A. Segal and Harold J. Spaeth, *The Supreme Court and the Attitudinal Model* (New York: Cambridge University Press, 1993), p. 66. The quotation is from Oliver Wendell Holmes, "The Path of the Law," *Harvard Law Review* 10 (1897): 461.

[19] See Segal and Spaeth, *The Supreme Court and the Attitudinal Model*, pp. 64–73.

[20] See Lawrence Baum, *The Supreme Court*, 5th ed. (Washington, D.C.: Congressional Quarterly Press, 1995), pp. 159–66; Baum, "Selection Effects and Judicial Behavior," pp. 11, 14.

[21] See Segal and Spaeth, *The Supreme Court and the Attitudinal Model*, pp. 214–60.

of a justice and are not good guides to the views of justices in specific areas of constitutional controversy.[22]

Segal and Spaeth are not overly concerned with these deficiencies given the weakness of the competing "legal" model of how the Supreme Court makes decisions. Among other points, they argue that the legal model cannot be formulated as a predictive theory and thus cannot be tested against the scientific accuracy of the attitudinal model.[23] The observations cited above concerning the Court's deviation from precedent and the liberal or conservative pattern of decisions also make political scientists in the behavioral tradition relatively confident that policy preferences rather than legal considerations drive case outcomes.[24]

Unfortunately, very few lawyers or scholars of jurisprudence would recognize the rather truncated and tendentious model that behaviorist political scientists attribute to them. One problem is that it is never clear in Segal and Spaeth's study and other similar studies whether the legal model is a jurisprudential theory or a statement of what constitutional lawyers and judges actually believe. Jurisprudential theories are highly abstract and can advocate revisions in the ordinary understanding of adjudication.[25] They are not necessarily followed by practicing lawyers and judges. If, on the other hand, political scientists are trying to test a model actually employed by lawyers and judges, they must do a great deal of empirical work to determine what that model is before they can declare with any confidence whether it can be formulated as a predictive theory. So far they have not done this.[26]

Another problem with Segal and Spaeth's study is that they rely on the naive idea that if judges really followed the legal model they would never disagree. Segal and Spaeth interpret disagreement over case outcomes as

[22] For this criticism, see Lawrence Baum, "The Critics," *Law and Courts: Newsletter of the Law and Courts Section of the American Political Science Association* 4 (1994): 3–5.

Segal and Spaeth also produce evidence that justices' votes correlate with the facts of cases. The problem here, as they admit, is that the legal model also predicts that the facts of individual cases will influence how the justices vote. See Segal and Spaeth, *The Supreme Court and the Attitudinal Model*, pp. 215–21.

[23] See Segal and Spaeth, *The Supreme Court and the Attitudinal Model*, pp. 64–65, 221.

[24] It should be noted that some political science studies provide evidence that both legal and extralegal factors play a role in the Court's decisions. See, e.g., Lee Epstein and Joseph F. Kobylka, *The Supreme Court and Legal Change: Abortion and the Death Penalty* (Chapel Hill: University of North Carolina Press, 1992); Tracey E. George and Lee Epstein, "On the Nature of Supreme Court Decision Making," *American Political Science Review* 86 (1992): 323.

[25] See, e.g., Steven J. Burton, *Judging in Good Faith* (New York: Cambridge University Press, 1992).

[26] For an exception, see J. Woodford Howard, Jr., *Courts of Appeals in the Federal Judicial System* (Princeton: Princeton University Press, 1981), pp. 159–88.

clear evidence that the legal model is a myth.[27] The model of adjudication actually followed by lawyers and judges of course allows for the possibility of strong disagreement in constitutional cases given, among other factors, the ambiguity of the clauses of the Constitution that are most frequently at issue.[28] The idea that the law provides clear black-letter answers for every dispute is a notion frequently held by first-year law students and it is one law professors make sure students abandon by graduation.

As we saw in the first section, it is questionable whether constitutional adjudication should be understood simply as another kind of judging. Many scholars, including political scientists, have viewed constitutional adjudication as a hybrid of law and politics.[29] There are any number of anecdotes of Supreme Court decisionmaking that support this idea. Two that seem especially relevant derive from the reflections of President Theodore Roosevelt and Justice Robert Jackson. In evaluating the qualifications of Justice Holmes, President Roosevelt remarked:

> In the ordinary and low sense which we attach to the words "partisan" and "politician," a judge of the Supreme Court should be neither. But in the higher sense, in the proper sense, he is not in my judgment fitted for the position unless he is a party man, a constructive statesman, constantly keeping in mind his adherence to the principles and policies under which this nation has been built up and in accordance with which it must go on; and keeping in mind also his relations with his fellow statesmen who in other branches of the government are striving in cooperation with him to advance the ends of government . . .[30]

When Jackson was under consideration for appointment to the New York Court of Appeals, he was told by Justice Benjamin Cardozo to accept the appointment. Cardozo said, "That's a lawyer's court. Those are the kind of problems you'll enjoy. Over on [the Supreme Court] there are two kinds of questions—statutory construction, which no one can make interesting, and politics." Jackson later stated, "Of course [Cardozo] didn't

---

[27] See Segal and Spaeth, *The Supreme Court and the Attitudinal Model,* pp. 17–18, 235–36.

[28] For an important jurisprudential theory that emphasizes the importance of theoretical disagreement in law, see Ronald Dworkin, *Law's Empire* (Cambridge: Harvard University Press, 1986), pp. 3–15.

[29] See Howard, *Courts of Appeals in the Federal Judicial System,* pp. 184–88; Stephen Macedo, *Liberal Virtues: Citizenship, Virtue, and Community in Liberal Constitutionalism* (New York: Oxford University Press, 1990), p. 162; Perry, *Deciding to Decide,* pp. 271–84; Doris Marie Provine, *Case Selection in the United States Supreme Court* (Chicago: University of Chicago Press, 1980), pp. 174–75. For a discussion from a legal point of view, see Henry P. Monaghan, "Constitutional Adjudication: The Who and When," *Yale Law Journal* 82 (1973): 1369–71.

[30] Quoted in Felix Frankfurter, *Mr. Justice Holmes and the Supreme Court* (Cambridge: Harvard University Press, 1938), pp. 21–22.

mean politics in the sense of party politics, but in the sense of public policy. There's a great deal of truth in that observation. Many of our cases really turn on your views of political policy, governmental policy."[31]

In describing Supreme Court decisionmaking, both Roosevelt and Jackson appealed to the idea that constitutional cases involve matters of high politics and public policy, issues that differ in significant respects from the more lawyerly questions considered by other courts. The account of American constitutionalism offered in chapter 1 also supports this idea. The model of constitutional adjudication actually employed by lawyers and judges thus mixes legal and political considerations together from the beginning. It is worth keeping in mind that by the standards of European civil law countries, whose judiciaries are composed of professional civil servants, the American federal judiciary is hopelessly politicized, no matter whether judges use legal or extralegal criteria to decide cases. While all federal judges are lawyers, they may be appointed directly from political positions without going through special judicial training, as is the case in civil law countries.[32] Supreme Court justices have been appointed from the Senate, governorships, the Department of Justice, and even law schools. This means that justices do not necessarily bring a strictly legalist perspective to the task of judging constitutional cases.

These considerations suggest that political science studies based on a sharp division between legal and extralegal methods of decisionmaking have misanalyzed the character of decisionmaking in constitutional cases. There is a more serious problem with the approach of behaviorist political scientists to Supreme Court decisionmaking, however. Political scientists tend to assume that models of adjudication must be predictive. We have already noted Segal and Spaeth's emphasis on predicting justices' votes in future cases. This approach does not necessarily tell us what we need to know about judicial decisionmaking. The point of the inquiry is presumably to discover how justices make decisions in constitutional cases. In order to do this, we must necessarily investigate how the justices themselves understand their role. We can call this an internal inquiry, because it seeks to understand the decisionmaking process from the perspective of the decisionmaker.

The problem is that the attitudinal model is not an internal theory of judicial decisionmaking. The attitudinal model is an external theory that aims at prediction, rather than seeking to understand the role of a justice as the justice understands it. Jurisprudential scholars have long appreci-

---

[31] Quoted in Dennis J. Hutchinson, "The Black-Jackson Feud," in Philip B. Kurland, Gerhard Casper, and Dennis J. Hutchinson, eds., *The Supreme Court Review, 1988* (Chicago: University of Chicago Press, 1989), p. 239.

[32] See Mirjan R. Damaska, *The Faces of Justice and State Authority: A Comparative Approach to the Legal Process* (New Haven: Yale University Press, 1986), pp. 32–46, 68.

ated that Holmes's predictive definition of law is inadequate to the task of explaining how judges decide cases. "Judges do not understand themselves to be explaining the psychological, social, or political causes of their own decisions, to be predicting what they themselves will do, or to be describable scientifically like rats."[33] A predictive theory of adjudication cannot explain what judges do because it does not describe or explain matters from their perspective. It ignores what H.L.A. Hart has called the internal aspect of law and legal rules.[34] This internal aspect is constituted by what legal rules mean to those who accept them as reasons for acting. Hart comments, "What the external point of view, which limits itself to the observable regularities of behaviour, cannot reproduce is the way in which the rules function as rules in the lives of . . . the officials, lawyers, or private persons who use them."[35]

Formulating an adequate internal theory of adjudication leads us toward the theories of interpretation we will discuss in the next chapter and away from the statistical studies of judicial votes and attitudes favored by behaviorist political scientists.[36] The deficiencies of an external approach to understanding constitutional adjudication should not, however, prevent us from taking account of the practical difficulties justices face when they decide cases and write opinions. Any adequate theory of constitutional adjudication must take account of the fact that the American judicial tradition provides the basis for several inconsistent approaches to judicial decisionmaking.

Some justices argue that decisions should be made on a case-by-case basis and stress the essential similarity between the Supreme Court and other courts.[37] Other justices such as Felix Frankfurter and Hugo Black implicitly rejected a case-by-case approach in favor of an overarching judicial philosophy that enabled them to claim the virtues of consistency and coherence across a wide range of constitutional provisions.[38] A third approach is evident in the careers of the justices who were arguably

---

[33] Burton, *Judging in Good Faith*, p. 147. For additional relevant discussion, see ibid., pp. 107–34.

[34] See H.L.A. Hart, *The Concept of Law* (Oxford: Oxford University Press, 1961), pp. 79–88.

[35] Ibid., p. 88. See also Burton, *Judging in Good Faith*, pp. 118–21.

[36] It should be noted that not all political scientists agree that such external studies are the best way to study constitutional adjudication. For an alternative approach, see Ronald Kahn, *The Supreme Court and Constitutional Theory, 1953–1993* (Lawrence: University Press of Kansas, 1994).

[37] See Lewis F. Powell, Jr., "What Really Goes On at the Supreme Court," in Mark W. Cannon and David M. O'Brien, eds., *Views From the Bench: The Judiciary and Constitutional Politics* (Chatham, N.J.: Chatham House Publishers, 1985), p. 73.

[38] See, e.g., G. Edward White, *The American Judicial Tradition* (New York: Oxford University Press, 1988), pp. 325–36.

most influenced by legal realism: William O. Douglas, Abe Fortas, and Byron White.[39] These justices appeared to regard the duty to decide a case as being of much greater importance than the task of justifying the decision in a careful, well-reasoned, "judge-like" opinion. Since justices in all three camps have their share of supporters in the legal community, it is apparent that there are multiple legitimate approaches to constitutional adjudication.

The debate over neutral principles of constitutional law initiated by the legal scholar Herbert Wechsler is another indication that important disagreements exist within the American judicial tradition over the proper method of constitutional adjudication. Wechsler argued that the Supreme Court should operate as an institution of principle, reaching decisions that rest on "reasons that in their generality and their neutrality transcend any immediate result that is involved."[40] Wechsler's thesis was taken to mean that the Court must always attempt to identify the general principle that decides a given case, state the principle clearly in the opinion, and continue to apply that principle in all similar cases in the future. Although the requirement of neutral principles appears to be a fairly minimal criterion, it has been subject to criticism on the ground that it demands too much of the justices.[41] It is at least implicitly at odds with the case-by-case approach to constitutional adjudication just mentioned. In any event, while a particular justice might be able to satisfy the criterion, it is questionable whether a majority in a given case can reach the consensus required on a principle sufficiently robust to give the criterion real meaning.[42]

These disagreements over the proper method of constitutional adjudication are the inevitable result of the mixed political-legal character of American constitutionalism that we analyzed in chapter 1. American constitutionalism requires that the Supreme Court settle matters of fundamental political importance with a set of legal tools that were not de-

---

[39] See ibid., pp. 384–420 (on Douglas); Laura Kalman, *Abe Fortas* (New Haven: Yale University Press, 1990), pp. 249–76 (on Fortas); "Perspectives on White: A Roundtable," *ABA Journal* (October 1993), p. 68 (on White).

For further commentary on Justice White's jurisprudence and approach to writing opinions, see David Savage, *Turning Right: The Making of the Rehnquist Supreme Court* (New York: John Wiley and Sons, 1992), pp. 93, 275; Allan Ides, "The Jurisprudence of Justice Byron White," *Yale Law Journal* 103 (1993): 419; William E. Nelson, "Justice Byron R. White: A Modern Federalist and a New Deal Liberal," *Brigham Young University Law Review* (1994): 313.

[40] Herbert Wechsler, "Toward Neutral Principles of Constitutional Law," *Harvard Law Review* 73 (1959): 19. For commentary on Wechsler's thesis, see Kent Greenawalt, "The Enduring Significance of Neutral Principles," *Columbia Law Review* 78 (1978): 982.

[41] See J. Skelly Wright, "Professor Bickel, The Scholarly Tradition, and the Supreme Court," *Harvard Law Review* 84 (1971): 769. See also Greenawalt, "The Enduring Significance of Neutral Principles," pp. 1001–4.

[42] See Greenawalt, "The Enduring Significance of Neutral Principles," pp. 1007–8.

signed in a constitutional context. This mismatch between the constitutional task and an inadequate set of adjudicative tools creates the tensions that are the source of these theoretical conflicts over the proper method of adjudication.

If political scientists tend to rely too heavily on external studies of the adjudicative process, the doctrinal commentary characteristic of legal scholarship is not necessarily more realistic about the process of decision-making at the Supreme Court. Political scientists are more mindful of the reality that the Court has to act as an institution and that individual justices can rarely win the approval of their colleagues for the kind of over-arching philosophy that will produce principled and coherent decisions in a wide range of cases.[43] Bargaining, compromise, and strategies for obtaining a majority of five are a necessary part of the adjudicative process for any justice who wishes to have an influence on how cases are decided.[44] Strong criticism of the consistency and coherence of the Court's reasoning is very common in legal scholarship, but it is not clear that such criticism can be justified once these institutional factors are taken into account.[45]

Unfortunately, neither legal scholars nor political scientists have done an adequate job assessing the implications of these institutional factors for evaluations of the Supreme Court's decisions. While legal scholars view the Court's opinions as incoherent and call for more principled reasoning, political scientists take poorly reasoned opinions as evidence that legal rules are irrelevant to case outcomes, thus justifying an external approach to the study of the Court's decisions. Both of these responses are problematic because they do not take account of the complexity of the internal, institutional context in which justices make their decisions.[46]

Most political scientists and legal scholars do, however, agree that justices take their role very seriously and attempt to follow the law in good faith.[47] Apart from the checks and balances in the Constitution,

[43] An important exception is the increasing application of positive political theory to constitutional law by legal scholars. See, e.g., William N. Eskridge, Jr. and Philip P. Frickey, "Foreword: Law as Equilibrium," *Harvard Law Review* 108 (1994): 26. For another example of a more realistic approach to Supreme Court decisionmaking by a legal scholar, see Cass R. Sunstein, "Incompletely Theorized Agreements," *Harvard Law Review* 108 (1995): 1733.

[44] See Walter F. Murphy, *Elements of Judicial Strategy* (Chicago: University of Chicago Press, 1964). See also Jeffries, *Justice Lewis F. Powell, Jr.,* p. 432.

[45] See Michael J. Gerhardt, "The Role of Precedent in Constitutional Decisionmaking and Theory," *George Washington Law Review* 60 (1991): 114–17.

[46] For relevant discussion, see Douglas Lind, "Constitutional Adjudication as a Craft-Bound Excellence," *Yale Journal of Law and the Humanities* 6 (1994): 353.

[47] For evidence from political scientists, see O'Brien, *Storm Center,* p. 141; Perry, *Deciding to Decide,* p. 207; Provine, *Case Selection in the United States Supreme Court,* pp. 174–75.

this role perception is the most important constraint on the Supreme Court. Although the debate over theories of constitutional interpretation is driven in part by the belief that the justices will only adhere to their proper place in the constitutional scheme if they follow the correct theory of interpretation, the justices' perception of their role is the true restraining influence. While some approach to constitutional interpretation is part of this role perception, the greater part is derived from the justices' understanding of how cases should be decided in appellate courts. When we ask what prevents justices from doing what they like, we should look first to these institutional and role considerations rather than any theory of interpretation.

Five

Theories of Constitutional Interpretation

ALTHOUGH modern constitutional theory began with the critical reaction to Supreme Court decisions of the *Lochner* era, the starting point of contemporary constitutional theory is *Brown v. Board of Education*.[1] While we live in a constitutional world in which a serious challenge to *Brown* is impossible for all practical purposes, this was not the case when the decision was announced in 1954. At mid-century, all constitutional judges and scholars of consequence accepted the validity of the Progressive critique of the *Lochner* era Court and saw the post-1937 retreat of the Court on matters of social and economic regulation as entirely justified.[2]

Brown posed grave problems for distinguished judges and scholars such as Learned Hand and Herbert Wechsler. *Brown* raised the possibility of a return to judicial activism, which some believed had been forsworn in the aftermath of the 1937 struggle between President Roosevelt and the Court. Further, since *Brown* was based on the Equal Protection clause of the Fourteenth Amendment, one of the most ambiguous clauses in the Constitution, the decision also indicated that the Court might be returning to a jurisprudence which emphasized reading substantive values into clauses that provided little interpretive guidance. If aggressive judicial intervention was appropriate against segregation, why was it not also appropriate against state and federal legislation that arguably violated property rights? What was the "neutral principle," applicable in future cases, that justified the result in *Brown*? These were some of the questions Hand and Wechsler posed for constitutional theorists.[3]

While Hand and Wechsler's criticisms of *Brown* represented a minority position, they nonetheless posed a challenge that theorists of the time felt compelled to answer.[4] Today, such direct criticisms of *Brown* would be

---

[1] 347 U.S. 483 (1954).

[2] For discussion, see Robert A. Burt, *The Constitution in Conflict* (Cambridge: Harvard University Press, 1992), p. 11.

[3] See Learned Hand, *The Bill of Rights* (Cambridge: Harvard University Press, 1958); Herbert Wechsler, "Toward Neutral Principles of Constitutional Law," *Harvard Law Review* 73 (1959): 19.

For relevant commentary, see Gerald Gunther, *Learned Hand: The Man and the Judge* (New York: Alfred A. Knopf, 1994), pp. 652–72; Morton J. Horwitz, *The Transformation of American Law 1870–1960* (New York: Oxford University Press, 1992), pp. 258–68.

[4] See, e.g., Alexander M. Bickel, *The Least Dangerous Branch: The Supreme Court at the Bar of Politics* (Indianapolis: Bobbs-Merrill, 1962).

dismissed out of hand. As is well known, however, the Warren Court did not rest on the laurels it earned from *Brown*. Decisions respecting school prayer, legislative reapportionment, civil rights, civil liberties, and especially criminal procedure were highly controversial, sparking debates that went far beyond the confines of the legal and scholarly communities. In the 1968 presidential election, Warren Court decisions regarding civil rights and criminal procedure became campaign issues.[5]

While the activism of the Warren Court posed many difficult questions, it did not lead to a fundamental change in the way scholars approached constitutional theory. It is questionable whether scholars in the 1960s saw constitutional theory as conceptually distinct from the task of commenting in a learned way on constitutional law. Although criticism of the Warren Court could be abstract, as well as sharp and caustic, scholarly commentary was dominated by the careful consideration of doctrine. Leading scholars tended to be respectful of *Brown* while still assuming the validity of the Progressive critique of Court activism and the need for the Court to elaborate the reasoning behind its decisions.

The decision that altered this state of affairs was *Roe v. Wade*.[6] Although the right of privacy used in *Roe* originated in *Griswold v. Connecticut*,[7] *Griswold* could be understood as an anomaly, the judicial invalidation of an outmoded and unenforced statute.[8] *Roe* made clear that the doctrine of substantive due process, thought to be discredited by the Progressive critique of the *Lochner* era, was back. The return of substantive due process and the political reaction to *Roe* posed a series of urgent questions for constitutional scholars. If substantive due process was again part of constitutional law, what was the answer to the Progressive critique of *Lochner*? If, on the other hand, substantive due process was unacceptable, was the Court without power when confronted by government intrusions into intimate decisions?[9]

The reaction to *Roe* also posed the issue of activism versus restraint across the entire range of constitutional law. In a widely read critique of *Roe*, John Hart Ely argued that academic criticism of the Court was too shallow. Ely believed that to fairly evaluate the Court's constitutional inferences, scholars needed to develop theories that analyzed decisions on a more rational basis.[10] In another article that developed the distinction be-

---

[5] See, e.g., Liva Baker, *Miranda: Crime, Law and Politics* (New York: Atheneum, 1985), pp. 245–49.

[6] 410 U.S. 113 (1973).

[7] 381 U.S. 479 (1965).

[8] See, e.g., Charles Fried, *Order and Law* (New York: Simon and Schuster, 1991), p. 79.

[9] For a relevant discussion, see John C. Jefferies, Jr., *Justice Lewis F. Powell, Jr.: A Biography* (New York: Charles Scribner's Sons, 1994), pp. 359–64.

[10] John Hart Ely, "The Wages of Crying Wolf: A Comment on *Roe v. Wade*," *Yale Law Journal* 82 (1973): 943–49.

tween "interpretivist" and "noninterpretivist" theories of judicial review, Thomas Grey called for an explicit theoretical defense of recent Court decisions.[11] *Roe* generated an ever-expanding scholarly literature that produced the academic field of constitutional theory as it exists today.

Constitutional theory is thus a reactive and episodic field of inquiry because it has been driven largely by controversial Supreme Court decisions. As scholars developed their arguments after *Roe*, however, they became dissatisfied with the narrowly legal and doctrinal character of their theories. Scholars became theoretically self-conscious, increasingly concerned with whether their theories of interpretation and judicial review were sound in light of relevant developments in academic disciplines such as philosophy, history, political science, and literary theory. This self-consciousness seemed to make constitutional theory a self-sustaining scholarly enterprise, independent to a certain extent from actual constitutional decisions.[12]

All of this scholarly effort did not result in a consensus on a theory that resolved the issues posed by the controversial decisions of the Warren and Burger Courts. In fact, the emphasis on theory appeared only to increase the division of opinion and to separate scholars into a number of hostile camps. The division of opinion was highlighted and accentuated by the contentious constitutional politics of the 1980s. Reagan Administration officials such as Edwin Meese and William Bradford Reynolds criticized the Warren Court and urged the adoption of a jurisprudence of original intent.[13] The nominations of Robert Bork and Clarence Thomas to the Supreme Court further sharpened scholarly divisions and made it difficult to conduct a meaningful theoretical dialogue.

The sheer size of the scholarly literature and the division of opinion that persists in the 1990s pose serious difficulties for any attempt to summarize and comment on the theoretical debate. The discussion in this chapter is organized around six broad topics: the presentation of a pluralist theory of constitutional interpretation that is connected with the theory of American constitutionalism advanced in chapter 1, an introduction to the con-

---

[11] Thomas C. Grey, "Do We Have an Unwritten Constitution?" *Stanford Law Review* 27 (1975): 705.

[12] For a sense of the scholarly debate during the 1980s, see the following symposia: Symposium, "Constitutional Adjudication and Democratic Theory," *New York University Law Review* 56 (1981): 259; Symposium, "Judicial Review Versus Democracy," *Ohio State Law Journal* 42 (1981): 1; Symposium, "Judicial Review and the Constitution—The Text and Beyond," *University of Dayton Law Review* 8 (1983): 443; "Interpretation Symposium," *Southern California Law Review* 58 (1985): 1.

[13] See Edwin Meese III, "Interpreting the Constitution," in Jack N. Rakove, ed., *Interpreting the Constitution: The Debate over Original Intent* (Boston: Northeastern University Press, 1990), p. 13.

temporary theoretical debate, the relation of American democracy to theories of interpretation, a discussion of the problem of history in constitutional interpretation, the interpretation of the Fourteenth Amendment and the problem of fundamental rights, and the concept of republicanism as a constitutional philosophy. While these topics address much of the theoretical debate that has occurred since *Brown*, it should be kept in mind that a comprehensive discussion would require a separate book.

A Pluralist Theory of American Constitutional Interpretation

A general theory of American constitutional interpretation would provide some guidance to interpreting any U.S. constitution, whether state or federal, no matter whether the person using the theory was a judge, lawyer, public official, or ordinary citizen. We will emphasize describing such a general theory in this section partly because the debate over theories of constitutional interpretation that has occurred during roughly the last four decades cannot be understood as the search for a general theory.[14] Instead, the debate has focused on the interpretive problems created by specific constitutional provisions such as the Due Process and Equal Protection clauses of the Fourteenth Amendment. These clauses are crucial to a large portion of contemporary Supreme Court jurisprudence, and the scholarly attention they have received is clearly warranted.

Nevertheless, the scholarly debate can give a misleading impression about how a theory of constitutional interpretation should be developed. The debate appears to be a contest of single-method theories in which originalism, textualism, fundamental rights, and other theories battle to be declared the most justified theory. Even if there were to be a victor in this struggle, however, we would not have a general theory of constitutional interpretation. We would simply have a theory useful to interpreting the particular clauses that are the grounds for the debate. Such a limited theory would not necessarily help us understand the entire Constitution.[15]

---

[14] Some scholars have offered theories that can be construed as general theories of constitutional interpretation. See Sotirios A. Barber, *On What the Constitution Means* (Baltimore: The Johns Hopkins University Press, 1984); William F. Harris II, *The Interpretable Constitution* (Baltimore: The Johns Hopkins University Press, 1993); Walter F. Murphy, "Who Shall Interpret? The Quest for the Ultimate Constitutional Interpreter," *Review of Politics* 48 (1986): 401.

[15] Although a general theory of American constitutional interpretation should include interpretive principles appropriate to state constitutions, we will leave this aside since the scholarly debate has focused overwhelmingly on the U.S. Constitution.

We will thus understand the theory of constitutional interpretation as a search for a truly general account of constitutional interpretation. In searching for a general theory, we must take account of two dimensions of theory evaluation: the descriptive-explanatory and the normative. In the descriptive-explanatory dimension, we ask how well the theory describes and explains the actual process of constitutional interpretation. Ideally, we should compare theories with the interpretive activities of all citizens and public officials. Most theories, however, concentrate on the activity of the Supreme Court, and we will accept this limitation. In the normative dimension, we ask whether the theory can be justified by critical standards of political morality, standards that are independent of those contained in the Constitution.

This last point can escape attention, so it deserves a separate discussion. We must always keep in mind that the Constitution is not an exhaustive statement of all politically relevant moral and ethical values. We might prefer a constitution with different values or one that assigns a different priority to the values the Constitution now recognizes. We have no way of determining this, however, unless we appreciate that the Constitution itself must be justified by reference to external critical standards of political morality. Requiring such a justification ensures that we will have a measure of critical distance from the Constitution and the values it endorses. Achieving this critical distance is salutary because it guards against the likelihood that we will take the Constitution as the inevitable baseline for evaluating present political practices and proposals for change.

It is not clear that the current scholarly debate takes proper account of the descriptive-explanatory dimension.[16] Theories of constitutional interpretation are usually evaluated along normative lines. But describing and explaining how the Supreme Court and other constitutional actors interpret the Constitution should be a matter of at least some interest. As we will see, investigating the descriptive-explanatory dimension may influence how we develop normative theories by suggesting the inherent limits and possibilities of constitutional interpretation. Investigating how the Court actually interprets the Constitution might make some theories of constitutional interpretation look less realistic.

In chapter 1, we described American constitutionalism as an instance of the interpenetration of law and politics. As the political conflicts of the 1790s raised questions as to the viability of the constitutional experiment, some members of the founding generation sought to preserve the original promise of constitutionalism by moving the courts into the forefront of constitutional interpretation and enforcement. The Constitution was le-

---

[16] For one scholar who recognizes its importance, see Richard H. Fallon, Jr., "A Constructivist Coherence Theory of Constitutional Interpretation," *Harvard Law Review* 100 (1987): 1231–32.

galized by the importation of interpretive principles used to construe ordinary legal documents to the constitutional sphere.[17]

The legalization of the Constitution can be seen clearly in the resolution of constitutional issues by the Marshall Court. Chief Justice Marshall and the justices who followed him did not attempt to develop a method of interpretation that squarely confronted the unique nature of the Constitution as a blend of law and politics. Instead, they enforced their understanding of the Constitution as law by employing methods of interpretation derived from the various sources of American law. Given the presence of multiple sources of law in the United States, the result was a pluralistic theory of constitutional interpretation.

Marshall and his contemporaries were familiar with a number of different sources of law besides the Constitution: the common law, the law of nations, civil law, and more specialized sources such as equity.[18] These sources of law formed the background against which the justices developed a number of different methods of constitutional interpretation. Justices looked to "the text of the Constitution, the plain or ordinary meaning of words, common-law definitions or principles, natural law, local practices and rules, principles of equity, and . . . 'general principles of republican government.'"[19] Common-law principles became especially important in constitutional interpretation. The task of constitutional interpretation was thought of in common-law terms, and the common law took on a broad meaning, "signifying the use of a discretionary methodology in which judges found, declared, and applied legal principles, employing a variety of sources."[20]

The key move of the founding generation was thus the use of interpretive principles appropriate to ordinary law to construe the Constitution. The Constitution was drawn into and made a part of an increasingly systematized American law. It should not be thought, however, that the methods of constitutional interpretation used in the nineteenth century matched the different sources of law precisely. Rather, the sources of law, especially the common law, formed the terrain in which interpretive arguments could meaningfully take place.[21] In addition, the understanding of the sources of law did not remain static. As American law changed, so did

[17] See Gordon S. Wood, "Judicial Review in the Era of the Founding," in Robert A. Licht, ed., *Is the Supreme Court the Guardian of the Constitution?* (Washington, D.C.: AEI Press, 1993), pp. 163–66; H. Jefferson Powell, "The Principles of '98: An Essay in Historical Retrieval," *Virginia Law Review* (1994): 689.

[18] See G. Edward White, *The Marshall Court and Cultural Change, 1815–1835* (New York: Macmillan, 1988), p. 112.

[19] Ibid., p. 114.

[20] Ibid., p. 119.

[21] For a contemporary theory of interpretation that emphasizes the point, see Philip Bobbitt, *Constitutional Interpretation* (Oxford: Basil Blackwell, 1991), p. 5.

the understanding of the sources of law and their relative importance for constitutional law. These changes had important implications for constitutional interpretation.

One change that has had a continuing influence on contemporary theories of interpretation was an increasing emphasis in the nineteenth century on statutory law and the emergence of a dispute as to whether constitutional law should be regarded as analogous to the common law or statutory law. While nineteenth-century constitutional theorists such as Theodore Sedgwick and John Pomeroy emphasized understanding the Constitution as a statute, other theorists argued that the development of a substantial body of precedent by the Supreme Court meant that the common law was a better model.[22]

The use of a statutory model, however, did not imply a reliance on the intention of the Framers, at least not in the sense we understand it today. After all, reliable evidence of what occurred at the Federal Convention was in short supply until the publication of Madison's notes in 1840.[23] Although looking to the intention of the Framers was regarded by most nineteenth-century theorists as the basic method of interpretation, this did not involve consulting historical records. Instead, Framers' intent was to be determined through a close reading of the text of the Constitution.[24] This nineteenth-century approach collapses the contemporary distinction between textualism and originalism. The idea of using the record of the Federal Convention as the legislative history of the Constitution was thus not an obvious method of interpretation and developed gradually over the course of the nineteenth century.[25]

The use of multiple methods of interpretation based on multiple sources of law by the Supreme Court, lawyers, and scholars continues in the present day.[26] Every first-year law student learns that in addition to the

---

[22] See Paul W. Kahn, *Legitimacy and History: Self-Government in American Constitutional Theory* (New Haven: Yale University Press, 1992), pp. 68–77. For Sedgwick's views, see Theodore Sedgwick, *A Treatise on the Rules which Govern the Interpretation and Application of Statutory and Constitutional Law* (New York: John S. Voorhies, 1857), p. 21 (hereafter cited as Sedgwick, *A Treatise*).

[23] For a relevant discussion, see James H. Hutson, "The Creation of the Constitution: The Integrity of the Documentary Record," *Texas Law Review* 65 (1986): 24–35.

[24] See Thomas M. Cooley, *A Treatise on the Constitutional Limitations Which Rest Upon The Legislative Power of the States of the American Union*, 8th ed. (Boston: Little, Brown, 1927), pp. 124–25; Sedgwick, *A Treatise*, pp. 231–32, 243, 382–83.

[25] For important general discussions, see Hans W. Baade, " 'Original Intent' in Historical Perspective: Some Critical Glosses," *Texas Law Review* 69 (1991): 1001; H. Jefferson Powell, "The Original Understanding of Original Intent," *Harvard Law Review* 98 (1985): 885.

[26] For a lawyerly summary of the different possible approaches to interpreting the Constitution, see Ronald D. Rotunda and John E. Nowak, *Treatise on Constitutional Law: Substance and Procedure*, 2d ed., vol. 4 (St. Paul: West Publishing, 1992), pp. 639–81.

Constitution, the common law and statutory law are the basic sources of law in the United States. The use of common-law doctrinal techniques and the search for legislative intent in constitutional law thus seem perfectly natural. Although the multiple methods of interpretation can be described in different ways, it is clear that the Court has never adopted a single preferred method of interpretation. Nor has the Court ever established a priority or ranking of the different methods of interpretation, or suggested that the multiple methods are reducible to one master method. The absence of a preferred method of interpretation suggests that the Court is using multiple methods of interpretation. The Court's use of such multiple methods can be fairly described as a pluralistic theory of constitutional interpretation.

The pluralism of methods in contemporary constitutional interpretation thus flows from the legalization of the Constitution and the multiple sources of American law. This approach illuminates both the Supreme Court's jurisprudence and academic theory. It is useful to see justices and constitutional theorists as influenced primarily by one particular kind of law. As was the case in the nineteenth century, some scholars are influenced by the model of adjudication represented by the common law and see controversial Court decisions as the legitimate application of common-law reasoning to constitutional provisions.[27] Other contemporary scholars such as John Hart Ely specifically deny that an analogy exists between constitutional law and the common law, continuing the debate begun in the nineteenth century.[28] Originalists base their approach to constitutional interpretation on principles drawn from the law of contracts and wills and from analogies to the use of legislative history in statutory interpretation.[29]

A pluralistic theory of interpretation thus helps us understand the debate over theories of constitutional interpretation that has occurred over the past several decades and the resiliency, despite many effective criticisms, of the different positions in the debate. Each theory of interpretation is grounded in a recognized source of law and draws strength from the authority of that source. Partisans of a particular theory can always

[27] See, e.g., Laurence H. Tribe and Michael C. Dorf, *On Reading the Constitution* (Cambridge: Harvard University Press, 1991), pp. 114–17; Harry H. Wellington, *Interpreting the Constitution* (New Haven: Yale University Press, 1990), pp. 77–88, Paul Brest, "The Misconceived Quest for the Original Understanding," *Boston University Law Review* 60 (1980): 228–29.

[28] See John Hart Ely, *Democracy and Distrust: A Theory of Judicial Review* (Cambridge: Harvard University Press, 1980), pp. 67–68. See also Henry P. Monaghan, "Our Perfect Constitution," *New York University Law Review* 56 (1981): 391–95.

[29] See, e.g., Raoul Berger, *Government by Judiciary: The Transformation of the Fourteenth Amendment* (Cambridge: Harvard University Press, 1977), pp. 363–67; Robert H. Bork, *The Tempting of America* (New York: Free Press, 1990), pp. 143–45.

take comfort in the fact that their theory is used somewhere in American law, whatever the doubts of critics. From a partisan perspective, this surely indicates that their theory is correct. And so, as in the nineteenth century, the debate continues.

What has been said thus far should establish pluralism as the best descriptive-explanatory account of constitutional interpretation. Pluralism is the most accurate description of American constitutional interpretation because the sources of American law are plural. Given the legalization of the Constitution by the founding generation, these sources of law have influenced constitutional interpretation and have produced the pluralism of interpretive methods and principles we now observe in the contemporary theoretical debate. With regard to the normative dimension of evaluation, a pluralistic theory is dependent ultimately on the desirability of the legalized Constitution. It is the effort to legalize the Constitution, after all, that produced a plurality of methods of interpretation. To the extent that the legalization of the Constitution was desirable, a pluralistic theory can be justified.[30]

The different methods of interpretation in contemporary constitutional law have been explored ably in the pluralistic theories of interpretation developed by Philip Bobbitt, Richard Fallon, and Robert Post.[31] Their theories converge around the following methods of interpretation: consulting the text of the Constitution, the intent of the Framers, precedent, inferences from the structure of the Constitution, and the national ethos or tradition. To these methods, Bobbitt argues we should add prudential argument, a category best represented by the approach of Justice Felix Frankfurter and the constitutional scholar Alexander Bickel.[32] We will describe each of these methods briefly.

As we saw in our discussion of nineteenth-century constitutional theory, an emphasis on the text has always been part of American constitutional interpretation.[33] Textualism is rooted firmly in the strain of American constitutionalism that stresses the importance of the fact that the Constitution is a written document. Justice Hugo Black renewed the

---

[30] This issue is taken up in the third section of chapter 6.

[31] See Philip Bobbitt, *Constitutional Fate* (New York: Oxford University Press, 1982); Bobbitt, *Constitutional Interpretation*; Fallon, "A Constructivist Coherence Theory of Constitutional Interpretation," Robert Post, "Theories of Constitutional Interpretation," *Representations* 30 (1990): 13.

The use of Bobbitt's pluralist theory does not imply endorsement of his philosophical position that the methods of interpretation are conventions that we have no option to accept or reject. See Bobbitt, *Constitutional Fate*, pp. 5–8.

[32] See Bobbitt, *Constitutional Fate*, pp. 59–73.

[33] See H. Jefferson Powell, "The Political Grammar of Early Constitutional Law," *North Carolina Law Review* 71 (1993): 952–64; Powell, "The Principles of '98: An Essay in Historical Retrieval," pp. 705–15.

textualist tradition for the twentieth century and there is reason to believe that textualism has a special status in contemporary constitutional law.[34] The Supreme Court seems to take care to link all constitutional doctrines and decisions to a specific clause of the Constitution. This may appear to be the only legitimate way to interpret the Constitution, but, as we shall see, studying the other methods of interpretation shows that this is not the case. The self-conscious contemporary belief that every constitutional doctrine must be rooted in a specific clause shows that, relative to past eras of constitutional interpretation, we are living in a textualist age.[35]

As these remarks suggest, the different methods of interpretation have not always had the same relative status they have today. History influences which methods of interpretation are popular at a given time. Originalist theories that look to the intent of the Framers as a guide to interpretation now appear on any list of important interpretive theories, but this was not always the case. The rejection of precedents founded partly on originalist appeals by the Supreme Court after 1937 and the rejection of states rights arguments also founded on originalist appeals made by southern segregationists during the 1950s and 1960s discredited originalism for a time as a genuine alternative to other interpretive approaches. It was in *Brown*, after all, that the Supreme Court stated that historical inquiry into the meaning of the Fourteenth Amendment was "inconclusive."[36] The Court went on to state that in resolving the question of whether segregation in public education was unconstitutional under the Fourteenth Amendment, "we cannot turn the clock back to 1868 when the Amendment was adopted. . . . We must consider public education in the light of its full development and its present place in American life throughout the Nation."[37]

It is not an accident that originalism reemerged as a respectable position only after the heyday of the Nixon Administration's "southern strategy" and the effective end of the civil rights movement. Raoul Berger's well-known work on the original meaning of the Fourteenth Amendment, a work that supported the position taken earlier by southern segregationists, received a far more respectful treatment from the scholarly community when it was published in 1977 than it would have received in 1957.[38]

---

[34] On Justice Black's contribution, see Bobbitt, *Constitutional Fate*, pp. 26–38.

[35] For relevant discussion, see Michael J. Perry, *The Constitution in the Courts* (New York: Oxford University Press, 1994), pp. 29–31. For a recent defense of a textualist theory, see Leslie Friedman Goldstein, *In Defense of the Text: Democracy and Constitutional Theory* (Savage, Md.: Rowman and Littlefield, 1991).

[36] 347 U.S. at 489.

[37] Ibid., pp. 492–93.

[38] See generally Berger, *Government by Judiciary*.

Although textualist and originalist theories have attracted much scholarly attention, there is little doubt that most Supreme Court decisions
are based on some sort of doctrinal test or appeal to precedent.[39] In
contrast to the situation faced by the Supreme Court in its early years,
the contemporary Court typically has a substantial and ever-growing
body of precedent to draw on in a given case.[40] The development of this
body of case law has no doubt contributed to the persuasive appeal of
theories that see a close relationship between constitutional law and the
common law.

The dominance of precedent as a method of constitutional interpretation and the scholarly debate over the relative merits of textualism and
originalism tend to obscure the potential importance of the remaining
methods. In particular, it is unfortunate that less attention is paid to structural argument.[41] Although the contemporary Court does not often employ structural arguments, it is possible that they were more popular in the
past. There is some evidence that the Supreme Court regularly employed
structural argument in the *Lochner* era. When the Court ruled various
social and economic measures unconstitutional, it did so less in the service
of an interpretation of a particular clause (such as the Due Process clause
of the Fourteenth Amendment), than a conception of the appropriate
scope of state legislative power. The Court appeared to believe that there
could be no meaningful constitutional check on the legislative branch unless it could formulate a doctrine specifying what acts were beyond the
power of the legislature. Formulating such a doctrine led the Court to
draw distinctions between constitutional and unconstitutional exercises of
the police power of the kind on display in the *Lochner* case.[42] Understanding this aspect of the *Lochner* era has perhaps been obscured by the assumption that textualism has always been as important as it is today. If the
Lochner era Court was advancing a structural argument, contemporary

[39] A recent study of the opinions of Justices William Rehnquist and William Brennan
showed that doctrinal argument is their dominant mode of constitutional interpretation.
See Glenn A. Phelps and John B. Gates, "The Myth of Jurisprudence: Interpretive Theory
in the Constitutional Opinions of Justices Rehnquist and Brennan," *Santa Clara Law Review* 31 (1991): 590–91.

For a discussion by a former Solicitor General that supports the approach taken here, see
Fried, *Order and Law*, pp. 66–68.

[40] For a good discussion of the use of precedent by the Supreme Court, see Michael J.
Gerhardt, "The Role of Precedent in Constitutional Decisionmaking and Theory," *George
Washington Law Review* 60 (1991): 68.

[41] For a contemporary presentation of the structural approach, see Charles L. Black, Jr.,
Structure and Relationship in Constitutional Law (Baton Rouge: Louisiana State University
Press, 1969).

[42] This is suggested by Horwitz, *The Transformation of American Law*, pp. 20–30. See
also Howard Gillman, *The Constitution Besieged: The Rise and Demise of Lochner Era Police
Powers Jurisprudence* (Durham: Duke University Press, 1993).

criticisms of *Lochner* rooted in a textualist approach to the Due Process clause are beside the point.[43]

It is likely that prudential argument is the newest form of constitutional argument, a form that did not exist in the nineteenth century. It is defined by Bobbitt as "constitutional argument which is actuated by the political and economic circumstances surrounding the decision."[44] Prudential argument is based on the conviction that when the Supreme Court reviews the complex policies approved by the activist federal government of the twentieth century, the Court's inquiry must pay close attention to the facts, the relevant experience with such government action, and the Court's own institutional position.[45] Prudentialists are more willing to acknowledge that constitutional law is an uneasy mix of law and politics.

Constitutional arguments based on a national ethos or tradition have received a great deal of scholarly attention since they have formed the basis of some of the Supreme Court's most controversial decisions. We will postpone the exploration of this method of interpretation, however, until later in the chapter when we discuss the interpretation of the Fourteenth Amendment.

Although the actual practice of the Supreme Court and the nature of American constitutionalism make a pluralistic theory the best candidate for a general theory of constitutional interpretation, this approach has not received much attention in the contemporary scholarly debate. This is due in part to the way the contemporary scholarly debate began. Many of the most controversial constitutional decisions since *Brown* have involved the Due Process and Equal Protection clauses of the Fourteenth Amendment. Scholars reacted to these decisions by attempting to criticize or defend them in terms of some theory such as originalism or fundamental rights. The theoretical debate came to be understood as a battle between such single-method theories of interpretation.

Nevertheless, almost all constitutional scholars accept a plurality of methods of interpreting the Constitution. The theories that have produced the most debate such as John Hart Ely's interpretivism and Robert Bork's originalism are in fact pluralistic theories in that they recognize at least two legitimate methods of interpretation—text and precedent—in addition to the particular methods (structural argument in Ely's case and originalist argument in Bork's) on which they lavish most of their attention.[46] Their theories have not been described as pluralistic, however, be-

---

[43] For an example of such a critique, see Ely, *Democracy and Distrust*, pp. 18–21.

[44] Bobbitt, *Constitutional Fate*, p. 61.

[45] Ibid., pp. 61–73. As this description suggests, prudential argument as a method of constitutional interpretation is closely related to the prudential arguments for judicial review we explored in chapter 3.

[46] See generally Bork, *The Tempting of America*; Ely, *Democracy and Distrust*.

cause of the narrow focus of the debate on clauses where the methods of text and precedent do not seem to be of much help.

One benefit of a pluralistic theory of constitutional interpretation is that it shifts attention away from the seemingly endless attempts of scholars to definitively justify their preferred theory and debunk rival theories. We concentrate instead on the actual practice of the Supreme Court and on the method of interpretation that best illuminates a particular clause and case. This chapter will therefore not offer any knockdown criticisms of the various theories that have been proposed by scholars. All of the theories are equally legitimate to the extent that they are rooted in the historical evolution of American constitutionalism. Theories can be criticized, however, when they make grandiose claims to being the most acceptable or the only possible method of interpretation. We will again take up the different methods of interpretation and describe them in greater detail in the section on the Fourteenth Amendment.

The Contemporary Theoretical Debate

The distinction between interpretive and noninterpretive accounts of constitutional interpretation has played a major role in the theoretical debate that has occurred over the past two decades. Constitutional theory in the 1980s was described as being divided into two camps: interpretivist and noninterpretivist.[47] Interpretive theories were those that stayed close to the Constitution by making clear inferences from the text and the intent of the Framers. Noninterpretive theories were those that moved beyond the text and original intent in favor of values not found within the document.[48] It appeared to follow that only interpretivist theories offered interpretations of the Constitution. Noninterpretivist theories simply added new values to the text.[49]

The distinction between interpretive and noninterpretive theories made its first appearance in a seminal article by Thomas Grey. Grey was responding to an outbreak of textualist criticism of Warren and Burger Court decisions respecting the Equal Protection clause and the right of privacy.[50] Grey defended these decisions by arguing that the Supreme Court had often proceeded in a noninterpretive mode by deciding cases on the basis of "basic national ideals of individual liberty and fair treat-

---

[47] See Richard Saphire, "Judicial Review in the Name of the Constitution," *University of Dayton Law Review* 8 (1983): 746.

[48] See Grey, "Do We Have an Unwritten Constitution?" pp. 703–7.

[49] See Michael J. Perry, *The Constitution, the Courts, and Human Rights* (New Haven: Yale University Press, 1982), pp. 10–11.

[50] See Grey, "Do We Have an Unwritten Constitution?" pp. 703–4.

ment, even when the content of these ideals is not expressed as a matter of positive law in the written Constitution."[51] If the Court tried to apply an interpretive model consistently, it would have to overturn many important decisions, including those involving substantive due process, the incorporation of various provisions of the Bill of Rights in the Fourteenth Amendment, voting rights under the Equal Protection clause, and prohibition of school segregation. Grey concluded that the drastic implications of the interpretive model counted against adopting it as the sole approach to constitutional interpretation.[52]

Grey's article is a useful point of departure because it contained in summary form a number of the ambiguities that ran through subsequent theoretical debates. The interpretive model he described appeared to allow appeals to the Constitution's text, history, and structure, but the tendency of this model to collapse into a theory which relied solely on original intent was already apparent.[53] This tendency resulted from the difficulty of distinguishing between interpretive and noninterpretive decisions. The distinction could not rest on the use of the text of the Constitution in interpretive decisions because decisions that seemed noninterpretive could also be characterized as textualist, given that they made good-faith attempts to interpret ambiguous constitutional clauses.[54] Since there was evidence that the Framers would have disapproved of particular controversial decisions, however, resting the interpretive model on an appeal to original intent meant that a clear distinction could be made. Grey's article thus foreshadowed the turn the theoretical debate would take toward emphasizing the distinction between originalism and nonoriginalism.

Grey's article also raised the troublesome issue of under what conditions very general constitutional clauses, such as the Due Process and Equal Protection clauses of the Fourteenth Amendment, could become part of the legalized Constitution. Grey rested the interpretive model on an appeal to the doctrine of popular sovereignty. Exercises of judicial review based on text and original intent were legitimate because they rested on an earlier constitutional judgment of the people as a whole.[55] Grey asserted that there was a fundamental difference between such interpretive decisions and decisions purporting to "interpret" general constitutional clauses on the basis of important national values. Such noninterpretive

---

[51] Ibid., p. 706.

[52] Ibid., pp. 710–14.

[53] See ibid., p. 706 n. 9. For an example of the collapse of interpretivism into originalism, see Earl Maltz, "Some New Thoughts On An Old Problem—The Role of the Intent of the Framers in Constitutional Theory," *Boston University Law Review* 63 (1983): 811.

[54] For this reason, Grey later rejected the interpretivist-noninterpretivist distinction. See Thomas C. Grey, "The Constitution as Scripture," *Stanford Law Review* 37 (1984): 1.

[55] See Grey, "Do We Have an Unwritten Constitution?" pp. 705–6.

decisions could not appeal to popular sovereignty for their legitimacy because there was no meaningful link between these decisions and an original constitutional judgment.[56]

This argument exposed an important fault line running through subsequent theoretical debates. To Grey, it was obvious that there was a difference between interpreting clauses of the Constitution that indicate the value they wish to protect (such as the Freedom of Speech clause of the First Amendment), and the Due Process and Equal Protection clauses of the Fourteenth Amendment that do not indicate a clear constitutional value.[57] To other theorists, it seemed equally obvious that interpreting such general clauses was no different in principle from interpreting more specific clauses. In both cases, interpretive arguments resting on the text, history, structure, and fundamental values of the Constitution were required to make sense of the clauses in question.[58]

The account of American constitutionalism offered in chapter 1 provides a useful perspective on this debate. As we noticed there, constitutional clauses framed in general language are not analogous to ordinary law. This disanalogy becomes obvious when controversial Supreme Court decisions direct attention to especially ambiguous clauses such as those in the Fourteenth Amendment. The line between law and politics that the legalized Constitution is supposed to establish grows dim in such cases, prompting constitutional scholars to advocate theories of interpretation that reestablish a clear difference between constitutional law and political value judgments.[59] Theorists that emphasize the essential similarity between interpreting ambiguous clauses and other constitutional provisions argue in effect for the partial dissolution of the legalized Constitution and for confronting the unique status of the Constitution as a fundamental law.

In any event, the distinction between interpretive and noninterpretive theories was misguided. The distinction was tendentious because it begged the question of the proper character of constitutional interpretation. Those theorists labeled noninterpretivists did not think they were offering noninterpretations of the Constitution. To the contrary, they insisted that their theories did count as constitutional interpretations.[60] This meant that the distinction was not a fair description of the boundary between competing

[56] Ibid., p. 710. Grey continued to emphasize this point in a later article. See Grey, "The Constitution as Scripture," pp. 13–17.

[57] The distinction was implicit, for example, in Robert H. Bork, "Neutral Principles and Some First Amendment Problems," *Indiana Law Journal* 47 (1971): 1.

[58] For a recent statement of this view, see Ronald Dworkin, *Life's Dominion* (New York: Alfred A. Knopf, 1993), pp. 129–31.

[59] See, e.g., Bork, *The Tempting of America.*

[60] See, e.g., Ronald Dworkin, "The Forum of Principle," *New York University Law Review* 56 (1981): 472.

theories. The interpretive-noninterpretive distinction itself assumed a controversial theory about what counts as a legitimate interpretation of the Constitution, and it was criticized effectively on this basis.[61]

The theoretical debate then turned toward describing theories of constitutional interpretation in terms of a dichotomy between originalism and nonoriginalism. This turn was in part the product of the public attention directed at a debate initiated by Attorney General Edwin Meese, who argued in the mid-1980s for a return to a jurisprudence of original intention, and the nomination of Judge Robert Bork, a noted exponent of original intent theory, in 1987.[62]

The originalism-nonoriginalism distinction is arguably more viable than the interpretive-noninterpretive distinction because the theory of original intent can be elaborated in a way that makes clear it is a distinctive position that some judges and scholars reject.[63] It is nonetheless misleading as a way to understand the debate among the different theories of constitutional interpretation. The distinction implies that nonoriginalist theories make no appeal to understanding the Constitution in a historical context, when in fact all theories of interpretation make some claim of this kind.[64] In addition, drawing such a dichotomy collapses without justification the distinctions among many different kinds of nonoriginalist theories, theories that are more usefully considered separately. The pluralist theory of constitutional interpretation offered earlier illustrates this point. Originalism and nonoriginalism are not truly general theories of constitutional interpretation, since they are inspired primarily by the debate over the interpretation of the Fourteenth Amendment. The distinctions we drew earlier between textual, doctrinal, and prudential approaches, among others, cannot be captured through any such dichotomy.

If the distinctions between interpretivism-noninterpretivism and originalism-nonoriginalism are misleading, however, why do they exert such a hold over the theoretical debate? As our discussion of the interpretive-

---

[61] Ibid., pp. 471–76.

[62] For a useful collection of articles relevant to this debate, see Rakove, ed., *Interpreting the Constitution: The Debate Over Original Intent*. After his nomination was defeated in the Senate, Bork published a book defending his theoretical position. See Bork, *The Tempting of America*.

[63] For a useful review of various forms of originalism and an argument that some are more defensible than others, see Gregory Bassham, *Original Intent and the Constitution: A Philosophical Study* (Lanham, Md.: Rowman and Littlefield, 1992).

[64] See the important critiques of the originalism-nonoriginalism distinction by David Couzens Hoy, "A Hermeneutical Critique of the Originalism/Nonoriginalism Distinction," *Northern Kentucky Law Review* 15 (1988): 479; Lawrence B. Solum, "Originalism as Transformative Politics," *Tulane Law Review* 63 (1989): 1599.

Hoy and Solum were criticizing the use of the distinction in Michael J. Perry, *Morality, Politics, and Law* (New York: Oxford University Press, 1988).

noninterpretive distinction suggests, the theoretical debate is driven by such dichotomies because a more fundamental dichotomy between law and politics stands in the background, motivating the parties to describe the debate as a choice between two positions—theories that preserve the law-politics distinction and those that challenge the distinction. The legal community is strongly committed to the project of legalizing the Constitution in order to draw a clear distinction between constitutional law and ordinary politics, a politics that is often perceived by legal scholars as a capricious, sordid, compromised affair.[65]

As we noted in chapter 4, however, the nature of constitutional adjudication forces the Supreme Court to challenge this distinction as it struggles to interpret the ambiguous clauses of the Constitution. This means that the first marker laid down in the theoretical debate is often an exhortation for the Court to return to an approach that reinforces the legalized Constitution and reassures the legal community that the law-politics distinction is meaningful. Thus the debate revolves around poles such as interpretivism and originalism as scholars respond to controversial Court decisions by continually seeking to reestablish the legalized Constitution.

The theoretical debates over interpretivism and originalism reveal more fundamental conceptual problems with the attempt to provide an adequate account of constitutional interpretation. In the course of their debates, lawyers and scholars typically mix descriptive-explanatory and normative arguments without sufficient attention to the implications of this mixing for the question of justification. For lawyers and legal scholars, this mixing is understandable because it is one of the chief characteristics of the practice of lawyering. Ronald Dworkin has argued persuasively that the arguments employed by lawyers and judges are not solely descriptive or normative, but a combination of both he calls interpretive.[66] Legal arguments do not distinguish sharply between reports of what the law is and appeals to what the law should be. This sort of legal argument is common in constitutional law. Scholars often argue, for example, that the Constitution and Supreme Court precedents have created rights that the Court has not yet recognized formally.

In scholarly and theoretical debates, however, the mixing of descriptive and normative arguments poses special difficulties. Unless great care is taken, failure to attend to the difference between the tasks of description and explanation on the one hand, and the task of normative evaluation on the other, can seriously degrade the quality of the arguments offered. Put briefly, the unjustified mixing of descriptive and normative arguments can

[65] See Stuart A. Scheingold, *The Politics of Rights* (New Haven: Yale University Press, 1974), p. 14.

[66] See Ronald Dworkin, *Law's Empire* (Cambridge: Harvard University Press, 1986), pp. 46–48, 87–90.

create two effects: it allows the status quo to masquerade as normatively desirable simply because it exists and allows proposals for radical change to masquerade as simple extensions of what has already occurred.

One must be on constant guard against the unjustified mixing of these different kinds of argument in constitutional theory. Constitutional theorists have characteristically been in the business of proposing that the Supreme Court should behave in a certain way or that constitutional law should go in a certain direction. Influenced by normal lawyering practice, it is all too easy for theorists to cut corners and fail to provide the kind of normative justification required by these theoretical projects. To avoid the former effect and prevent an unjustified normative halo from forming around the status quo, justification must by provided by a normative theory that is independent of the Constitution, since the Constitution itself is part of the status quo. The way to guard against proposals for radical change from assuming the aspect of the status quo is to make sure that the line between the status quo and significant change is marked clearly.

The discussion of prudential arguments for and against judicial review in chapter 3 is an example of scholars creating an unjustified normative halo around the status quo. Whether scholars criticize judicial review for being inconsistent with American democracy or praise it for being consistent with American constitutionalism, the theoretical error is the same. In both cases, judicial review is assessed against a largely undefined and completely undefended normative standard. The problem is created by the assumption that the democratic and constitutional status quo is inherently desirable. This enables a description of the status quo to masquerade as a critical normative standard capable of condemning or defending a controversial practice. By substituting a description for an evaluation, scholars make their task much easier at the expense of proper theoretical justification.

The typical presentation of originalism as a theory of constitutional interpretation is a good example of a proposal for radical change masquerading as the status quo. Originalists often start from the assumption that originalism has been the primary method of constitutional interpretation followed by courts and commentators from the beginning of the republic.[67] Originalism thus appears to be the status quo. Any deviation from originalist practice is seen as grounds for criticism, not as evidence that

[67] See, e.g., Bassham, *Original Intent and the Constitution*, pp. 1–7; Berger, *Government by Judiciary*, pp. 363–72; Richard S. Kay, "Adherence to the Original Intentions in Constitutional Adjudication: Three Objections and Responses," *Northwestern University Law Review* 82 (1988): 226–29; Monaghan, "Our Perfect Constitution," pp. 374–81. The historical discussion that is offered in these works is anachronistic because there is no attempt to distinguish between the different versions of originalism that have existed during different historical periods.

other methods of interpretation have been employed by the Supreme Court or that originalism itself has assumed different forms at different times. Our discussion of pluralism in constitutional interpretation, however, showed that the contemporary version of legislative intent originalism was not the common practice in the early nineteenth century. Furthermore, the different sources of American law inspired different methods of constitutional interpretation.

Originalists thus do not typically focus on the actual interpretive practice of the contemporary Supreme Court, except as an object of criticism. Without rooting their theory firmly in an accurate description of past and present interpretive practice, however, originalists have no way to demonstrate that their assumption that originalism is the status quo is correct. If the adoption of originalism by the Court as the sole or primary method of constitutional interpretation would therefore be a significant departure from the status quo, originalists must assume a heavy normative burden. They must show why such a departure would be justified in terms of its overall consequences on past precedent and future cases. If Grey is right that originalism would require abandoning many significant precedents that give constitutional law much of its present stability, then the burden of justification may be impossible to meet.

For all the emphasis on theory in the debate over controversial Supreme Court decisions, it seems that some basic theoretical errors run through much of contemporary scholarship. As the foregoing discussion suggests, one source of the trouble is insufficient attention to the difference between scholarship that is based on the values of lawyering and scholarship that seeks to preserve a clear distinction between the different tasks of description and evaluation. The latter sort of scholarship may not produce insights that are immediately useful to lawyers, but it addresses theoretical questions that are important in their own right.

There is thus a strong connection between our conception of what constitutional theory is for and our ability to pursue the truth about the theoretical aspects of constitutionalism. If we do not make the former explicit, we may have trouble achieving the latter. Is the primary purpose of constitutional theory to assist lawyers and judges in their real-world tasks or is it an effort to discern the truth, however unpalatable or irrelevant to immediate constitutional concerns? The great error of the contemporary theoretical debate is to think that a choice need not be made. The failure to choose produces proposals for the recognition of new constitutional rights and revisionary views about the basis for controversial decisions masquerading as theories of the status quo. These theories neither describe how justices make judgments or provide adequate normative justifications for the revisions they advocate. Scholarship that aims to be truly theoretical must attempt both tasks.

Democracy and Theories of Interpretation

We saw in chapter 3 how the Supreme Court fashioned a new role for itself in the post-1937 era with the help of the *Carolene Products* footnote.[68] This footnote has also been important to the debate over theories of constitutional interpretation. A continuing element in the scholarly debate is the use of the *Carolene Products* footnote to develop theories of interpretation, especially theories that illuminate the Equal Protection clause of the Fourteenth Amendment.[69]

In John Hart Ely's well-known theory, the *Carolene Products* footnote is used as the foundation of a structural argument concerning how the most ambiguous clauses of the Constitution should be interpreted. Ely poses an interpretive problem—given that the Constitution contains clauses that cannot be interpreted solely by means of examining the text or the intent of the Framers, how should such clauses be construed?[70] Ely identifies the Ninth Amendment and the Privileges or Immunities and Equal Protection clauses of the Fourteenth Amendment as the provisions in question.[71] Ely's solution to this problem is structural because it draws on the "general themes of the entire constitutional document" in order to specify how these clauses should be interpreted.[72]

Ely's interpretive solution draws on the second and third provisos of the *Carolene Products* footnote. The Supreme Court should interpret the ambiguous clauses of the Constitution, particularly the Equal Protection clause, to ensure that the democratic process is kept open to all and that prejudice against particular minority groups does not contaminate legislation that affects them.[73] This solution is supported by three arguments: the nature of the Constitution, particularly in light of the amendments ratified in the twentieth century, shows that it is devoted largely to considerations of representative government, that a *Carolene Products* approach is consistent with the principles of American democracy, and that courts are in a better position than elected officials to make the sorts of judgments called for by such an approach.[74] Ely then goes on to show in detail how various decisions made by the Warren Court can be defended

---

[68] See *United States v. Carolene Products Co.*, 304 U.S. 144, 152–53 n.4 (1938).

[69] See Ely, *Democracy and Distrust*; Cass R. Sunstein, *The Partial Constitution* (Cambridge: Harvard University Press, 1993).

[70] See Ely, *Democracy and Distrust*, pp. 12–13.

[71] Ibid., pp. 22–41. On the other hand, Ely denies that the Due Process clause, source of the doctrine of substantive due process, is such an open-ended provision. Ibid., pp. 14–21.

[72] Ibid., p. 12. For the description of Ely as a structuralist, see Bobbitt, *Constitutional Interpretation*, p. 133.

[73] See Ely, *Democracy and Distrust*, pp. 75–77.

[74] Ibid., pp. 87–88.

as efforts to implement the second and third provisos of the *Carolene Products* footnote.[75]

Despite the democratic appeal of Ely's theory, it has been criticized severely and abandoned as a dead end by most constitutional theorists.[76] One serious problem was created by the way Ely distinguished his theory from rival theories. Ely endorsed the interpretivist-noninterpretivist distinction and claimed that his theory was interpretivist in that it did not ask courts to make controversial value judgments.[77] In Ely's view, theories that attempted to interpret ambiguous constitutional clauses by means of fundamental values were clearly noninterpretivist, since such values could only be found outside the Constitution.[78]

Unfortunately, since Ely's theory clearly relied on certain political values to give content to ambiguous clauses, he was open to the charge of inconsistency.[79] The distinction between theories of interpretation that are supported by controversial substantive values and Ely's theory, justified by an appeal to a supposedly nonsubstantive process, was untenable, just as the interpretivist-noninterpretivist distinction was untenable for the reasons we noticed earlier. Another point that puzzled scholars was how Ely could think that the Constitution is devoted primarily to concerns of process, when the Constitution's commitment to values such as religious freedom and equality seems manifest.[80]

For all of the problems with Ely's theory, there seems to be something relatively robust about the *Carolene Products* approach. Other scholars, most notably the political theorists Robert Dahl and Michael Walzer, have reached conclusions similar to Ely's through independent arguments. For the reasons that we explored in the third section of chapter 3, Dahl is doubtful that the "quasi guardianship" (as he calls it) of judicial review can actually operate to protect fundamental rights.[81] If judicial review is

[75] Ibid., pp. 105–79.

[76] For representative criticisms, see the symposia cited in note 12. See also David Lyons, "Substance, Process, and Outcome in Constitutional Theory," *Cornell Law Review* 72 (1987): 745; "Symposium on Democracy and Distrust: Ten Years Later," *Virginia Law Review* 77 (1991): 631.

[77] See Ely, *Democracy and Distrust*, pp. 1–4, 73–77, 87–88.

[78] Ibid., p. 43.

[79] See, e.g., Paul Brest, "The Fundamental Rights Controversy: The Essential Contradictions of Normative Constitutional Scholarship," *Yale Law Journal* 90 (1981): 1093–94; Laurence H. Tribe, "The Puzzling Persistence of Process-Based Constitutional Theories," *Yale Law Journal* 89 (1980): 1067–77.

[80] See Tribe, "The Puzzling Persistence of Process-Based Constitutional Theories," pp. 1065–67. See also Erwin Chemerinsky, "The Price of Asking the Wrong Question: An Essay on Constitutional Scholarship and Judicial Review," *Texas Law Review* 62 (1984): 1220–26.

[81] Robert A. Dahl, *Democracy and Its Critics* (New Haven: Yale University Press, 1989), pp. 187–91.

adopted, however, Dahl argues that it can be made consistent with democratic principles if it is limited to enforcing "rights and interests integral to the democratic process."[82] Walzer also argues that judicial review must be limited to "enforcing first of all the basic political rights that serve to sustain the character of . . . [the democratic] assembly and protecting its members from discriminatory legislation. They are not to enforce rights beyond these, unless they are authorized to do so by a democratic decision."[83] As Dahl and Walzer note, the role they assign to judicial review is similar to that advocated by Ely.[84]

In addition, it is not clear that the objections to Ely's theory are inherent in the *Carolene Products* approach. A better version of a *Carolene Products* theory would offer an explicit defense of the theory's orientation toward the democratic process in terms of fundamental substantive values and institutional considerations. Cass Sunstein, for example, argues that the commitment of the Framers to a form of deliberative democracy and the institutional and enforcement problems associated with judicial review help justify a *Carolene Products* approach.[85] The point is not that Sunstein has advanced a flawless theory, but that some of the objections directed against Ely's theory are not fatal to the general project of limiting judicial enforcement of ambiguous constitutional clauses to instances where such enforcement would promote democratic values.

It should also be noted that Ely never purported to advance a general theory of constitutional interpretation in the sense we defined above. Ely's theory was not intended to provide guidance into the interpretation of any provision of the Constitution. Ely's particular concern was to argue that if the ambiguous clauses of the Constitution were interpreted in accordance with the *Carolene Products* footnote, then this would be consistent with interpretivism.[86] Ely did not argue that all constitutional provisions had to be interpreted in accordance with *Carolene Products*; he argued rather that the emphasis of the Constitution on establishing the procedures and values important to representative government showed the way to give content to these troublesome clauses.[87]

There can be a legitimate argument over whether, in pursuing such a structural approach, one should look to the entire Constitution or to the

---

[82] Ibid., p. 191.

[83] Michael Walzer, "Philosophy and Democracy," *Political Theory* 9 (1981): 397.

[84] See Dahl, Democracy and Its Critics, p. 359 n. 9; Walzer, "Philosophy and Democracy," p. 399 n. 21.

[85] See Sunstein, *The Partial Constitution*, pp. 133–53. See also Sunstein's remarks on Ronald Dworkin's theory of judicial review in ibid., pp. 374–75 n. 35.

For a unified treatment and criticism of Ely and Sunstein, see James E. Fleming, "Constructing the Substantive Constitution," *Texas Law Review* 72 (1993): 211.

[86] See Ely, *Democracy and Distrust*, pp. 12–13, 87–88.

[87] Ibid., pp. 87–104.

most important provisions of the document, as revealed by precedent. In responding to Ely's structural argument, scholars such as Laurence Tribe emphasized those portions of the Constitution that have been the basis for most of the constitutional doctrine developed by the Supreme Court. The Court's enforcement of such substantive values thus showed the fundamental character of the Constitution itself.[88] Tribe gave no weight, as Ely did, to a consideration of principled constitutional change; that is, how Article V has been employed, particularly in the twentieth century, to reinforce the values of the democratic process.[89] This dispute over the fundamental character of the Constitution is a good example of a conflict between the structural and doctrinal forms of constitutional argument.

In any event, Ely's attempt to interpret ambiguous constitutional clauses by means of democratic principles embodied a challenge to rival theories that has never been assessed properly. Ely's challenge is how to justify granting the institutional power to recognize rights that are not explicitly mentioned in the Constitution (and thus do not fall within the ambit of the first paragraph of the *Carolene Products* footnote) and have nothing to do with improving the democratic process or protecting minorities from the effects of prejudice.[90] One may concede that the ideas of defending the democratic process and protecting minorities from prejudice may be elaborated in different ways without blunting the force of the challenge. It may also be the case that Supreme Court decisions employing the right of privacy, such as the abortion decisions, can be justified under a *Carolene Products* rationale.[91] This still leaves us with the question posed by Ely's challenge.

The force of the challenge derives from the kind of argument that would have to be made to justify such a grant of power. Giving the judiciary (or any other institution) the power to recognize new constitutional rights seems inconsistent both with constitutionalism and democracy. Constitutional norms are violated to the extent that power is granted without being subject to a written standard. Further, the backstop that recognition of new rights is necessary to preserve democracy is unavailable by hypothesis. Such a grant of power could only be supported on the ground that the judiciary has the superior insight to discern the fundamental rights that deserve protection. It is doubtful that anyone (except, perhaps, judges and their scholarly cohorts) would agree that judges have

---

[88] See Tribe, "The Puzzling Persistence of Process-Based Constitutional Theories," pp. 1065–67.

[89] See Ely, *Democracy and Distrust*, pp. 98–99.

[90] This challenge is also suggested by Walzer's discussion in "Philosophy and Democracy," pp. 382–93.

[91] See, e.g., Sunstein, *The Partial Constitution*, pp. 270–85.

a special moral and political insight given to no one else. It may be conceded that judges have an expertise in legal matters that ordinary citizens do not, but this does not affect the argument. Without postulating such a special insight, however, there is no basis for giving the judiciary the power to recognize new rights.

Something like this argument appears to move Ely, Sunstein, Dahl, and Walzer to conclude that there is no basis for judicial review of ambiguous constitutional clauses outside rationales that connect in some way with democratic principles. This conclusion, however, does not necessarily have dramatic consequences for the justification of Supreme Court decisions based on controversial doctrines such as the right of privacy. Although Ely and others have criticized the doctrine of substantive due process on which the right of privacy is based, the decisions reached on the basis of this doctrine can still be justified if a democratic rationale for the result can be found. As we have observed, Sunstein and other scholars believe that at least some substantive due process decisions can be justified on democratic grounds. On the other hand, numerous scholars believe that the substantive due process doctrine makes sense and should remain a part of the law, regardless of whether it is consistent with democratic principles.[92] For these scholars, Ely's challenge poses a problem that has not been faced squarely.

It should not be thought, however, that Ely's challenge is decisive, for advocates of a *Carolene Products* approach have left a number of debts. One important debt that remains is the presentation of the full theory of democratic principles that is needed to support the argument for judicial review limited to a *Carolene Products* rationale. Sunstein has gestured in the direction of such a theory, but he tends to rely on the generalization that the Framers meant to establish a deliberative democracy.[93] Ely certainly does not supply such a theory, as many scholars have noted.[94]

Another point that needs clarification is whether the *Carolene Products* approach is one that the Supreme Court already follows, at least in certain respects, or whether its consistent adoption would constitute a radical reform of constitutional doctrine.[95] If a *Carolene Products* approach repre-

[92] See, e.g., Fleming, "Constructing the Substantive Constitution."

[93] See Sunstein, *The Partial Constitution*, pp. 133–34.

[94] See, e.g., Lyons, "Substance, Process, and Outcome in Constitutional Theory," pp. 754–56.

[95] For an argument that rationales drawn from the Carolene Products footnote have not driven the Supreme Court's decisions, see L. A. Powe, Jr., "Does Footnote Four Describe?" *Constitutional Commentary* 11 (1994): 197. See also Daniel A. Farber and Philip P. Frickey, "Is *Carolene Products* Dead? Reflections on Affirmative Action and the Dynamics of Civil Rights Legislation," *California Law Review* 79 (1991): 685.

sents radical reform, this increases the burden of justification on its advocates. As we have seen, however, this approach continues to exert a hold on the contemporary debate because its strengths have yet to be appreciated fully.

The Problem of History in Constitutional Interpretation

The preceding chapters should have made it apparent that it is impossible to understand American constitutionalism without an appreciation of American constitutional history. All theories and methods of constitutional interpretation, not just originalism, operate in a historical context and make appeals to history in their arguments. There appears to be a close relationship between the study of constitutional history and the practice of constitutional law.

This relationship, however, is far more problematic than it first appears. There is an inherent quarrel between constitutionalism and history. As we saw in chapter 1, the ceaseless forces of political, economic, social, and cultural change pose difficult problems for those who aspire to adopt a permanent set of constitutional principles and have those principles enforced through the centuries. Historical change forces a decision between continually amending the document as the government is compelled to deal with new problems and allowing change to occur through ordinary political and judicial means. Constitutionalists often respond to this dilemma by insisting that the Constitution established a set of timeless first principles to which the nation must return in order to fulfill its ideals.[96]

The quarrel between constitutionalism and history becomes apparent in the contrasting ways lawyers and historians approach historical events. Constitutional historians have often been quite critical of the use of history by judges. In a well-known article, historian Alfred Kelly made the point that Supreme Court justices often resort to what he called "law-office" history to justify their decisions.[97] Law-office history is advocacy history in which the Court selects historical evidence in order to show that only one possible position is correct. Constitutional historians, by contrast, are interested in a broad assessment of the relevant evidence and establishing the proper context in which that evidence can be understood

---

[96] For a relevant discussion, see Gordon S. Wood, "The Fundamentalists and the Constitution," *New York Review of Books*, February 18, 1988, p. 33.

[97] See Alfred H. Kelly, "Clio and the Court: An Illicit Love Affair," in Philip B. Kurland, ed., *Supreme Court Review 1965* (Chicago: University of Chicago Press, 1965), p. 122. For a general study, see Charles A. Miller, *The Supreme Court and the Uses of History* (Cambridge: Harvard University Press, 1969).

and explained. Kelly concluded that the Court "has confused the writing of briefs with the writing of history."[98] The perspectives of the lawyer and judge on the one hand, and the historian on the other, are fundamentally different and not complementary.[99]

Lawyers and historians thus do not study historical events in the same ways for the same purposes. The code of ethics, for example, requires lawyers to represent their clients zealously within the bounds of the law.[100] The client relationship determines the boundaries of the lawyer's inquiry into the past. In writing briefs to appellate courts such as the Supreme Court, lawyers are justified in presenting the historical evidence that best favors their client's position. They are not required to research primary sources (other than relevant precedents) and the adversary system discourages them from arguing that the evidence they find is ambiguous or irrelevant. As Kelly argued, this advocacy orientation also influences the way justices write opinions. It appears that the justices do not perceive a problem with the selective use of historical evidence.[101]

What lawyers and judges tend to ignore is that constitutional history is more of an ongoing argument than a set of received understandings. The conception of history promoted by the adversary system is that every historical question has a definite answer. If the historical evidence points in a variety of directions, lawyers and judges typically distort the evidence until it can be separated into two camps, with one camp proclaimed the victor. The idea that there may be contemporary issues that history cannot answer is not considered. As constitutional historians recognize, however, the evidence available may simply be too ambiguous to admit of a clear answer. This third alternative is usually ignored in the theoretical debates that have occurred over the meaning of ambiguous constitutional clauses. From a lawyer's perspective, history must provide one right answer and it is this orientation that separates lawyers from constitutional historians.[102]

---

[98] Kelly, "Clio and the Court: An Illicit Love Affair," in Kurland, ed., *The Supreme Court Review*, p. 155.

[99] For a valuable recent discussion, see Martin S. Flaherty, "History 'Lite' in Modern American Constitutionalism," *Columbia Law Review* 95 (1995): 526–27 n. 16, 551–55.

[100] This language is taken from Canon 7 of the American Bar Association's Model Code of Professional Responsibility. Although the Model Code has been replaced in many states by the ABA Model Rules of Professional Conduct, the new rule has been interpreted as consistent with Canon 7. See Stephen Gillers and Roy D. Simon, Jr., *Regulation of Lawyers: Statutes and Standards* (Boston: Little, Brown, 1995), pp. 40, 474.

[101] See Kelly, "Clio and the Court," in Kurland, ed., *The Supreme Court Review*, pp. 155–58.

[102] See the discussion in William E. Nelson, *The Fourteenth Amendment: From Political Principle to Judicial Doctrine* (Cambridge: Harvard University Press, 1988), pp. 1–12; Michael Les Benedict, "Book Review," *Law and History Review* 10 (1992): 377.

The problem of history in constitutional interpretation goes deeper than the selective use of historical evidence by lawyers and judges. American constitutional law implicitly embodies a presentist bias, what historians call a Whig theory of history.[103] As historian Joyce Appleby remarks, "Like the history of science, the history of the United States Constitution has been largely written as the history of its progress."[104] The story of American constitutional law is typically presented as a narrative of moral progress, of a continuous closer approximation of the ideals of the founding generation, culminating in the desirable democratic order of the present, with its valuable and historically rooted set of civil rights and civil liberties. This story stresses the continuities between past and present, rather than the discontinuities that have also contributed to the present constitutional order.[105]

The fallacy of presentism is the reading of the present back into the past, as if the purpose of the past was to produce inevitably the circumstances of the present.[106] This fallacy colors many arguments of constitutional law. In his history of the Marshall Court, G. Edward White remarks on the "prehistoricist sensibility" of early constitutional figures such as Justices Marshall and Story.[107] Historical change was thought of "as the progressive unfolding of first principles rather than as a continuous, dynamic process."[108] Although White says that this sensibility is not a modern one, there are strong elements of this lack of historical consciousness in contemporary American constitutionalism. Judges and scholars speak of the founding generation as if they were our contemporaries and continue the search for the first principles that will return America to its proper course.[109] This way of thinking may be understandable

[103] See Herbert Butterfield, *The Whig Interpretation of History* (New York: W. W. Norton, 1965); David Hackett Fischer, *Historians' Fallacies: Toward a Logic of Historical Thought* (New York: Harper and Row, 1970), pp. 139–40. For a discussion with specific reference to constitutional law, see Saul Cornell, "Moving Beyond the Canon of Traditional Constitutional History: Anti-Federalists, the Bill of Rights, and the Promise of Post-Modern Historiography," *Law and History Review* 12 (1994): 5–12.

[104] Joyce Appleby, "The American Heritage: The Heirs and the Disinherited," in David Thelen, ed., *The Constitution and American Life* (Ithaca: Cornell University Press, 1988), p. 146.

[105] See Scheingold, *The Politics of Rights*, pp. 37–38; Wood, "The Fundamentalists and the Constitution," pp. 39–40.

[106] See Fischer, *Historians' Fallacies*, pp. 135–40.

[107] White, *The Marshall Court and Cultural Change*, p. 360. See also ibid., pp. 974–75.

[108] Ibid., p. 360.

[109] See, e.g., Hadley Arkes, *Beyond the Constitution* (Princeton: Princeton University Press, 1990); Christopher Wolfe, *The Rise of Modern Judicial Review* (New York: Basic Books, 1986). The fallacy of presentism is a special problem for theories of constitutional interpretation that appeal to the "aspirations" of the Constitution. See, e.g., Barber, *On What the Constitution Means*, pp. 154–59.

in that it seeks a usable past, but it also involves an impossible escape from historical change.

The legalized Constitution and the presentism inherent in the American constitutional tradition powerfully reinforce one another to produce the widespread view that the Constitution is without significant flaws and has changed very little since its adoption. A variation on this view is that if significant changes have occurred, they can be shown to be consistent with the original purpose or spirit of the Constitution.[110]

This constitutional perfectionism is deeply misleading, as the theory of constitutional change advanced in chapter 1 and the above remarks demonstrate. The idea of a perfect, ever-progressing Constitution has a certain circularity that appears to make it impervious to refutation. If significant, even radical constitutional changes occur, they can always be reinterpreted as inevitable realizations of abstract founding principles. The price of such perfection, however, is the absence of intellectual content. If there is no such thing as constitutional imperfection, then the idea of perfection has no meaning. More concretely, unless meaningful criteria for constitutional imperfection or failure are specified by those who see the Constitution as perfect, then the idea of perfection is exposed as wishful thinking.

In point of fact, there have been serious discontinuities in the American constitutional tradition, as the preceding chapters have shown. The constitutional disaster of the Civil War, the constitutional revolution of the New Deal, and the shift to a more democratic form of government in the twentieth century are all examples of such discontinuities. In particular, the presentist, perfectionist Constitution somehow does not take the Civil War very seriously. If the Civil War does not count as a constitutional failure, it is difficult to see what does. Understanding American constitutionalism in a historical context requires accepting its discontinuities and crises and abandoning the idea of the Constitution as a perfect framework for government.

These differences between constitutional law and the practice of history have several implications for our discussion of theories of constitutional interpretation. First, we should be wary of appeals to history as substitutes for normative justifications. When historical evidence is presented to justify a result in the present, a contemporary normative standard is the real engine driving the argument. Such a standard can only be justified by a normative argument, not by the selective editing of history to support a

---

[110] See, e.g., Jeffrey K. Tulis, *The Rhetorical Presidency* (Princeton: Princeton University Press, 1987), pp. 6–9; Morton Keller, "Powers and Rights: Two Centuries of American Constitutionalism," in Thelen, ed., *The Constitution and American Life*, p. 15; Jeffrey K. Tulis, "The Constitutional Presidency in American Political Development," in Martin L. Fausold and Alan Shank, eds., *The Constitution and the American Presidency* (Albany: State University of New York Press, 1991), p. 133.

predetermined conclusion. Appeals to history in constitutional interpretation serve to conceal the need for normative justification, although, as we shall note below, such appeals may be justified for other reasons.

Second, originalism has serious difficulties to the extent that it is presented as a method of interpretation that relies on the ordinary practice of historians and has a direct and uncomplicated relationship with the past.[111] Historians as different as Gordon Wood, Forrest McDonald, and Leonard Levy have all denied that the intent of the Framers has any meaning as a historical concept.[112] Originalists obtain clear historical answers to contemporary constitutional questions by employing canons of legal interpretation to reduce the likelihood that they will find the historical evidence ambiguous or irrelevant.[113] Again, while such interpretation may be justified on nonhistorical grounds, originalists cannot claim the mantle of history.

Third, some of the most important debates in contemporary constitutional theory are based on historical anachronisms. We noticed one such anachronism in chapter 3 when we elaborated the difference between the modern institution of judicial review and eighteenth-century conceptions of the judicial power. There is no point in asking whether the founding generation endorsed judicial review because the various understandings and institutional commitments that structure modern judicial review did not exist in the eighteenth century.

Similarly, the debate over how to distinguish *Lochner* from *Roe* involves the fallacy of anachronism. As we noted in chapter 3, *Lochner* was justifiable by the standards prevailing at the turn of the century. Although the approach of the majority in *Lochner* was abandoned after the New Deal, this does not mean that the return of substantive due process in *Griswold* and *Roe* was the return of *Lochner*. The new substantive due process doctrine was used for different purposes and operated in a fundamentally different political, legal, and social context. To ask how *Roe* can be justified if *Lochner* was unjustified thus makes the anachronistic assumption that the normative standards and relevant background did not change between 1905 and 1973.

For all the difficulties caused by the use of history in constitutional

[111] For an example of such an originalist theory, see Berger, *Government by Judiciary*, pp. 5–10. For commentary on this problem with originalism, see H. Jefferson Powell, "Rules for Originalists," *Virginia Law Review* 73 (1987): 659.

[112] See Leonard W. Levy, *Original Intent and the Framers' Constitution* (New York: Macmillan, 1988); Forrest McDonald, *Novus Ordo Seclorum: The Intellectual Origins of the Constitution* (Lawrence: University Press of Kansas, 1985), p. 224; Wood, "The Fundamentalists and the Constitution," pp. 39–40.

[113] See the discussion in Mark Tushnet, *Red, White, and Blue: A Critical Analysis of Constitutional Law* (Cambridge: Harvard University Press, 1988), pp. 36–39; Benedict, "Book Review," pp. 380–81.

interpretation, the actual practice of the Supreme Court arguably shows that its use is inevitable and perhaps desirable. American constitutionalism rests on the legalized Constitution, a distinctive practice that involves applying ordinary legal methods of interpretation to constitutional law. Since ordinary law rests on appeals to precedent and seeks a meaningful connection with the past, it is understandable that constitutional lawyers and judges search constantly for a usable past. This search may play a useful role in guiding and restraining constitutional arguments.[114] To the extent that the use of history, selective or not, does play this role, it may be justified on normative grounds in the same way as other desirable political practices. It is doubtful, however, that it can be justified as history.

Interpreting the Fourteenth Amendment

We have noted a number of times that the debate over theories of constitutional interpretation tends to center on the ambiguous clauses of section one of the Fourteenth Amendment. This is partly because these clauses are the basis of many of the important decisions by the Supreme Court in the latter half of the twentieth century, including *Brown* and *Roe*. But it is also because of the widespread opinion in the legal community that the reasoning of the Court in a number of these decisions is seriously deficient and the theoretical problems that arise when scholars attempt to construct better rationales for these controversial decisions.

The Due Process and Equal Protection clauses pose special theoretical problems because two standard methods of interpretation, looking to the text of the Constitution and consulting relevant precedents, appear to be of little help. The wording of these clauses is too ambiguous and, as just noted, the reasoning of the relevant precedents is in question. It is almost by default, then, that the theoretical debate revolves around the other methods of interpretation that we outlined in the first section of this chapter. In interpreting these clauses, judges and scholars have appealed to the intent of the Framers of the Fourteenth Amendment, the structure of the Constitution and the political order it was meant to establish, and the national ethos or tradition.

In this section we will examine the intricate web of argument spun by the Supreme Court and legal scholars with respect to the Fourteenth Amendment. This discussion will also serve to illustrate the more general points made in the preceding sections. We will begin by discussing the approach the Court has taken in a number of important cases to the inter-

[114] See Wood, "The Fundamentalists and the Constitution," pp. 39–40. See also the insightful commentary by Cass R. Sunstein, "The Idea of a Useable Past," *Columbia Law Review* 95 (1995): 601.

pretation of the Due Process clause and then move to the scholarly debate, which is dominated by a division between the proponents of fundamental rights and their originalist critics.

Our point of departure is the dissent by Justice John Harlan in *Poe v. Ullman*.[115] Harlan's dissent had a significant influence on subsequent thinking about how the Court should develop substantive due process jurisprudence and, more generally, on how the Court should go about inferring fundamental rights from ambiguous constitutional clauses.[116] Harlan denied that due process could be "reduced to any formula," for him it represented "the balance which our Nation, built upon postulates of respect for the liberty of the individual, has struck between that liberty and the demands of organized society."[117] In striking this balance, judges must consult "what history teaches are the traditions from which [this country] developed as well as the traditions from which it broke."[118] Harlan continued:

> [T]he full scope of the liberty guaranteed by the Due Process Clause cannot be found in or limited by the precise terms of the specific guarantees elsewhere provided in the Constitution. This "liberty" is not a series of isolated points pricked out in terms of the taking of property; the freedom of speech, press, and religion; the right to keep and bear arms; the freedom from unreasonable searches and seizures; and so on. It is a rational continuum which, broadly speaking, includes a freedom from all substantial arbitrary impositions and purposeless restraints.[119]

It became apparent only in subsequent cases that Harlan's method of interpreting the Due Process clause pointed in two directions. Harlan spoke of looking to history and tradition to discover which rights were fundamental to liberty, but he also emphasized that "the supplying of content to this Constitutional concept [due process] has of necessity been a rational process."[120] Inferring the existence of new fundamental rights along Harlan's "rational continuum" did not necessarily involve an appeal to history and tradition. As we shall see, in subsequent cases some justices preferred to rely on history and tradition to assess whether a new fundamental right should be recognized, while other justices preferred inferring the existence of fundamental rights from provisions of the Bill of Rights and the structure of the constitutional order.

In *Griswold*, Justice Douglas drew on Harlan's idea of a rational con-

---

[115] 367 U.S. 497 (1961).
[116] See, e.g., Tribe and Dorf, *On Reading the Constitution*, pp. 76–79.
[117] 367 U.S. at 542.
[118] Ibid.
[119] Ibid., p. 543.
[120] Ibid., p. 542.

tinuum of rights to argue that "specific guarantees in the Bill of Rights have penumbras, formed by emanations from those guarantees that help give them life and substance."[121] Citing several provisions in the Bill of Rights, Douglas contended that they created zones of privacy from which an independent right of privacy could be derived.[122] While somewhat influential in its libertarian appeal, Douglas's opinion did not have as important an impact on the scholarly debate as Justice Arthur Goldberg's concurrence.[123]

Goldberg cited the Ninth Amendment as evidence that "the Framers did not intend that the first eight amendments be construed to exhaust the basic and fundamental rights which the Constitution guaranteed to the people."[124] This appeal to a specific textual provision was highly suggestive to the future scholarly debate. In a textualist age, Goldberg's approach appeared to have an anchor in the Constitution that Douglas's did not. Like Harlan, Goldberg appealed to tradition and reason to explain how judges should determine which rights were truly fundamental.[125]

Justice Harry Blackmun's opinion for the majority in *Roe* has been criticized severely and has not been a strong reference point for the subsequent theoretical debate. In part, that is because Blackmun did not address the crucial challenge of substantive due process jurisprudence that Harlan, Douglas, and Goldberg all faced—how to derive new fundamental rights and specify their content. Blackmun relied on precedent to show the existence of the right of privacy and stated simply that it "is broad enough to encompass a woman's decision whether or not to terminate her pregnancy."[126] In effect disregarding Harlan's approach, Blackmun did not connect the history of abortion regulation set out in his opinion with the rationale for extending the right of privacy to cover abortion, nor did he explain how the right to terminate a pregnancy could be inferred by the method of reason from other guarantees in the Bill of Rights.

As the Court inclined in a conservative direction, the idea of using history and tradition to decide whether new fundamental rights should be recognized took on an increased importance. In *Moore v. City of East Cleveland*, Justice Lewis Powell argued that "the Constitution protects the sanctity of the family precisely because the institution of the family is deeply rooted in this Nation's history and tradition."[127] In *Bowers v.*

---

[121] 381 U.S. at 484.

[122] Ibid., pp. 484–85.

[123] For discussion, see Kent Greenawalt, "Dualism and Its Status," *Ethics* 104 (1994): 494–95.

[124] 381 U.S. at 490 (footnote omitted).

[125] 381 U.S. at 493–94.

[126] 410 U.S. at 153.

[127] 431 U.S. 494, 503 (1977) (footnote omitted).

Hardwick, Justice Byron White cited this formulation in ruling that the Due Process clause did not provide a basis for recognizing "a fundamental right [for] homosexuals to engage in sodomy."[128]

Hardwick constituted a sharp break in fundamental rights jurisprudence. Justice Harlan's dissent in *Poe* established fundamental rights jurisprudence on the basis of a progressively evolving libertarian tradition. As new violations of fundamental rights were brought to the attention of the Court, it would take action to preserve the rational continuum of fundamental rights. In *Hardwick*, however, Harlan's approach was used to support a refusal to apply the right of privacy, an established fundamental right, to a new situation. Justice White argued that "[t]he Court is most vulnerable and comes nearest to illegitimacy when it deals with judge-made constitutional law having little or no cognizable roots in the language or design of the Constitution."[129] The Court should therefore offer "great resistance to expand the substantive reach" of the Due Process clause.[130]

The case of *Michael H. v. Gerald D.* further illustrated the consequences of deriving fundamental rights from history and tradition.[131] In *Michael H.*, as in *Moore* and *Hardwick*, Harlan's rational continuum of fundamental rights did not appear in the majority opinion. Justice Antonin Scalia insisted that a fundamental right must be "an interest traditionally protected by our society."[132] The purpose of the substantive due process doctrine "is to prevent future generations from lightly casting aside important traditional values—not to enable this Court to invent new ones."[133] For Scalia, the method of history and tradition consisted largely of an inquiry into whether the common law protected the right in question. The broad sweep of Harlan's appeal to the history and tradition of the nation was now confined to the history of the common law in England and the United States.[134]

The transformation of Harlan's method of history and tradition into a barrier to the recognition of new fundamental rights shows that Harlan's interpretation of the Due Process clause was based on an implicit view of the Court's proper role. Harlan appeared to believe that the Court should always stand ready to remedy the violation of fundamental rights by the states.[135] Justices White and Scalia, by contrast, argued that the Court

---

[128] 478 U.S. 186, 190, 192 (1986).
[129] Ibid., p. 194.
[130] Ibid., p. 195.
[131] 491 U.S. 110 (1989).
[132] Ibid., p. 122 (footnote omitted).
[133] Ibid., p. 122 n. 2.
[134] See ibid., pp. 124–26.
[135] For discussion, see Fried, *Order and Law*, pp. 72–75.

should rarely exercise the power of judicial review to create new fundamental rights. But White and Scalia did not have to offer a new method for
interpreting the Due Process clause because history and tradition could be
construed as a limit on the recognition of new rights.[136]

It is noteworthy, then, that in *Planned Parenthood of Southeastern
Pennsylvania v. Casey*, Justices Sandra Day O'Connor, Anthony Kennedy,
and David Souter adopted Harlan's rational continuum approach instead
of relying on history and tradition to provide the basis for the right to
terminate a pregnancy.[137] Quoting extensively from Harlan's dissent in
Poe, the three justices emphasized that courts have always exercised "reasoned judgment" to decide cases, and that substantive due process cases
were no different.[138] In addition to Harlan's dissent, the three justices
relied on precedents involving individual autonomy and the right of privacy and a moral argument that the liberty protected by the Fourteenth
Amendment must include matters "involving the most intimate and personal choices a person may make in a lifetime, choices central to personal
dignity and autonomy" in order to avoid granting the state the power to
define these "attributes of personhood."[139]

Along with important cases interpreting the Equal Protection clause,
these opinions addressing the proper interpretation of the Due Process
clause created the terrain of the contemporary theoretical debate. That
debate can be divided between those who basically support the approach
taken by Justice Harlan and the three justices in *Casey*, and those who
criticize that position in favor of some form of originalism.

The Fundamental Rights Perspective

Justice Harlan's approach in *Poe* and the *Casey* opinion demonstrate that
we must add to our list of the methods of constitutional interpretation
offered in the first section. The method of reason or reasoned judgment,
as ambiguous as those terms may be, merits a place on the list as an alternative to appeals to a national ethos or tradition.[140] As we shall see, however, it is difficult to keep the two methods separate in practice. We will
examine three approaches to fundamental rights jurisprudence: the

---

[136] See Rebecca L. Brown, "Tradition and Insight," *Yale Law Journal* 103 (1993):
201–2.

[137] 112 S.Ct. 2791, 2805 (1992). For a discussion of this sequence of cases, see Fleming,
"Constructing the Substantive Constitution," pp. 268–73.

[138] *Casey*, 112 S.Ct. at 2806.

[139] Ibid., p. 2807.

[140] In this regard, see the discussion in J. M. Balkin and Sanford Levinson, "Constitutional Grammar," *Texas Law Review* 72 (1994): 1771.

method of history and tradition, the method of reason, and appeals to the common-law tradition of judging. We should keep in mind that our chief purpose is not to support or condemn these methods of interpretation, but to provide a framework in which they can be understood and assessed. The account of American constitutionalism set out in chapter 1 is the most important element of this framework.

As we saw in our examination of the Supreme Court's use of Harlan's appeal to history and tradition in *Poe*, this method of interpretation was given life by Harlan's implicit belief that American constitutionalism embodied a progressive tradition of the Court moving to protect rights when they were threatened by some new form of government activism. As such, the method of looking to the nation's history and tradition to justify fundamental rights is a good example of the influence of a Whig interpretation of history on American constitutionalism. Morally repugnant traditions such as slavery, white supremacy, the extermination of Indian tribes, and so on are ignored in favor of traditions that show American history to be the gradual and inevitable realization of founding principles such as liberty, equality, and the protection of human rights.[141] In order for the method of history and tradition to be persuasive, fundamental rights must be based on traditions that are morally acceptable.

Harlan recognized the need to use tradition selectively when he stated in *Poe* that judges must take into consideration the traditions that played a role in the nation's development, while setting aside those traditions that had been discarded.[142] This means that the primary engine in an argument that uses history and tradition is a normative standard that enables judges to select those traditions that are most relevant. To avoid a circular argument, such a normative standard obviously stands in need of justification on a basis that is independent of the appeal to tradition.

The normative standard that enables justices to ignore unacceptable traditions is usually invisible in substantive due process cases. The justices do not sift carefully through the conflicting traditions in American history to determine which tradition has been dominant. They simply invoke an attractive tradition that seems relevant to the case at hand. Justices do argue, however, over the level of specificity at which a tradition should be described.

This dispute emerged clearly in the *Michael H.* case. Justice Scalia contended that in deciding whether or not to recognize a new fundamental right, the Supreme Court should examine "the most specific level at which a relevant tradition protecting, or denying protection to, the asserted

---

[141] See the criticism of the method of tradition in Ely, *Democracy and Distrust*, pp. 60–63.

[142] *Poe*, 367 U.S. at 542.

right can be identified."[143] Scalia argued that unless the tradition was assessed at a specific level, the Court would usually end up recognizing the right in question, given that if very general traditions such as "protecting family relationships" were invoked in support of the right, evidence of traditional protection would always be produced with ease.[144] In dissent, Justice William Brennan responded that the Court would not have been able to justify the rulings in *Griswold* and other cases if Scalia's standard had been applied.[145]

This debate illustrates that the traditions the Court invokes do not select themselves. Justice Scalia, for example, argued for his version of the method of tradition on the ground that it ensures that society, not the judge, controls the result in the case.[146] This normative standard appeals to a certain conception of judging and the Court's institutional role in the constitutional system. Since such a normative standard can only be justified on the basis of normative reasons, however, we appear to have moved from the method of tradition to the method of reason.

The idea of a method of reason is not well defined but we will regard it here as arguing for the recognition of fundamental rights on the basis of justified first principles. The validity of such an approach obviously depends greatly on how the first principles are derived. There are two main theories, one based on what may be called conventional normative standards (or conventional morality) and the other based on critical normative standards (or abstract theories of morality and politics). The former theory often involves an appeal to a societal value consensus and the latter often appeals to ideas of natural law and natural rights that were current at the time the Constitution was adopted.

Theories that rely on conventional morality or a value consensus to ground fundamental rights are especially popular with judges. Justice Brennan, for example, declares that "[w]hen Justices interpret the Constitution they speak for their community, not for themselves alone. The act of interpretation must be undertaken with full consciousness that it is . . . the community's interpretation that is sought. . . . Justices must render constitutional interpretations that are received as legitimate."[147] The attraction of searching for the value consensus of the national community seems clear enough in these remarks. Such a consensus provides a basis for

---

[143] *Michael H.*, 491 U.S. at 128 n. 6.

[144] Ibid., pp. 127–28 n. 6.

[145] Ibid., pp. 139–40.

[146] Ibid., p. 128 n. 6. For criticism of Scalia's approach, see Tribe and Dorf, *On Reading the Constitution*, pp. 97–117.

[147] William J. Brennan, Jr., "The Constitution of the United States: Contemporary Ratification," in Rakove, ed., *Interpreting the Constitution: The Debate over Original Intent*, p. 25.

arriving at first principles that are widely agreed upon. Decisions based on such principles will presumably not be open to the charge that the judge has used his or her own values to decide the case.[148]

Judith Shklar has called legalism an "ideology of agreement," and this is easy to see in constitutional theories that elaborate a method of reason to derive fundamental rights.[149] Even in theories that are based on a critical morality, there is usually some appeal to values that are widespread in society. Yet the very idea of using societal values to support fundamental rights has been questioned, most notably by Ely. Ely asks how minorities can be protected effectively by values that are founded on the beliefs of the majority.[150] Ely's criticism seems borne out by cases such as *Hardwick*, in which societal prejudice toward homosexuals was used as grounds to deny them the right of privacy. If a statute is generally good evidence as to the content of societal values, it seems unlikely that those same values could be invoked to rule the statute unconstitutional as a violation of fundamental rights.

Ely's criticism is telling, but it is not necessarily decisive. To see why, we must keep in mind the context in which the new fundamental rights jurisprudence arose in the 1960s. One of the most important accomplishments of the Warren Court was the invalidation of state statutes in the South that perpetuated racial segregation. In making such decisions, the Court was not necessarily acting against the wishes of a national majority. As we observed in chapter 3, the nation's federal structure makes it possible for the Court to act in service of majority sentiment even as it upholds the rights of minorities in particular states.

In light of this experience with the Warren Court, the consensus theorists can be understood to be arguing that the Court should strike down state statutes that are out of step with national values. While this may be a plausible position, the nature of the values involved is often somewhat vague. If, for example, a national consensus cannot be summoned in favor of a right to abortion due to the controversial politics of this issue, the focus is shifted, as it was in *Casey*, to a consensus that citizens must be able to protect their personal dignity and autonomy on important life choices. This shift to a higher level of generality suggests that a national value consensus can be summoned in favor of almost any right that a particular groups thinks desirable. It also suggests that this way of approaching the

---

[148] For academic examples of this approach, see Wellington, *Interpreting the Constitution*, pp. 83–94; Brest, "The Misconceived Quest for the Original Understanding," pp. 226–27; Owen M. Fiss, "Foreword: The Forms of Justice," *Harvard Law Review* 93 (1979): 11–17.

[149] See Judith N. Shklar, *Legalism: Law, Morals, and Political Trials* (Cambridge: Harvard University Press, 1986), pp. 88–110.

[150] See Ely, *Democracy and Distrust*, pp. 68–69.

method of reason has the same level of generality difficulty that we saw in the method of tradition. Since the point of looking for an interpretive method under the Due Process clause is to guide (and presumably restrain) judicial decisions, this level of generality problem undermines the credibility of consensus theories.[151]

In contrast to consensus theories, theories that appeal to a critical morality do not have to accept values simply because they are widely held in society. Critical theories provide an independent perspective from which proposals for the recognition of new fundamental rights can be evaluated. At first glance, however, such theories would seem to have little to do with the Constitution. There are many different critical theories of morality and politics, developed in a wide variety of historical, social, and political contexts. The selection of any one theory, no matter how compelling, to illuminate the Constitution seems to be inconsistent with the idea of the Constitution as a rule of law.

On the other hand, those theories that emphasize the importance of basic rights and liberal and republican political principles arguably have a special claim on our attention. In this regard, the famous words of the Declaration of Independence have proven very suggestive for the American constitutional tradition: "We hold these truths to be self-evident: that all men are created equal; that they are endowed, by their Creator, with certain unalienable rights; that among these are life, liberty, and the pursuit of happiness." Following Abraham Lincoln's reflection that the Constitution was meant to fulfill the purposes of the Declaration, it has seemed apparent to many that the Constitution was brought into being to secure the rights of which the Declaration speaks.[152] On this account, every American possesses a set of unalienable rights that preexist the constitutional order and constitute a set of normative standards that may be invoked to judge and improve that order. At the opening of the hearings on the nomination of Judge Robert Bork to the Supreme Court, for example, Joseph Biden, the Chairman of the Senate Judiciary Committee, stated:

> I believe all Americans are born with certain inalienable rights. As a child of God, I believe my rights are not derived from the Constitution. My rights are

---

[151] See the discussion in Tushnet, *Red, White, and Blue*, pp. 133–37.

[152] Lincoln commented that the principle "'Liberty to all'" recognized in the Declaration "was *the* word, '*fitly spoken*' which has proved an 'apple of gold' to us. The *Union* and the *Constitution*, are the *picture* of *silver*, subsequently framed around it. The picture was made, not to *conceal*, or *destroy* the apple; but to *adorn*, and *preserve* it. The *picture* was made *for* the apple—*not* the apple for the picture." Quoted in Walter Berns, *Taking the Constitution Seriously* (New York: Simon and Schuster, 1987), pp. 18–19. For commentary, see ibid., pp. 16–20; Gary Jeffrey Jacobsohn, *Apple of Gold: Constitutionalism in Israel and the United States* (Princeton: Princeton University Press, 1993), pp. 3–4.

not derived from any government. My rights are not de[rived] from any majority. My rights are because I exist. They were given to me and each of my fellow
citizens by our creator and they represent the essence of human dignity.[153]

Since the Declaration of Independence refers also to "the laws of nature and of nature's God," ideas of natural law and natural rights that were
invoked frequently in political debates before and after 1776 appear to
provide an appropriate context for a critical theory capable of providing a
basis for fundamental rights.[154] Accordingly, scholars have searched the
historical record in order to demonstrate several points—that the founding generation believed that there were rights and principles that pre-
existed the establishment of the Constitution, that while some of these
basic rights were protected in the Bill of Rights, others were not, and that
these unenumerated rights could be protected by judicial review.[155] The
appeal of this argument from a legal point of view is that it shows that
contemporary fundamental rights jurisprudence is rooted securely in the
intent of the Framers and English and American precedents. Yet every
aspect of this argument is the subject of serious historical dispute.[156]

While the use of ideas of natural law and natural rights during the
founding period cannot be doubted, we are some distance away from having a secure historical understanding of the context in which such ideas
were offered, their relationship to other ideas, such as that first principles
should be reduced to written form before they can be enforced, and
whether the concept of judicial review was sufficiently far advanced so
that appeals to such ideas by judges of the early republic is relevant to
the contemporary problems presented by substantive due process juris-

[153] Nomination of Robert H. Bork to be Associate Justice of the Supreme Court of the
United States: *Hearings Before the Senate Comm. on the Judiciary*, 100th Cong., 1st Sess. 97
(1987)(opening statement of Chairman Joseph R. Biden, Jr.).

[154] See, e.g., Stephen Macedo, *Liberal Virtues: Citizenship, Virtue, and Community in
Liberal Constitutionalism* (New York: Oxford University Press, 1990), pp. 172–75.

For an original and compelling argument that the Declaration was referring to scientific
principles just as much as universal moral laws, see I. Bernard Cohen, *Science and the Founding Fathers: Science in the Political Thought of Jefferson, Franklin, Adams and Madison* (New
York: W. W. Norton, 1995), pp. 108–21.

[155] See, e.g., Thomas C. Grey, "Origins of the Unwritten Constitution: Fundamental
Law in American Revolutionary Thought," *Stanford Law Review* 30 (1978): 843; Suzanna
Sherry, "The Founders' Unwritten Constitution," *University of Chicago Law Review* 54
(1987): 1127.

[156] See, e.g., Howard Gillman, "Preferred Freedoms: The Progressive Expansion of State
Power and the Rise of Modern Civil Liberties Jurisprudence," *Political Research Quarterly*
47 (1994): 626–32; Philip A. Hamburger, "Natural Rights, Natural Law, and American
Constitutions," *Yale Law Journal* 102 (1993): 907; Helen K. Michael, "The Role of Natural Law in Early American Constitutionalism: Did the Founders Contemplate Judicial Enforcement of 'Unwritten' Individual Rights?" *North Carolina Law Review* 69 (1991): 421;
Powell, "The Political Grammar of Early Constitutional Law," pp. 964–68.

prudence.[157] We previously explored two problems with the use of history by constitutional scholars that are relevant here. As we saw in chapter 3, the modern institution of judicial review did not exist in the late eighteenth century. It is thus difficult to see how the very different judicial practices that existed during the founding period can help justify the substantive due process jurisprudence that began in the 1960s. In addition, the debate suffers from the assumption we noted in the preceding section that there are only two possible answers to the question of the relevance of natural law and natural rights to constitutional law. The possibility that the founding generation may not have needed or been able to reach a collective judgment on this question is usually ignored.[158]

Even if the historical relevance of natural law and natural rights were established, it is not clear how the argument for this method of reason proceeds. Since it is unlikely that eighteenth-century theories of natural law and natural rights support the contemporary right of privacy, it must be shown that such theories can be reproduced in a form acceptable today and that they can generate the fundamental rights protected by the Supreme Court.[159] While there are many contemporary theories of natural law and natural rights, none of them have sufficient acceptance to serve the Court as a public basis for fundamental rights jurisprudence.[160] In addition, while contemporary theories are capable of producing sound arguments for the existence of particular fundamental rights, they tend not to take account of the need to resolve conflicts between rights and the problems involved in the enforcement of rights, matters that are crucial to any system of constitutional law.[161]

---

[157] For examinations by historians of the importance of natural law and natural rights to the founding generation that illustrate the limitations of the contemporary theoretical debate, see John Phillip Reid, *Constitutional History of the American Revolution: The Authority of Rights* (Madison: University of Wisconsin Press, 1986), pp. 87–95; G. Edward White, *The Marshall Court and Cultural Change*, pp. 129–30 n. 190, 674–740; Morton White, *The Philosophy of the American Revolution* (New York: Oxford University Press, 1978); Gordon S. Wood, *The Creation of the American Republic, 1776–1787* (New York: W. W. Norton, 1969), pp. 291–305; Knud Haakonssen, "From Natural Law to the Rights of Man: A European Perspective on American Debates," in Michael J. Lacey and Knud Haakonssen, eds., *A Culture of Rights: The Bill of Rights in Philosophy, Politics, and Law—1791 and 1991* (New York: Cambridge University Press, 1991), p. 19.

[158] For a particularly relevant article on this point, see James Q. Whitman, "Why Did the Revolutionary Lawyers Confuse Custom and Reason?" *University of Chicago Law Review* 58 (1991): 1321.

[159] See the discussion in Powell, "Rules for Originalists," p. 672.

[160] For a helpful collection of recent essays on natural law and natural rights, see Robert P. George, ed., *Natural Law Theory: Contemporary Essays* (New York: Oxford University Press, 1992).

[161] See the discussion in Rex Martin, *A System of Rights* (New York: Oxford University Press, 1993), pp. 124–26.

Another route to justifying the use of critical theories of morality is more direct. It can be argued that certain provisions of the Constitution provide a textual basis for the recognition of fundamental rights. Justice Goldberg's appeal to the Ninth Amendment in *Griswold* has been influential in this respect. The Ninth Amendment provides: "The enumeration in the Constitution, of certain rights, shall not be construed to deny or disparage others retained by the people." Justice Goldberg emphasized that although the Ninth Amendment was not a source of rights, it could be viewed as a textual confirmation that the rights protected in the Bill of Rights did not exhaust the rights retained by the people, rights that could be recognized under the Due Process clause.[162] On this understanding, refusing to protect unenumerated rights under the Due Process clause would operate to "deny or disparage" those rights relative to enumerated rights.[163]

Ronald Dworkin's distinction between abstract political "concepts" and "conceptions" of those concepts has been influential in developing this approach.[164] Dworkin argues that terms in the Fourteenth Amendment such as "liberty" and "equal protection" are most naturally read as referring to the abstract political values of liberty and equality. These general concepts can only be given meaning through competing interpretive conceptions that spell out their implications in detail. Such specific interpretive conceptions will draw on the best contemporary moral and political theories as a matter of course.[165] Although Dworkin has been criticized for not producing evidence that the Framers intended that these clauses be read in this fashion, his argument does not have to be construed as an appeal to history.[166] It can be understood as a textualist argument that when a constitution uses general concepts such as liberty, private prop-

---

[162] See 381 U.S. at 488–93. For scholarly theories that makes the same point, see, e.g., Ely, *Democracy and Distrust*, pp. 34–41; Tribe and Dorf, *On Reading the Constitution*, pp. 54–55, 110–11. For a helpful collection of readings on the Ninth Amendment, see Randy E. Barnett, ed., *The Rights Retained by the People: The History and Meaning of the Ninth Amendment* (Fairfax, Va.: George Mason University Press, 1989).

Some scholars have also argued that the Privileges or Immunities clause of the Fourteenth Amendment provides a textual basis for the recognition of fundamental rights. See, e.g., Ely, *Democracy and Distrust*, pp. 22–30.

[163] This reading of the Ninth Amendment has been disputed on historical grounds. See, e.g., Earl M. Maltz, *Rethinking Constitutional Law* (Lawrence: University Press of Kansas, 1994), pp. 50–55; Thomas B. McAffee, "The Original Meaning of the Ninth Amendment," *Columbia Law Review* 90 (1990): 1215.

[164] See Ronald Dworkin, *Taking Rights Seriously* (Cambridge: Harvard University Press, 1978), pp. 134–37.

[165] Ibid., p. 149.

[166] For examples of this criticism, see Tushnet, *Red, White, and Blue*, pp. 30–31; Stephen R. Munzer and James W. Nickel, "Does the Constitution Mean What it Always Meant?" *Columbia Law Review* 77 (1977): 1037–41.

erty, freedom of speech, and so on, it is best interpreted as referring to the abstract political concepts these terms evoke.[167]

Dworkin is willing to press this argument as far as it will go. Since the concepts of liberty and equality protected by the Fourteenth Amendment "in our political culture are the two major sources of claims of individual rights," it follows that there will never be a need for additional constitutional amendments to protect individual rights that can be based on these concepts.[168] Dworkin accepts the common view, supported by the discussion in chapter 1, that amendment is an impractical means of adapting the Constitution to historical change.[169] Note, however, the consequences of this point of view for the theory of constitutional interpretation. On this understanding, there would be nothing improper in having the Court in effect adopt the rejected Equal Rights Amendment by holding that classifications based on gender deserve strict scrutiny under the Equal Protection clause. This stance dissolves any difference between interpreting and amending the Constitution. The difficulty of amendment thus appears to encourage the conclusion that the terms of the Constitution ought to be read as broadly as possible.

As we noted above in the section on the contemporary theoretical debate, theories that sweep as broadly as Dworkin's in effect challenge the legalized Constitution. To critics of this approach, it seems obvious that the use of contemporary critical theories would be inconsistent with the idea of the Constitution as a rule of law. Such theories have no legal status and, as with contemporary theories of natural law and natural rights, lack the public acceptance necessary for the Supreme Court to legitimately employ them to resolve cases. The Ninth Amendment and the American natural law tradition may direct our attention beyond the Constitution, but this does not resolve the political problem that would be created by the Court's use of contemporary critical theories that are not widely accepted by the public.

It therefore appears that it is hard to elaborate the method of tradition without recourse to contemporary standards and it is hard to justify a method of reason without recourse to values that are widely accepted. While it is thus doubtful that each of the methods can stand on its own, this should not prevent us from seeing that different justices and scholars may be more attracted to one method and, in the process, downplay the method they find less useful to the task at hand.

---

[167] See Dworkin, *Life's Dominion*, pp. 127–28. See also the discussion in David Lyons, "Constitutional Interpretation and Original Meaning," *Social Philosophy and Policy* 4 (1986): 85–88.

[168] Dworkin, *Life's Dominion*, p. 128. For a critique of this point of view, see Monaghan, "Our Perfect Constitution," pp. 356–74.

[169] Dworkin, *Life's Dominion*, p. 145.

The last approach to fundamental rights jurisprudence we will examine appeals to the method of the common law. While Justice Harlan did not have the luxury of relying on a well-developed set of precedents elaborating the content of substantive due process, contemporary theorists, operating more than twenty years after *Roe*, have this advantage. Appeals to common-law adjudication rest not only on the accumulated precedents respecting the right of privacy, but offer an attractive way to combine the methods of tradition and reason in one framework.[170] The idea is that the evolution of substantive due process doctrine can be understood in the same way as the evolution of common-law doctrines. The Supreme Court tends to make decisions one at a time, with due consideration for past precedents, the likely impact of its decisions, and mindful of societal traditions and values. It is not necessary to consider the question of legitimacy each time a new case is brought because legitimacy is provided by the process of adjudication, not by a definitive theoretical statement in one case.

The appeal to common-law adjudication thus buys the Court some relief from charges that its reasoning in the substantive due process cases has been inadequate. If the overall direction the Court takes is sound and the precedents are relatively consistent, the precise reasoning offered matters less. As we noted in the first section of this chapter, however, there is a long-standing dispute over whether common-law forms of reasoning should be applied to constitutional law. There is no counterpart in the common law of the unique political and legal authority of the Constitution. The text of the Constitution and the intent of the Framers stand as independent sources of legitimacy and critique no matter what the Court says. Originalist critics of substantive due process are thus unlikely to be satisfied no matter how many precedents are based on the right of privacy. From an originalist perspective, if the right of privacy is not enumerated in the Constitution or supported by the historical record, there is no basis for judicial recognition of such a right.

The Originalist Perspective

There are a number of different versions of originalism and a number of different ways to construe the possible reach of an originalist theory of interpretation. We criticized several versions of originalism in the preceding sections. To the extent that originalism is presented as the only legitimate general theory of constitutional interpretation, it is vulnerable to the

---

[170] See the sources cited in note 27. See also the helpful essay by Kathleen M. Sullivan, "Law's Labors," *The New Republic*, May 23, 1994, p. 42.

objection that a pluralist theory is a superior descriptive-explanatory and normative alternative for the reasons we presented in the first section. As we noticed in the second section, to the extent that proponents of originalism assume that it does not require a normative justification, they allow a controversial theory to masquerade as the status quo. If originalism is presented as a theory that is based on a simple appeal to historical fact, it is vulnerable to the objection that the processes of lawyering and adjudication are different from the practice of history. Finally, we criticized the division of theories of interpretation into originalist and nonoriginalist camps. We will not revisit these criticisms in this section.[171]

It is therefore important to keep in mind that we review originalism here as one method of constitutional interpretation among others, not as an all-purpose solution to the problems of constitutional interpretation. We will understand originalism as the major theoretical alternative to the jurisprudence of fundamental rights in interpreting the ambiguous clauses of section one of the Fourteenth Amendment. Originalists reject the reasoning of the Supreme Court in some or all of the cases we reviewed at the beginning of this section. They advocate consulting the intent of the Framers of the Fourteenth Amendment instead of the national ethos or tradition to deal with the problems of interpretation presented by these troublesome clauses. Originalist theorists do not agree on what that intent demonstrates; they do, however, usually argue that the doctrine of substantive due process is not grounded in the Framers' intent and that the Equal Protection clause should be given a more restrictive meaning than it has been given by the Court.[172] Once again, our purpose is not to support or condemn this method of interpretation, but to understand it within the context of American constitutionalism.

We saw that Justice Harlan's approach to substantive due process doctrine rested on an implicit view of the Supreme Court's proper role in defending individual rights against the government. Originalism is also animated by such a background view, although it tends to be obscured by the assumption, common to originalist theories, that originalism is the status quo. Central to that view is the idea of the legalized Constitution, of which originalists are the defenders *par excellence*. As Justice Scalia comments, "[T]he Constitution, though it has an effect superior to other laws, is in its nature the sort of 'law' that is the business of the courts—an enactment that has a fixed meaning ascertainable through the usual de-

---

[171] For a useful review of the debate over originalism in the 1980s, see Daniel A. Farber, "The Originalism Debate: A Guide for the Perplexed," *Ohio State Law Journal* 49 (1989): 1085. See also the articles in Rakove, ed., *Interpreting the Constitution: The Debate over Original Intent.*

[172] See, e.g., Bork, *The Tempting of America*, pp. 31–32, 143–60.

vices familiar to those learned in the law."[173] An appeal to the intent of the Framers is, of course, a usual device of legal interpretation. Other elements common to the background view that supports originalism include an appeal to democratic values and a conception of the proper role of judges in constitutional cases. Originalists argue that their view supports democratic values by adhering to the considered judgments of the people embodied in the Constitution, judgments that should not be reversed by the judiciary. Originalists argue also that recourse to the intent of the Framers prevents judges from resorting to their own policy preferences in deciding cases.[174]

The concept of the intent of the Framers can be understood in many different ways. The Framers of the Fourteenth Amendment, for example, could be understood as all members of the Congress that approved the amendment, as only those members who voted in favor of the amendment, as the state legislators who had to ratify the amendment, the public as a whole, or some combination of these groups. The intent of these groups could be understood as a mental state or as the public principles and understandings these groups agreed to in approving the amendment (this is sometimes understood as the difference between subjective and objective intent, respectively). We could include also public understandings of the amendment's meaning that developed soon after it was adopted. We could construe evidence of intent in light of the rules appropriate to assessing legislative history in statutory interpretation or proceed in the manner of historians, immersing ourselves in the thinking and assumptions of the period in order to understand the full context in which the Framers acted.

These different options are often cited by critics of originalism to show the difficulties posed by this method of interpretation.[175] Originalists, however, do not regard these difficulties as insuperable. These options show merely that the idea of the intent of the Framers must be further specified and clarified.[176] While originalists do not agree on how to choose among these options, it must be remembered that the defenders of fundamental rights jurisprudence also do not agree on how to carry out the methods of tradition and reason.

In pursuing the project of specifying an adequate account of originalism, its proponents and critics alike have produced dense webs of increasingly esoteric analysis. Strong originalism has been distinguished from weak originalism, strict intentionalism from moderate intentionalism, in-

---

[173] Antonin Scalia, "Originalism: The Lesser Evil," *University of Cincinnati Law Review* 57 (1989): 854. See also Berger, *Government by Judiciary*, pp. 288–99.

[174] See, e.g., Scalia, "Originalism: The Lesser Evil," pp. 862–64.

[175] See, e.g., Dworkin, *Life's Dominion*, pp. 133–34.

[176] See the discussion in Maltz, *Rethinking Constitutional Law*, pp. 20–36.

terpretive intentions from substantive intentions, and subjective intentionalism from public-understanding originalism.[177] These distinctions have been developed by scholars searching for the most defensible form of originalism, but it is not clear that they have improved our understanding of this method of constitutional interpretation. Originalism, after all, is not a philosophical theory but one method of interpretation among others that judges employ to decide cases. These distinctions are not grounded, as they should be, in the actual practice of the Supreme Court.

The deliberations of the Supreme Court in *Brown* show more clearly the options realistically open to judges regarding the intent of the Framers.[178] The Court had three options with respect to the intentions of the Framers of the Fourteenth Amendment. First, the Court could rely on the specific intent of the Framers regarding the effect of the amendment on segregated schools. Evidence of specific intent seemed to indicate that segregated schools were consistent with the purpose of the amendment. Second, the Court could focus on the more general intent of the Framers, rooted in antebellum abolitionist thought, that all unequal racial classifications should be prohibited by the Constitution. Third, the Court could have reasoned, as it seemed to do in its opinion, that as educational institutions served a fundamentally different purpose in the twentieth century than in the nineteenth, the real question was the counterfactual one of what the Framers would have concluded about the constitutionality of twentieth-century segregated schools.[179]

The third option is especially attractive because it explicitly takes into consideration the reality of historical change and that studying the intent of the Framers may not yield a clear answer due to the different circumstances in which they lived. It is difficult, however, to regard this as a true variation of looking to the intent of the Framers. This option is often described as one of translating the intent of the Framers into the circumstances of the present.[180] But no matter how hard we try to engage in counterfactual speculation about what the Framers would have thought of the present, this does not change the fact that we, not the Framers, are carrying out the translation. While the translation process may maintain

---

[177] See, e.g., Bassham, *Original Intent and the Constitution*, pp. 17–65; Brest, "The Misconceived Quest for the Original Understanding," pp. 222–24.

[178] See the discussion in Mark V. Tushnet, *Making Civil Rights Law: Thurgood Marshall and the Supreme Court, 1936–1961* (New York: Oxford University Press, 1994), pp. 196–216.

[179] See *Brown*, 347 U.S. at 492–93.

[180] For discussion of this option see Brest, "The Misconceived Quest for the Original Understanding," pp. 218–21; Lawrence Lessig, "Fidelity in Translation," *Texas Law Review* 71 (1993): 1165; Lawrence Lessig, "Understanding Changed Readings: Fidelity and Theory," *Stanford Law Review* 47 (1995): 395.

some link with the past, it is driven ultimately by contemporary values in the same manner as the methods of tradition and reason.

This leaves us with the conflict between understanding the intent of the Framers at a specific or a more general level. This conflict, often called the "level of generality" problem, has provoked many scholarly discussions.[181] The problem of what level of generality to use in assessing the intent of the Framers with respect to the Equal Protection clause is similar to the problem of describing the relevant tradition in interpreting the Due Process clause. As we saw above, Justices Scalia and Brennan debated this issue in the *Michael H.* case. One important difference, however, is that the *Michael H.* debate was about how to read precedents, not the intent of the Framers. The possibility of a split between the specific and general intent of the Framers means that the history of the Equal Protection clause and whether *Brown* was a justifiable interpretation of that clause have special importance for originalism. It is generally thought that originalists must show how the intent of the Framers can be reconciled with *Brown* to maintain the credibility of their approach.[182]

The problem of justifying *Brown* is a good example of the lack of agreement among originalists on how to elaborate this method of interpretation. Some originalists believe that there is no reasonable way to justify the decision, given the specific intent of the Framers that segregated schools were constitutional.[183] Other originalists, including former Judge Robert Bork, insist that the intent of the Framers can be construed to support the decision.[184] Bork argues that the general intent of the Framers to foster equality under law should be understood as the "primary goal" of the Equal Protection clause and hence should override any specific intent to allow segregated schools.[185] Bork solves the level of generality problem "by finding the level of generality that interpretation of the words, structure, and history of the Constitution fairly supports."[186]

It is not clear that Bork's suggested solution is an adequate response to the level of generality problem. The problem is created by evidence of a conflict in the various intentions of the Framers with respect to the Fourteenth Amendment. This means that the relevant history supports more than one reasonable interpretation. If this is the case, the problem

---

[181] See, e.g., Bork, *The Tempting of America*, pp. 147–51; Maltz, *Rethinking Constitutional Law*, pp. 22–23; Brest, "The Fundamental Rights Controversy," pp. 1090–92; Dworkin, "The Forum of Principle," pp. 476–500.

[182] See, e.g., Henry Paul Monaghan, "Stare Decisis and Constitutional Adjudication," *Columbia Law Review* 88 (1988): 723.

[183] Ibid., p. 728.

[184] See Bork, *The Tempting of America*, pp. 81–82; Maltz, "Some New Thoughts on an Old Problem," pp. 846–50.

[185] Bork, *The Tempting of America*, p. 82.

[186] Ibid., p. 150.

cannot be wished away by assuming that the evidence points toward only one conclusion.[187] This is what Bork's suggested solution seems to do. The idea that we should find the appropriate level of generality by consulting the history of the Fourteenth Amendment is no help because it is that history that creates the problem in the first place. The problem can be solved only by indicating how following one particular intent best fulfills the goals of originalism. Such an argument may indeed be possible, but it would be based on values that are independent of the intent of the Framers.[188]

The difficulty with Bork's solution is related to one of the standard objections to originalism we mentioned above. As we saw, there are many different ways to construe the idea of the intent of the Framers. While critics think that this poses a problem for originalism, originalists often answer by describing a form of originalism that is specific enough to decide among the various options. The underlying point made by some critics, however, is that any specific form of originalism will be based on the normative reasons supporting that form, not on the intent of the Framers. Originalists can describe a specific form of originalism, but the issue is whether they can justify that choice on originalist grounds. If they cannot, originalism is based ultimately on contemporary moral and political values.[189]

It is important to see that this criticism is not unique to originalism. In substance, this is the same criticism we advanced above against the different ways of elaborating the methods of tradition and reason. We observed that versions of the level of generality problem also pose difficulties for the fundamental rights perspective. Why does this problem plague attempts to interpret the Fourteenth Amendment?

All of the theories just discussed attempt to provide a method of law to cabin the broad sweep of the Due Process and Equal Protection clauses. They are efforts to legalize these clauses and show how they can be doctrinally elaborated in a way that provides meaningful guidance to judges and prevents arbitrary decisions. Each theory, however, is structurally unsound unless contemporary moral and political values are employed to point the way. The theories of interpretation commonly employed in the law do not help because these clauses do not appear to embody conventional legal standards. Indeed, they seem to point beyond the law. Cer-

---

[187] Bork further undermines his solution by refusing to engage in any substantial historical inquiry concerning the intentions of the Framers of the Fourteenth Amendment. See the discussion in ibid., pp. 148–51.

[188] See the discussion in Tribe and Dorf, *On Reading the Constitution*, pp. 79–80.

[189] See the discussion in Ronald Dworkin, "Bork's Jurisprudence," *University of Chicago Law Review* 57 (1990): 657; Lyons, "Constitutional Interpretation and Original Meaning," pp. 77–78.

tainly the Supreme Court's jurisprudence of these clauses, with its constant invocation of the history and tradition of the nation, tends to confirm this.[190]

The account of American constitutionalism advanced in chapter 1 helps us understand why these theories fail unless they reach beyond the law to principles of morality and politics. As our discussion established, there are significant disanalogies between constitutional and ordinary legal standards. Constitutionalism is characterized by the interpenetration of political and legal considerations. Within this terrain, lawyers and judges maneuver to protect the autonomy of the law by maintaining the legalized Constitution. Their attempts to do so are more or less successful depending on the constitutional clause at issue. With extremely general clauses, such as those in the Fourteenth Amendment, the pressure to maintain the legalized Constitution is acute and produces the constant stream of theorizing we have just reviewed.

Our discussion of the fundamental rights and originalist perspectives does not end, then, with the judgment that one perspective is superior to the other. Both perspectives have a place on the constitutional terrain as efforts to preserve the legalized Constitution. Both appeal ultimately to background views rooted in constitutional history as well as different sets of moral and political values, but the conflict between them is not reducible to these. As long as the legalized Constitution retains meaning for American lawyers and judges there will be room for both perspectives and their contest of arguments.

Republicanism and Constitutional Philosophy

The theories of interpretation we have examined work by applying a method of legal interpretation from other areas of the law to constitutional law. There is, however, another important way to understand the Constitution that has influenced constitutional scholarship. One might construct a constitutional philosophy out of the materials provided by the intellectual history of the American Revolution and the Constitution and weave these materials together with relevant contemporary theories of philosophy, politics, and jurisprudence. The idea is to provide an overarching scheme to justify the Constitution in a normative sense, understand its basic purposes, and guide interpretation of the text.[191]

---

[190] For discussions of the role of values and value choices in constitutional law, see Tribe and Dorf, *On Reading the Constitution*, pp. 65–80; Erwin Chemerinsky, "Foreword: The Vanishing Constitution," *Harvard Law Review* 103 (1989): 89–96.

[191] David Richards is probably the foremost contemporary exponent of this way of understanding the Constitution. See David A. J. Richards, *Toleration and the Constitution* (New

Such constitutional philosophies have not been very influential with lawyers and judges because they appear to approach the Constitution from a nonlegal perspective. Those who work with the legalized Constitution are usually wary of theories that seem excessively abstract and freighted with political and ideological considerations.[192] Nevertheless, overarching constitutional philosophies have their place in the American constitutional tradition. They reflect the ability of the Constitution to inspire inquiry into the ultimate purposes of the American constitutional order and how those purposes should guide our response to contemporary constitutional issues. Lincoln's Gettysburg Address is a good example of the high order of political reflection the American constitutional tradition can inspire.[193]

The most significant constitutional philosophy in recent American constitutional theory has been some form of republicanism. Republicanism has had a wide influence among scholars of history, politics, and law as a master concept for understanding the American Revolution and the political order established by the Constitution. According to this republican understanding, the purpose of the Constitution was not to establish a liberal order of self-seeking market opportunists, but to found a dignified republic of statesmen along the lines suggested by the political orders of classical antiquity.[194] Historians have debated whether eighteenth-century republicanism constituted a real alternative to the liberal political order that eventually took hold in the nineteenth century, the extent to which republicanism survived the founding generation, and the influence of republican ideology as an alternative to market capitalism.[195]

While these historical debates are quite intricate, our interest is the

---

York: Oxford University Press, 1986); id., *Foundations of American Constitutionalism* (New York: Oxford University Press, 1989); and id., *Conscience and the Constitution: History, Theory, and Law of the Reconstruction Amendments* (Princeton: Princeton University Press, 1993).

[192] For relevant discussion, see Douglas Lind, "Constitutional Adjudication as a Craft-Bound Excellence," *Yale Journal of Law and the Humanities* 6 (1994): 369–92; Cass R. Sunstein, "Incompletely Theorized Agreements," *Harvard Law Review* 108 (1995): 1752–53.

[193] See Garry Wills, *Lincoln at Gettysburg: The Words That Remade America* (New York: Simon and Schuster, 1992). For criticism of Wills's reading of the Gettysburg Address and an alternative reading, see Phillip Shaw Paludan, *The Presidency of Abraham Lincoln* (Lawrence: University Press of Kansas, 1994), pp. 228–30.

[194] For a discussion of republicanism in the eighteenth century, see Gordon S. Wood, *The Radicalism of the American Revolution* (New York: Alfred A. Knopf, 1992), pp. 95–109.

[195] See the interesting discussion in Daniel T. Rodgers, "Republicanism: The Career of a Concept," *Journal of American History* 79 (1992): 11. For a comprehensive discussion, see Paul A. Rahe, *Republics Ancient and Modern: Classical Republicanism and the American Revolution* (Chapel Hill: University of North Carolina Press, 1992).

strong influence republicanism has had on contemporary constitutional theory. Advocates of republicanism have recommended it as a constitutional philosophy that has a meaningful link with the thought of the founding generation, especially as expressed in *The Federalist*, yet can be elaborated in a way that is consistent with contemporary political theory. The version of republicanism proposed by constitutional scholars calls for a commitment to deliberative government and the common good, reflects a belief in public values that can be rationally ascertained and debated, and sets itself against theories that understand American politics in terms of bargaining among pluralistic interest groups.[196]

This last aspect of contemporary republicanism is especially interesting, because it suggests some of the forces driving legal scholars to represent their constitutional philosophy as republican rather than liberal. As advocated by these scholars, republicanism is in fact a form of contemporary liberalism.[197] John Rawls's well-known liberal theory of justice, for example, is compatible with most of the normative commitments of scholars who advocate republicanism.[198] Rawls's insistence that the common good can be represented through the conditions on argument that make up his original position is particularly suggestive for republican theorists.[199]

The turn of constitutional scholars toward republicanism is driven more by developments in contemporary legal theory than by any animus against liberalism. Because of the prominence of the debate between the libertarian and skeptical form of liberalism represented by the law and economics movement and the egalitarian politics represented by the critical legal studies movement, forms of liberalism that are alternatives to both movements tend to be ignored. On the other hand, both movements cannot dismiss republicanism so easily, at least in the constitutional context, since this appears to involve repudiating a key element of the philosophy of the founding generation. Accordingly, constitutional scholars who want to distance themselves from both movements have been attracted by the promise of republicanism as a third alternative.

Contemporary liberal republicanism is valuable in that it reminds us that there are forms of liberalism that are compatible in a broad sense with some aspects of the thought of the founding generation. To set aside

---

[196] See, e.g., Sunstein, *The Partial Constitution*, pp. 18–24; Frank I. Michelman, "Foreword: Traces of Self-Government," *Harvard Law Review* 100 (1986): 4; Frank I. Michelman, "Law's Republic," *Yale Law Journal* 97 (1988): 1493; Cass R. Sunstein, "Beyond the Republican Revival," *Yale Law Journal* 97 (1988): 1539.

[197] Cass Sunstein, a leading theorist of contemporary republicanism, in fact refers to the theory as "liberal republicanism." Sunstein, "Beyond the Republican Revival," p. 1541.

[198] See John Rawls, *A Theory of Justice* (Cambridge: Harvard University Press, 1971); John Rawls, *Political Liberalism* (New York: Columbia University Press, 1993).

[199] See Sunstein, "Beyond the Republican Revival," p. 1567.

the danger of anachronism for a moment, the founding generation appeared to believe strongly in objective, impartial moral and political values, deliberation and dialogue as methods of governance, and opposed efforts to see politics solely as a matter of self-interest and the dispiriting clash of powerful private interests. All of these commitments remain attractive today and remind us that the constitutional order was not fashioned against a twentieth-century background of pluralist politics. Whether these original commitments have survived the erosive force of constitutional change is a difficulty that republican theorists have perhaps not yet faced.

Six

Constitutional Crisis and Reform

WATERGATE was not mentioned at Richard Nixon's funeral.[1] At Nixon's death, President Bill Clinton urged Americans to remember the former president as "a statesman who sought to build a lasting structure of peace."[2] Although Nixon was the only president ever to have resigned his office in disgrace, the significance of Watergate was obscured in the commentary that followed his death. Members of the legal community saw Watergate as a permanent stain on Nixon's presidency, while many members of the foreign policy community tended to downplay its significance.[3]

Watergate has been called "the nation's most sustained political conflict and severest constitutional crisis since the Great Depression," but Nixon's death showed that its significance remains unclear for many Americans.[4] Was it the defining event of Nixon's presidency or a scandal of minor importance? Was it a severe but isolated crisis produced by the particular circumstances of Nixon's presidency or part of a larger constitutional drama?

One reason Americans may have difficulty coming to grips with constitutional crises is that they challenge the widely held notion that the Constitution is without significant flaws. If Watergate was a product of Nixon's personality, then the troubling thought that it revealed long-standing structural weaknesses in American constitutionalism may be avoided. To see American constitutionalism whole, however, we must consider the idea that periods of constitutional crisis and reform are just as much a part of the constitutional story as periods of relative stability. To judge by the quantity of scholarly commentary, for example, *Roe v. Wade* was a far more important constitutional event than Watergate.[5] Yet the

---

[1] See Maureen Dowd, "Nixon Buried on Note of Praise and Reconciliation," *New York Times*, April 28, 1994, p. A21.

[2] "Text of President Clinton's Statement on Nixon's Death," *New York Times*, April 23, 1994, p. 13.

[3] See B. Drummond Ayres Jr., "In Death as in Life, Nixon Provokes Strong Passions," *New York Times*, April 23, 1994, p. 13; William E. Schmidt, "Nixon's Darkest Chapter, By Those Who Lived It," *New York Times*, April 26, 1994, p. B9.

[4] Stanley I. Kutler, *The Wars of Watergate* (New York: Alfred A. Knopf, 1990), p. 9.

[5] See *Roe v. Wade*, 410 U.S. 113 (1973).

scholarly attention paid to *Roe* is more a sign of how constitutional theory has been traditionally conceived than it is an accurate measure of Watergate's importance for American constitutionalism.

In this chapter we will concentrate on the contemporary constitutional scene and consider the theoretical questions raised by periods of constitutional crisis and reform. We will attempt first to define the idea of a constitutional crisis and assess the evidence that crises have occurred repeatedly in the post–New Deal period. Next we will consider the questions raised by recent proposals for constitutional reform such as term limits and the balanced budget amendment. The final section offers some concluding reflections on the themes of this book and the future of American constitutionalism.

While the questions considered in this chapter have been relatively neglected by constitutional theorists, they are of first importance for understanding American constitutionalism. As the United States moves into its third century under the Constitution, it is arguable that the most important and pressing constitutional issues have very little to do with the constitutional doctrines developed by the Supreme Court and everything to do with the challenges posed by events such as Watergate.

Constitutional Crisis

While it is relatively easy to identify periods of American history that have been called constitutional crises, the idea of a constitutional crisis is not well defined. Certainly the secession crisis leading to the Civil War and the conflict between President Andrew Johnson and the Republican Congress during Reconstruction qualify. We might also add the conflict between President Roosevelt and the Supreme Court in 1937, as well as Watergate and perhaps the Iran-Contra affair in the Reagan Administration. Perhaps some constitutional scholars might argue for the inclusion of the period of massive resistance to desegregation in the South that culminated in the defiance of federal court orders by Arkansas Governor Orval Faubus and the subsequent use of federal troops by President Eisenhower.[6] The question is whether there are any similarities among these periods that would give us insight into the nature of constitutional crises generally.

In these periods, the branches of the national government and the different layers of the federal government find themselves at odds over issues that raise fundamental constitutional questions and that resist solution

---

[6] See, e.g., Tony Freyer, *The Little Rock Crisis: A Constitutional Interpretation* (Westport, Conn.: Greenwood Press, 1984).

through ordinary political and legal means.[7] As we saw in chapter 2, for example, the secession crisis was preceded by many abortive efforts at compromise. Once ordinary political mechanisms break down, the situation moves to a plane of uncertainty that may be appropriately called a constitutional crisis. The participants perceive a crisis because familiar political and legal markers disappear or are ineffective. In such crises, there are usually key periods in which matters are brought to a head and decisive action is taken, such as the firing on Fort Sumter in April 1861.

We will explore the idea of a constitutional crisis by returning to the discussion of American political development begun in chapter 2 and examining the circumstances that produced the uneasy politics of the 1990s and the current round of calls for constitutional reform.

The Contemporary Constitutional System in Crisis

The designation of constitutional crisis may be appropriate also in situations when the apparently normal operation of the constitutional system produces a continual sense of political uncertainty and unease. In such a situation, matters do not necessarily reach a decisive moment, but there are indications throughout the constitutional system that something is fundamentally wrong with the way the system is operating as a whole. We will examine the validity of this suggestion by investigating the relationship of the Constitution and American political development in the post–New Deal era.

There is an intuitive case to be made that the constitutional system should have experienced increasing difficulty after the advent of the activist national state. The Constitution was not written in the context of activist government. To the contrary, it was designed in an age when the activities of the national government were quite limited. As the national government took on substantial responsibilities in the twentieth century, there was an increasing likelihood that there would be a mismatch between the institutions designed by the Constitution and the new requirements of governing. One might expect a crisis to develop as the constitutional system attempted to adjust to these new circumstances.

The story of the constitutional system since the New Deal can be understood in this light. The national government's assumption of responsibility for regulating the economy during the New Deal had pro-

---

[7] See the suggestive discussion in Arthur Bestor, "The American Civil War as a Constitutional Crisis," in Lawrence M. Friedman and Harry N. Scheiber, eds., *American Law and the Constitutional Order: Historical Perspectives* (Cambridge: Harvard University Press, 1978), p. 220.

found implications for American politics. The activism of the government encouraged citizens to look routinely to national politics for solutions to social problems.[8] Once the constitutional and attitudinal barriers to the expansion of the national political agenda were removed, there were no limits on the range of issues the national state might consider.

This meant that political issues that had previously been considered state and local matters would have to be confronted by the national state. More generally, issues that had been mediated within civil society would now be projected into the national political arena. This made it easier for the political interests of civil society to shape the structure of the national state. This process moved the national state from being democratic in form to having to accommodate a full-fledged national democratic politics for the first time in American history.

The turbulent politics of the Populist-Progressive eras, the ethno-cultural tensions of the 1920s, and the class divisions sharpened by the Great Depression suggested that a national democratic politics would be far from harmonious. Yet the full implications of the new national politics were initially concealed by the exigencies of the Depression and the political consensus necessary to fight World War II. A bipartisan consensus in foreign policy continued after the war given the widely perceived threat of international communism. A significant degree of consensus also appeared to exist in domestic politics during the 1950s, as the political issues introduced by the New Deal continued to dominate the national agenda.[9]

The turmoil in American politics after the 1950s and the contentious politics of European democracies during the twentieth century suggests, however, that there is no such thing as a democratic politics of consensus as a normal state of affairs. Thus when a consensus exists on a wide range of policy issues in a democracy, it is reasonable to infer that it is being maintained by an unusual external threat (such as during a war), or is the result of a constricted political agenda produced by economic, social, or legal restrictions on the political activity of citizens. The Cold War produced a bipartisan consensus in foreign affairs because an external threat was perceived clearly by elites and the public. It also had an important effect in limiting the further extension of the New Deal domestic policy agenda, as unions and other liberal organizations were forced on the defensive during the virulent anticommunist period of the late 1940s

---

[8] See, e.g., Barry D. Karl, *The Uneasy State: The United States from 1915 to 1945* (Chicago: University of Chicago Press, 1983), pp. 226–27; Sidney M. Milkis, *The President and the Parties: The Transformation of the American Party System since the New Deal* (New York: Oxford University Press, 1993), p. 150.

[9] See William H. Chafe, *Unfinished Journey: America Since World War II* (New York: Oxford University Press, 1986), p. 185.

and 1950s.[10] In addition, the restrictions on the electorate enacted in the Populist-Progressive eras remained in force.[11] All of these circumstances maintained the World War II consensus long after the fighting had ended.

In the 1960s the politicization of civil society increased rapidly, the legal restrictions on the electorate were for the most part abolished, and the United States experienced a full-fledged national democratic politics for the first time in its history. The bipartisan consensus in foreign policy permanently cracked under the strain of fighting a war that the U.S. could not win.[12] The civil rights movement was instrumental in democratizing American politics and encouraging a wide range of social groups to mobilize and seek political solutions to their problems.[13] The reach of civil society into the national state was extended greatly, as more organizations began to lobby Washington.[14]

By the early 1970s, all the issues that now occupy national politics were present in some form. The politicization of civil society and the democratization of the state had enormously expanded the scope of the national policy agenda.[15] The range of interests the national state now had to take into account approximated much more closely the range of interests in society. But there had been no fundamental change in the ability of the national state to wield public authority and govern these contending interests. The consequence of this mismatch between the demands of various interest groups and an inadequate state structure, exacerbated by the breakdown of consensus in foreign policy, was a constitutional crisis.

The basic difficulty was the sudden appearance of a contentious national democratic politics in a wartime situation. From a traditional point of view, wartime demands a patriotic consensus, as any dissent might undermine the war effort. But the Vietnam War was far more ambiguous in its implications for political dissent. President Lyndon Johnson decided deliberately not to mobilize the nation for war. Moreover, the restraints on politics that were operative in the anticommunist period of the early 1950s no longer existed. In the absence of consensus on the war, it could be criticized in the same way as any other controversial government pol-

[10] Ibid., p. 79.

[11] See Earl Black and Merle Black, *Politics and Society in the South* (Cambridge: Harvard University Press, 1987), p. 112.

[12] See Allen J. Matusow, *The Unraveling of America: A History of Liberalism in the 1960s* (New York: Harper and Row, 1984), pp. 376–77.

[13] See Eddie N. Williams and Milton D. Morris, "Is the Electoral Process Stacked against Minorities?" in A. James Reichley, ed., *Elections American Style* (Washington, D.C.: Brookings Institution, 1987), p. 137.

[14] See Kay Lehman Schlozman and John T. Tierney, *Organized Interests and American Democracy* (New York: Harper and Row, 1986), p. 387.

[15] See Barbara Sinclair, *The Transformation of the U.S. Senate* (Baltimore: Johns Hopkins University Press, 1989), pp. 54–57.

icy. Such criticism, however, then put in question the makeshift constitutional arrangements of the post–New Deal period by casting doubt on the
legitimacy of the extraordinary power of the president in foreign affairs.[16]

Another important cause of the crisis was the way the new democratic
politics was expressed. The existing political parties were unable to chan-
nel the demands of the new groups and so elections could not play an
important role in settling conflicts with established groups and institutions. The new politics was one of social movements and protest rather
than of political parties and peaceful elections. The consequence was a
dramatic increase in political violence and a series of breakdowns in public
order.[17] Political scientist Theodore Lowi notes that from 1965 to the end
of 1968, "there were 179 federal interventions using 184,133 federal
troops, to combat racial disorders and civil rights demonstrations, menac-
ing strikes, neighborhood riots, student marches, and the like."[18]

From the traditional wartime consensus perspective held by Presidents
Johnson and Nixon, any significant political protest undermined their authority to prosecute the war, whether it was aimed directly at the war or
not. The tensions inherent to a wartime situation were exacerbated in the
Nixon administration because of the division in party control between the
presidency and the Congress. Nixon was the first president in the twentieth century to face an opposition Congress in his first term in office.[19]
Without even the weak parties to bridge the gaps between the branches,
the separation of institutions mandated by the Constitution and the conflicting objectives of the parties began to rip the national policymaking
process apart. President Nixon's sweeping plan to reorganize the executive branch, the unprecedented scale of his impoundment of funds authorized by Congress, and the failed Supreme Court nominations of
Judges Haynsworth and Carswell, the first nominations rejected by the
Senate since 1930, were all examples of the increased conflict produced by
divided government.[20]

The constitutional crisis of Watergate resulted when Nixon began to
conduct the kind of surveillance operations normally carried out by the
intelligence agencies from inside the White House. The wiretapping and
illegal break-ins carried out by such groups as the Special Investigative
Unit (the "Plumbers") were justified by Nixon and his aides on the

---

[16] See the discussion in Michael Foley, *The Silence of Constitutions* (London: Routledge, 1989), pp. 40–42.

[17] See G. Bingham Powell, Jr., *Contemporary Democracies: Participation, Stability, and Violence* (Cambridge: Harvard University Press, 1982), pp. 22, 130–31.

[18] Theodore J. Lowi, *The End of Liberalism*, 2d ed. (New York: W. W. Norton, 1979), p. 114.

[19] See Kutler, *The Wars of Watergate*, pp. 126–27.

[20] Ibid., pp. 133–54.

ground that they were legitimate wartime responses to acts of domestic subversion. By this logic, the effort by the FBI to investigate the June 1972 Watergate arrests could be obstructed by the CIA on grounds of national security, given the need to preserve secrecy in carrying out intelligence operations. Congressional efforts to probe the White House activities behind the arrests were naturally seen as politically motivated attempts to undermine an opposition administration.[21]

From the summer of 1973 until Nixon's resignation in August 1974, the national policymaking process was frozen, as Nixon lost the capacity to govern.[22] The near impeachment and conviction of President Nixon marked the symbolic end of the permanent wartime presidency. While a newly assertive Congress did not gain parity with the president in foreign affairs, presidents accustomed to the power held during the Cold War found even ineffective restraints such as the War Powers Resolution to be unacceptable.[23]

Perhaps Watergate's most troubling legacy was its contribution to the massive loss of public confidence in government, a problem that remains serious today.[24] As the politicization of society increased and the wartime consensus began to break down during the mid-1960s, the American public grew increasingly alienated from politics. From 1964 onward, many citizens ceased believing that they had the power to influence politics and stopped trusting the government. Although Watergate undoubtedly contributed to this trend, it was a broad reaction to the state of national politics and government and continued into the 1980s.[25]

Survey research suggests that a significant proportion of the American public was unprepared for a full-fledged democratic politics. Most of the public was satisfied with political institutions during the period of artificial consensus after World War II. True to its Progressive heritage, the public disliked social and political conflict of any kind. Since democratic politics in a diverse society inevitably involves conflict, the politicization of society and increase in the scope of the national policy agenda in the 1960s led to a permanent increase in the level of conflict in American politics. Without any institutions to mediate this change, the public grew disillusioned with politics and government.[26]

[21] Ibid., pp. 79, 101, 218, 227–35.

[22] Ibid., pp. 260–62, 307–11, 335–38, 380.

[23] Ibid., pp. 601–2.

[24] See generally Alan I. Abramovitz, "The United States: Political Culture under Stress," in Gabriel Almond and Sidney Verba, eds., *The Civic Culture Revisited* (Boston: Little, Brown, 1980), p. 177; James L. Sundquist, "The Crisis of Competence in Our National Government," *Political Science Quarterly* 95 (1980): 183.

[25] See Seymour Martin Lipset and William Schneider, *The Confidence Gap* (Baltimore: Johns Hopkins University Press, 1987), pp. 3, 18, 419, 425.

[26] Ibid., pp. 368, 404–5.

The decline of confidence in government and increase in alienation had a direct influence on policymaking in the American state after the mid-1970s by contributing to an unwillingness on the part of voters to support increased taxes.[27] In many ways, a fiscal crisis has served as a stand-in for a crisis of legitimacy. Distrust in government contributed to support for such tax revolt measures as California's Proposition 13 in 1978. Such fiscal limits enabled voters to affect an unresponsive policymaking process that appeared to be dominated by interest groups.[28] Voter reluctance to support increased taxes continues to contribute to the inability of the federal government to make significant progress on reducing the federal budget deficit.[29]

Watergate was thus not an isolated constitutional incident, but one of a series of events that showed the constitutional system to be in increasing difficulty in the post–New Deal period. We analyzed some of the structural background of these events in chapter 2. The need to wage war and combat communism effectively created the need for continuous presidential leadership in foreign policy. In addition, the president controlled new institutions such as the National Security Council and the Central Intelligence Agency that gave him increased control over the means by which policies were carried out. Congress and the Supreme Court tended to defer to the president in matters of foreign policy. Nevertheless, the constitutional system of separated institutions sharing power remained. The president could not always obtain what he wanted from Congress yet, from his perspective, he had been elected as national leader invested with the power to make decisions for the United States as a whole.[30] This conflict between unchanged constitutional institutions and the political and policy demands on the president created the circumstances for Watergate and the subsequent Iran-Contra affair in the Reagan Administration.[31]

It is important to understand that these constitutional problems cannot be solved simply by exhorting Congress and the Supreme Court to assert themselves and play a meaningful role in checking presidential power. Such exhortations were heard increasingly from constitutional scholars after Watergate, often in analyses of the expansion of specific presidential powers, such as the war power.[32] Unless the structural origins of these

[27] Ibid., pp. 342, 349–50.

[28] See John J. Kirlin, *The Political Economy of Fiscal Limits* (Lexington, Mass.: Lexington Books, 1982), pp. 30–33.

[29] See Rudolph G. Penner and Alan J. Abramson, *Broken Purse Strings: Congressional Budgeting 1974 to 1988* (Washington, D.C.: Urban Institute Press, 1988), p. 64.

[30] See Milkis, *The President and the Parties*, p. 211.

[31] See the constitutional analysis of Iran-Contra in Theodore Draper, *A Very Thin Line: The Iran-Contra Affairs* (New York: Hill and Wang, 1991), pp. 478–598.

[32] See, e.g., Michael J. Glennon, *Constitutional Diplomacy* (Princeton: Princeton University Press, 1990), pp. 285–86.

problems are confronted, however, these exhortations are beside the point. The structure of power and decisionmaking in Congress as it is presently organized make it impossible for all practical purposes for the legislative branch to assume a truly coequal role in foreign policy. The constitutional separation of institutions is in inherent conflict with the practical requirement that the United States speak with a single voice in foreign policy. It is therefore likely that crises such as Watergate and Iran-Contra will continue to recur as long as the underlying constitutional problems go unaddressed.

The other salient aspect of the post–New Deal constitutional crisis is the long-term trend toward increased distrust of politicians and government. This trend has become an increasingly important factor in national politics, one that apparently exists independently of dissatisfaction with the government's performance on policy issues. Signs of increasing dissatisfaction toward national politics and institutions became evident in the wake of a number of disillusioning events in the late 1980s and early 1990s—the Iran-Contra affair, the savings and loan scandals, President George Bush's reversal on his campaign pledge not to raise taxes in the 1990 budget negotiations, the House of Representatives bank scandal, and the Senate's bungling of Anita Hill's charges against Judge Clarence Thomas. A sense of alienation and distrust of governing institutions was likely responsible for Ross Perot's surprisingly strong showing in the 1992 presidential election.[33]

The emergence of a significant group of citizens who are profoundly alienated from politics and government and feel powerless to affect ostensibly democratic institutions is the most disturbing aspect of the contemporary constitutional system. Widespread distrust, alienation, and

[33] See the series "The Trouble With Politics" in the *New York Times.* Michael Oreskes, "America's Politics Loses Way as Its Vision Changes World," *New York Times,* March 18, 1990, p. 1; Robin Toner, "'Wars' Wound Candidates and the Process," *New York Times,* March 19, 1990, p. A1; Richard L. Berke, "An Edge for Incumbents: Loopholes That Pay Off," *New York Times,* March 20, 1990, p. A1; Michael Oreskes and Robin Toner, "Swamp of Political Abuse Spurs a New Constituency, for Change," *New York Times,* March 21, 1990, p. A1.

On the 1990 budget negotiations and congressional elections, see Jane Gross, "Voters Feel Electoral Process Has Failed," *New York Times,* November 7, 1990, p. A16; Roberto Suro, "Viewing Chaos in the Capital, Americans Express Outrage," *New York Times,* October 19, 1990, p. A1.

On the situation before and after the 1992 and 1994 national elections, see Dan Balz and Richard Morin, "A Tide of Pessimism and Political Powerlessness Rises," *Washington Post,* November 3, 1991, p. A1; Adam Clymer, "Citing Rise in Frustration, Dozens of Lawmakers Quit," *New York Times,* April 5, 1992, p. 1; Janet Hook, "Voters' Hostility Is Shaping The Business of Congress," *Congressional Quarterly,* April 2, 1994, p. 785; Isabel Wilkerson, "Paradox of '94: Gloomy Voters in Good Times," *New York Times,* October 31, 1994, p. A1; Katharine Q. Seelye, "Voters Disgusted with Politicians as Election Nears," *New York Times,* November 3, 1994, p. A1.

hostility toward government are not healthy for any constitutional order. Such attitudes are by no means part of the historic skepticism toward government that many Americans have always had. They are of a different order and potentially place the entire constitutional system at risk.[34] Since such attitudes originated in the 1960s and have outlasted any specific event or issue, it seems appropriate to speculate that there may be a deep mismatch between the expectations many Americans have about politics and the ability of a fractious, newly democratic system to satisfy those expectations.

The increasing dissatisfaction with government has generated an impetus for many different kinds of constitutional reform, including constitutional amendments. Although governing elites have advanced their own suggestions for improving the constitutional system, it is noteworthy, as we shall see in the next section, that the proposals that are receiving the most attention have a popular base and are generally criticized by scholars and public officials.

Constitutional Reform

Well-meaning, closely argued, and ineffectual proposals for fundamental constitutional reform have been part of the American constitutional tradition for at least a century.[35] The 1980s saw the formation of the Committee on the Constitutional System, a group composed of members of Congress and former government officials concerned that constitutional deficiencies at least partially contributed to the policy difficulties experienced in the preceding two decades.[36] On the other hand, distinguished groups of lawyers, judges, and academics gathered by the American Academy of Political and Social Science in 1976 and the American Assembly in 1987 concluded that despite the vast changes of the twentieth century and the numerous problems of governance facing the United States, no changes in the Constitution were necessary or wise.[37]

[34] See the discussion in Garry Wills, "The New Revolutionaries," *New York Review of Books*, August 10, 1995, p. 50.

[35] See the valuable study by John R. Vile, *Rewriting the United States Constitution: An Examination of Proposals from Reconstruction to the Present* (New York: Praeger Publishers, 1991).

[36] See Donald L. Robinson, ed., *Reforming American Government: The Bicentennial Papers of the Committee on the Constitutional System* (Boulder: Westview Press, 1985).

[37] See Herbert Wechsler, "Reflections on the Conference," in *The Revolution, the Constitution, and America's Third Century: The Bicentennial Conference on the United States Constitution, Conference Discussions* (Philadelphia: University of Pennsylvania Press, 1980), pp. 451, 458; "Final Report of the Seventy-third American Assembly," in Burke Marshall, ed., *A Workable Government? The Constitution After 200 Years* (New York: W. W. Norton, 1987), pp. 235–36.

The proposals by the Committee on the Constitutional System generally followed the time-honored tradition of criticizing the desirability of
the separation of powers and advocating constitutional amendments, such
as to allow members of Congress to serve in the president's Cabinet, that
would enable our system to obtain some of the advantages of the British
parliamentary system.[38] There are two main arguments that usually drive
such critiques. It is argued that the separation of powers, especially when
combined with divided government (where the executive and legislative
branches are controlled by rival political parties), make it too difficult to
address serious policy problems in a meaningful way. It is argued also that
the separation of powers diffuses governmental responsibility for policy in
a way that makes it difficult for citizens to hold public officials accountable
for their actions. This undermines the democratic character of the constitutional system by reducing the importance of elections and in turn dis-
couraging citizen participation in politics.[39]

Since the scholars who advance these critiques often turn to the British
parliamentary system for inspiration on how to solve the problems of
American government, the discussion often moves quickly to a debate of
the merits of that system. It should be noted, however, that the validity of
the critique of the separation of powers (really the separation of governing
institutions) is not dependent on the viability of any particular solution. In
any case, very few proponents of fundamental constitutional change advocate the wholesale adoption of a parliamentary form of government. The
idea is to improve the ability of the government to solve policy problems
and to promote accountability by adopting particular elements of parliamentary government. Taken literally, the idea of adopting another form
of government is absurd. A different form of government such as the British parliamentary system is not merely a means to an end but expresses an
entirely different conception of the relationships among politics, society,
the economy, and the state. The relevant question is whether a given reform inspired by the parliamentary system would fit well into the American constitutional order.[40]

---

[38] See generally Robinson, ed., *Reforming American Government*. See also Vile, *Rewriting the United States Constitution*, pp. 129–34, 157–58.

[39] See, e.g., Lloyd N. Cutler, "To Form a Government," in Robinson, ed., *Reforming
American Government*, p. 11. There is an extensive literature examining the causes and
consequences of divided government. See, e.g., Morris P. Fiorina, *Divided Government*
(New York: Macmillan, 1992); Charles O. Jones, *The Presidency in a Separated System*
(Washington, D.C.: Brookings Institution, 1994); David R. Mayhew, *Divided We Govern:
Party Control, Lawmaking, and Investigations, 1946–1990* (New Haven: Yale University
Press, 1991); Gary W. Cox and Samuel Kernell, eds., *The Politics of Divided Government*
(Boulder: Westview Press, 1991).

[40] For an excellent review of recent proposals for constitutional reform, see James L.
Sundquist, *Constitutional Reform and Effective Government* (Washington, D.C.: Brook-

A general problem with proposals for fundamental constitutional reform is that the justification for change rarely matches the significance of the change advocated. American government is said not to be working well, or to be ineffective and gridlocked in addressing important national policy issues, but these concepts are seldom defined clearly. The proposals often seem to assume that ordinary politics does not apply to reform issues. But any proposal for reform will be evaluated against the background of the current constellation of policy problems, interest groups, relationships between the Democratic and Republican parties, the executive and legislative branches, and so on. As we noticed in chapter 1, passing any constitutional amendment requires an extraordinary degree of national consensus. Proposals for reform must somehow help solve important policy problems over which the major parties probably bitterly disagree while obtaining bipartisan support. It is difficult to see how this can happen simultaneously.

The kind of proposals just discussed are typically advanced by elite groups of academics and public officials. While they are advanced with some persuasive force, they appear to have no resonance with the general public. The proposals for constitutional reform that are presently receiving the most attention—term limits on elected officials and the balanced budget amendment—have been criticized severely by many scholars. Nevertheless they are among the leading proposals for constitutional amendments because they have strong popular support. The populist appeal of term limits, for example, has kept this proposal for constitutional amendment alive despite the opposition of most elected officials.[41]

The support for amendments providing for term limits and a balanced budget is motivated in part by the general dissatisfaction with government we explored in the previous section. Those who favor term limits argue that Congress and state legislatures are held captive by political careerists who use the perks of incumbency to perpetuate themselves in power. Setting limits on how long legislators can serve will end the reign of perpetual incumbents and improve electoral competition.[42] Most proposals for term limits, however, do not set an upper limit on how many years a given individual can serve in local, state, or federal elected office. This is what would be required if proponents of term limits were interested

---

ings Institution, 1992). For a comprehensive set of studies comparing government institutions in advanced democracies, see R. Kent Weaver and Bert A. Rockman, eds., *Do Institutions Matter? Government Capabilities in the United States and Abroad* (Washington, D.C.: Brookings Institution, 1993).

[41] See Sundquist, *Constitutional Reform and Effective Government*, pp. 180–82.

[42] See, e.g., Kenneth Jost, "Judgment Time for Term Limits," *ABA Journal*, November 1994, p. 80.

in ending political careerism and restoring the "citizen legislature" once and for all. Otherwise, political careers would still be possible as incumbents moved from office to office. In any event, opponents of term limits often respond by pointing to the advantages of having experienced incumbents in the legislature. Experience means that legislators are better prepared to decide complex policy issues, better able to negotiate with interest groups, and are trained to resist the encroachments of the executive branch.[43]

There is some irony in the public support for a balanced budget amendment since one of the reasons the executive and legislative branches failed repeatedly to reduce the federal budget deficit significantly in the 1980s was public resistance to higher taxes. Nevertheless, the failure of the elected branches to reduce the deficit was probably an important contributor to the belief of some citizens that the federal government was unwilling to deal forthrightly with major issues of public concern. The actual effect of a balanced budget amendment, were it to be approved by Congress and the states, is highly uncertain.[44] The legalistic push toward deficit elimination that the amendment would presumably supply might not be enough to overcome the forces that have consistently produced budget deficits in the 1980s and 1990s. In such a situation, the Constitution itself might be discredited. More likely, however, public confidence in Congress would sink to new lows. In addition, the Supreme Court and the President might acquire unusual power over the budget process in the wake of a congressional failure. Such an unprecedented intrusion of the judicial and executive branches into a key legislative process could have far-reaching implications for the constitutional system.

Both term limits and the balanced budget amendment have been criticized on the ground that their goals can be achieved within the present structure of government. That is, nothing prevents voters from using the ballot to informally enforce term limits on their representatives and there is no legal barrier to Congress adopting a balanced budget. This is a theoretically interesting argument, because it raises the question of why we should have a constitution in the first place. In the same vein, we might argue that as long as voters are unwilling to allow presidents to have a third term, there is no point in having the Twenty-second Amendment. Or as long as Congress is willing to be restrained in its exercise of power,

[43] See Fiorina, *Divided Government*, pp. 53–58; Sundquist, *Constitutional Reform and Effective Government*, pp. 183–84.

[44] See, e.g., Andrew Taylor, "Amendment Remains a Gamble Despite Its Popularity," *Congressional Quarterly*, January 14, 1995, p. 141; Andrew Taylor, "In Historic Turn, House Passes Balanced-Budget Amendment," *Congressional Quarterly*, January 28, 1995, p. 266.

there is no point to the enumeration of congressional powers in Article I. Or, again, as the Federalists argued in the debate over ratification of the Constitution, as long as no one assumes that Congress has the power to abridge the freedom of speech, there is no point to having the First Amendment.

The appropriate response to this argument should be evident. The normal operation of politics may guarantee that a certain desirable rule is respected, but then again it may not. If we consider the rule to be sufficiently important, we may wish to place it in the Constitution so that we will not be tempted to violate it in the future. In the terms of rational choice theory, we may wish to precommit ourselves to a rule in anticipation that ordinary democratic politics will fail to guarantee outcomes we think desirable.[45] Amendments providing for term limits or a balanced budget are no different in this respect from the other rules in the Constitution.

Although term limits and a balanced budget amendment may be unwise, we should bear in mind that the door to such proposals was opened by the signal failure of political elites to provide leadership on matters of public concern, significantly reform the Congress, and anticipate the populist reaction to these failures. Constitutional scholars also bear responsibility for failing to take such reform efforts seriously and being far too complacent about issues of congressional and constitutional reform. If political elites and constitutional scholars are dismayed by the adverse potential of these proposals for constitutional change, they have no one to blame but themselves.

Proposals for constitutional reform are often criticized on the ground that the Constitution has worked quite well over time and that there is therefore no pressing need for fundamental change. As we noted in chapter 5, however, testimonials to the Constitution's success mean very little unless the criteria for failure are specified clearly. Since such criteria are rarely, if ever, provided, this raises the suspicion that those extolling the Constitution cannot conceive of the possibility of failure. If this is the case, this criticism begs the question because it implies a standard of perfection no proposal for change could ever satisfy. In point of fact, the Constitution has been formally amended, indicating that it does have flaws and is not perfect. The general impression that the Constitution has been a success should not, therefore, discourage us from taking proposals for reform seriously and being willing to examine the Constitution in a critical light.

[45] See Cass R. Sunstein, *The Partial Constitution* (Cambridge: Harvard University Press, 1993), p. 21.

The Future of American Constitutionalism

As stated in chapter 5, the normative justification of the pluralistic theory of constitutional interpretation presented there depended on the desirability of the legalized Constitution. However, the question of whether the legalized Constitution is in fact desirable was not addressed. We should now face this question squarely, although it is a difficult issue to discuss. For lawyers and judges, after all, the legalized Constitution *is* the Constitution. From this perspective, asking whether the legalized Constitution is desirable is akin to asking whether the Constitution has been a success. As we have just seen, this is a slippery question. For lawyers and judges, the Constitution provides the grounds for the justification of political practices. As a fundamental law, it does not itself stand in need of justification.[46]

While this view may be questionable as a jurisprudential matter, it is difficult to see what practical difference it would make if we formulated a set of standards to judge the Constitution and then concluded that it was unjustified. The Constitution, legalized or not, is a key element of our political system and it is most unlikely that it will be significantly changed through formal amendment in the foreseeable future. Nevertheless, it is important to understand the difference the legalized Constitution makes to the operation of the constitutional system. Although the legalized Constitution provides the framework in which lawyers and judges work, it is not the whole story.

Constitutional crises are useful in demonstrating the limits of the legalized Constitution.[47] The legalized Constitution may well contribute to the inability of the public and elected officials to come to grips with the constitutional implications of Watergate and the Iran-Contra affair. With regard to Watergate, for example, there is a tendency to reduce the broad implications of Nixon's actions for the constitutional system to the question of whether he committed a crime. But Nixon should be judged by the special standards of the Constitution, not by ordinary law. The tendency to interpret those standards in the light of ordinary law frustrates the purpose of creating those standards in the first place. The reduction of profound constitutional issues to questions of ordinary criminality reflects an inability, encouraged by the legalization of the Constitution, to grasp the unique dimension of constitutionalism.

The chief defender of the legalized Constitution is the federal judiciary, especially the Supreme Court. As was shown in chapter 1, the Court po-

[46] For an example of this view, see Robert H. Bork, *The Tempting of America* (New York: Free Press, 1990), pp. 171–76.

[47] For a related discussion, see Foley, *The Silence of Constitutions*, pp. 39–40.

lices a limited constitutional domain. The Court is prevented from pressing the legalized Constitution to its logical limits by external and internal constraints. In order for the Court to be able to enforce the entire Constitution, it would have to become the most powerful branch of government. The executive and legislative branches are unlikely to allow this, thus creating an external constraint on the Court. The need to act as an appellate court and decide cases according to the law, understood in conventional terms, is the internal constraint. Since not all constitutional disputes can be resolved according to principles drawn from ordinary law, the Court must refuse to decide cases that would bring it too close to matters of politics, lest it lose its status as a court of law.

It is possible to question, however, whether the Court has been able to adhere to the internal constraint in light of the judicial activism that has occurred in the post-*Brown* period. Chapters 4 and 5 argued that the Court is forced to abandon the internal constraint when it is asked to interpret ambiguous constitutional clauses, such as those in the Fourteenth Amendment. The constitutional doctrines developed by the contemporary Court to interpret such clauses are certainly not regarded as clear, coherent, or consistent by scholarly commentators.[48] It is likely that contemporary constitutional doctrines are not significantly more coherent or consistent than the *Lochner* era jurisprudence they replaced.[49] This does not mean we should bring back the *Lochner* era, only that we should recognize that contemporary constitutional law and *Lochner* era jurisprudence are both products of the unresolved political and legal conflicts of their time.

The importance of the *Carolene Products* footnote, discussed in chapters 3 and 5, to contemporary constitutional theory should not obscure the reality that it has not served as the unifying theory for the Court in the post-*Brown* era. The recent important opinion by Justices O'Connor, Kennedy, and Souter in *Planned Parenthood v. Casey*, which we reviewed briefly in chapter 5, is far more representative of how the contemporary Court understands its role in American democracy.[50] The opinion trum-

---

[48] See, e.g., Rebecca L. Brown, "Separated Powers and Ordered Liberty," *University of Pennsylvania Law Review* 139 (1991): 1513 (separation of powers doctrine); Pamela S. Karlan, "The Rights to Vote: Some Pessimism about Formalism," *Texas Law Review* 71 (1993): 1705 (voting rights doctrine); Richard S. Kay, "Constitutional Cultures: Constitutional Law," *University of Chicago Law Review* 57 (1990): 311 (constitutional doctrine in general); Robert C. Post, "The Constitutional Concept of Public Discourse: Outrageous Opinion, Democratic Deliberation, and *Hustler Magazine v. Falwell*," *Harvard Law Review* 103 (1990): 603 (First Amendment doctrine).

[49] This is suggested by the argument in Howard Gillman, *The Constitution Besieged: The Rise and Demise of Lochner Era Police Powers Jurisprudence* (Durham: Duke University Press, 1993), pp. 195–205.

[50] 112 S.Ct. 2791 (1992).

pets the primacy of the legalized Constitution: "The root of American governmental power is revealed most clearly in the instance of the power conferred by the Constitution upon the Judiciary of the United States and specifically upon this Court."[51] The opinion thus asserts that the Court is at the center of the American constitutional universe; that its actions best embody the essence of American constitutionalism.

The purpose of the long opinion in *Casey* is not to justify the right to abortion as a matter of democratic principle, but to defend the substantive due process doctrine as an exemplar of the proper role of the Supreme Court. As we saw in chapter 5, the opinion invokes Justice Harlan's dissent in *Poe v. Ullman* rather than the *Carolene Products* footnote.[52] The opinion declares that overruling *Roe v. Wade* would undermine the legitimacy of the Court and "[i]f the Court's legitimacy should be undermined, then, so would the country be in its very ability to see itself through its constitutional ideals."[53] The opinion sees *Roe* as a case of fundamental importance to constitutional law because it possesses that "dimension present whenever the Court's interpretation of the Constitution calls the contending sides of a national controversy to end their national division by accepting a common mandate rooted in the Constitution."[54]

There is more than a tinge of arrogance here, regardless of the ultimate persuasiveness of the *Casey* opinion on the specific issue of abortion. These passages implicitly raise the justices to the status of the timeless symbols of justice and great historical figures of the law represented in the artwork of the Supreme Court building. Only such figures of majesty and authority would have the ability to reveal the essence of the nation's constitutional ideals and end a bitter national division at one stroke. Unfortunately, political reality intrudes on this Olympian fantasy. *Roe* did not settle the national controversy over abortion, but intensified it. The murderous outbreaks of violence that occurred after *Casey* was decided certainly indicate that the Court has not stilled the controversy.

It is important to see, however, that it is likely that many lawyers and scholars found this part of the *Casey* opinion, written by Justice Souter, to be expressive of their deepest aspirations for the Constitution and the Supreme Court.[55] The ability of the Court to enforce that part of the Constitution under its care gives constitutional rights a special political force in the United States that is still lacking in too many countries. For these lawyers and scholars, this achievement represents the best of Ameri-

[51] Ibid., p. 2814.

[52] See *Poe v. Ullman*, 367 U.S. 497 (1961).

[53] *Casey*, 112 S.Ct. at 2816.

[54] Ibid., p. 2815.

[55] See David J. Garrow, "Justice Souter Emerges," *New York Times Magazine*, September 25, 1994, p. 36.

can constitutional democracy and the institution that protects this achievement deserves respect and deference.

The ability of the Supreme Court to meaningfully enforce constitutional rights is indeed of great importance and by itself provides an adequate justification for the legalized Constitution. Nevertheless, we should appreciate again that this is not the whole story. As we observed in chapter 3, the past several decades have shown that the executive and legislative branches can also implement constitutional guarantees, at times far more effectively than the Court. Democratic processes can work to create, revise, and enforce individual rights, despite the apparent countermajoritarian character of such rights. If democratic politics can combine with democratic institutions to create and maintain rights of fundamental importance, then these institutions also deserve a measure of respect.

We should recognize as well that the Court is limited in the extent to which it can protect constitutional rights. Here again the *Casey* opinion is helpful in understanding the role of the Court in contemporary American constitutionalism. In *Casey*, the Court is aggressive in protecting its institutional role, but falters when it comes to implementing Warren Court–style fundamental rights. The Court assumes a bold stance while eviscerating the right to terminate a pregnancy as a *fundamental* right, thus breaking with the substantive due process tradition as it maneuvers to protect itself from a strong political counterattack. Despite its protestations to the contrary, the *Casey* Court could not avoid being influenced by the political storm over abortion.[56]

The Court's defense of the legalized Constitution has thus become increasingly problematic. The apparent extension of the legalized Constitution that was the consequence of the judicial activism of the Warren and Burger Courts resulted instead in an increased politicization of the judicial sphere. Rather than producing a new consensus, judicial activism instead introduced deep political conflicts into the constitutional arena. The divisive battles over nominations to the Court, the Court's retreat on fundamental rights, and the inability of the Court to satisfy even minimal standards of coherence and consistency provide clear evidence of this politicization.

While it is likely that constitutional scholars will continue to focus on the Supreme Court, the analysis in this chapter suggests that the most significant challenges to American constitutionalism as the Constitution enters on its third century lie elsewhere. In particular, the widespread public dissatisfaction with government in the United States suggests that the system of representation established by federal and state constitutions is

---

[56] See the discussion of the content of the right to abortion in *Casey*, 112 S.Ct. at 2816–21.

under serious strain. This is perhaps the most serious challenge to American constitutionalism at present. Elections come and go, officials are reelected or not, but the public remains frustrated with the way the system works. It is hard to see how this could be the case if the system of representation were working well. Elections ought to give voters a sense that they have a measure of control over their government. They provide a system of incentives and disincentives normally sufficient to give officeholders the motives necessary to address the voters' concerns. Yet whether the public continues to elect incumbents or votes to remove them from office, they remain disillusioned and demoralized with Washington and politics in general.[57]

At the same time, it would be wrong to conclude that the federal government is somehow out of touch with the people. Another important cause of the strain on the system of representation is the constant bombardment of pleas, demands, and ultimatums from an ever-increasing number of interest groups using a variety of media to create their own version of direct democracy. While this hyperdemocracy certainly does not represent the interests of all citizens, it makes a claim to legitimacy that competes effectively with the electorally based claims of Congress.[58] At the state level, this impetus toward direct democracy has encouraged an increasing use of initiatives to legislate by means of the ballot. Yet it is not at all clear that the use of initiatives has produced more confidence in state government.

The displacement of political authority, discussed in chapter 2, is another source of the trouble with the system of representation. The consistent use of independent agencies and the courts to make important policy decisions makes elections less relevant to policymaking and may increase the sense citizens have that they have no control over what government does. It may seem odd that contemporary American constitutionalism tends to work to undermine the importance of elections, but that appears to describe what is happening to the system of representation.

However we make sense of these trends in American constitutionalism, it is important to recognize that significant changes can occur in the constitutional order even in the absence of formal amendments or judicial decisions. We should resist the view, encouraged by the legalized Constitution, that seeking to reform the Constitution is dangerous because of

---

[57] In another sign that the system is under stress, members of Congress return the favor by holding a low opinion of the public. See "Congress isn't thrilled with voters, either," *New Orleans Times-Picayune*, April 5, 1992, p. A-3 (Associated Press). See also the articles cited in note 33 on the recent retirement of many members of Congress.

[58] See, e.g., Robin Toner, "The Art of Reprocessing the Democratic Process," *New York Times*, September 4, 1994, sec. 4, p. 1; Michael Wines, "Washington Really Is in Touch. We're the Problem," *New York Times*, October 16, 1994, sec. 4, p. 1.

the permanence of the document and the stability of the institutions it established. As we saw in chapter 1, the constitutional order has changed in significant respects without the use of amendments or judicial decisions, and it will continue to do so.

The question for the future is whether we have the confidence of the founding generation that we can rationally diagnose fundamental problems of our political order and then act to change them, whether through amendments or legislation. It is possible that we know more about our political order than the founding generation knew of theirs, but it is understandable that this may inspire caution rather than confidence in our ability to improve the Constitution. If this observation stifles reform, however, then we should be candid that we are abandoning constitutionalism as a meaningful political ideal. Not in the sense that the Constitution is irrelevant to the present political order, for clearly it is quite relevant. It is in the sense of admitting that we no longer believe we are able to exercise deliberate control over politics. Scholars often issue calls to renew American constitutionalism, but our present difficulties are not solved so easily. If we cannot renew American constitutionalism through theory, we can at least understand it.

Index